FORT MACON
a history

FORT MACON
a history

by PAUL BRANCH

Best wishes,
Paul

The Nautical & Aviation Publishing
Company of America
Charleston, South Carolina

Library of Congress Catalog Card Number: 97-29772

ISBN: 1-877853-45-3

Printed in the United States of America.

Front cover photograph by Paul Branch.
Back cover illustration from *Frank Leslie's Illustrated Newspaper.*

Library of Congress Cataloging-in-Publication Data

    Branch, Paul.
      Fort Macon: A History / by Paul Branch.
          p.   cm.
      Includes bibliographical references and index.
      ISBN 1-877853-45-3
      1. Fort Macon (N.C.)—History.   I. Title.
    F264.F67B68   1997
    975.6'197—dc21   97-29772
                                    CIP

TABLE OF CONTENTS

ACKNOWLEDGMENTS

There are a number of people who have helped make this book possible and I would like to express my grateful thanks to them. The staffs of the Military Reference Branch of the National Archives and the North Carolina State Archives have always been very helpful in locating documents during my many visits. In particular Michael Meier, formerly of the Military Reference Branch of the National Archives, deserves special thanks for his assistance over a period of years in locating obscure documents for me. Special thanks also goes to Annette Davis of the Carteret Community College Library for processing countless interlibrary loans and providing assistance over the years. Also, special thanks goes to William S. Powell of the University of North Carolina at Chapel Hill who will always be "Mr. North Carolina History." His assistance and inspiration have been a tremendous benefit to me for more than twenty years. I would also like to thank Doug Wolfe of Morehead City for first suggesting me to the folks at Nautical and Aviation for a book on Fort Macon. Special thanks go to Thomas J. Adams of Beaufort for making the aerial photographs of Fort Macon possible. Thanks also go to the following persons and organizations for permission to use items from their collections: David F. Dean, Rochester, NY; the Southern Historical Collection and North Carolina Collection of the University of North Carolina Library, Chapel Hill, NC; Mrs. Joseph D. Sebes, Beaufort, NC; Thomas McKeon, Hazlet, NJ; Earl Greg Swem Library, College of William and Mary, Williamsburg, VA; and the Casemate Museum, Fort Monroe, VA. I would also like to thank the staff of Fort Macon State Park, past and present, with whom I have worked for the last sixteen years. Also, I must include a special thanks to my family, especially my wife Paula, for her patience and understanding for all those yearly research trips to the National Archives. And of course, thanks to Mom and Dad.

Paul Branch

GLOSSARY OF FORT TERMS

BANQUETTE: A raised area of earth behind a parapet forming a platform on which soldiers may stand and fire at an enemy.

BARBETTE, or **EN BARBETTE:** A method of mounting cannons in a fort to fire over the top of a wall or parapet.

BASTION: A salient wall of four sides usually projecting from the angles of the main rampart of a fortification to provide flanking fire along the length of the rampart walls.

BREASTHEIGHT: The interior wall of a parapet.

CASEMATE: A vaulted room or chamber in a fort, heavily constructed to provide protection against enemy gunfire and intended to provide quarters and shelter to a garrison during attack. Casemates are usually provided with gun ports and embrasures to allow the garrison to fire out.

CITADEL: The main or central defensive structure located within a fortification. It commands the entire fortification and provides a sheltered strongpoint for a defending garrison.

CORDON: A projecting ledge or course of stone or masonry crowning a wall of a fortification to provide an obstacle to enemy escalade.

COUNTERFIRE GALLERIES: Interior defense galleries or casemates under a counterscarp wall to command the ditch or moat of a fort with reverse, or counter, fire.

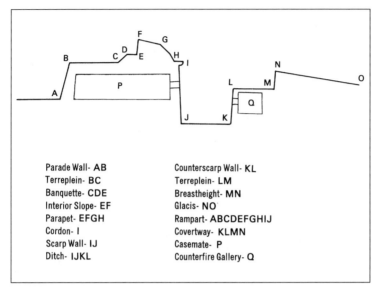

Parade Wall- **AB**	Counterscarp Wall- **KL**
Terreplein- **BC**	Terreplein- **LM**
Banquette- **CDE**	Breastheight- **MN**
Interior Slope- **EF**	Glacis- **NO**
Parapet- **EFGH**	Rampart- **ABCDEFGHIJ**
Cordon- **I**	Covertway- **KLMN**
Scarp Wall- **IJ**	Casemate- **P**
Ditch- **IJKL**	Counterfire Gallery- **Q**

Profile of a fortification.

COUNTERFORT: A short, buttress wall built behind a main wall to provide strength.

COUNTERSCARP WALL: The outer wall of a fort's ditch or moat facing the scarp, or main inner wall.

COVERTWAY, or **COVERED WAY:** An encircling road or battlement along the top of the Counterscarp Wall which in part forms an outer defensive area of a fort. It is protected in front by a parapet and provides a protected, or "covered" defensive area around a fort. It also serves to hide and shield a fort's troops and defenses from direct enemy view ("covert").

DITCH: An excavated area in front of or within a fortification designed to provide an obstacle to assault. The Ditch can be dry or filled with water ("wet ditch") for intensifying the difficulty for an attacker.

EMBRASURE: A gun port or opening in a wall or parapet which allows a cannon to fire out.

ENFILADE FIRE: A very destructive mode of gunfire which rakes or sweeps down the length of a battleline or fortification from the side or rear.

FASCINES: Long, cylindrical bundles of sticks and saplings tightly bound which are used to provide fill in building or strengthening fortifications.

GLACIS: A gentle slope of earth inclining outward away from the walls of a fortification. Its purpose is to cover and protect the walls of a fortification from direct fire. It alsoprovides an open, coverless, unprotected approach to a fortification over which an attacker will be fully exposed to defensive fire in an assault.

HOT SHOT FURNACE: A masonry structure used to heat cannonballs red hot for the purpose of setting fire to wooden ships.

INTERIOR SLOPE: The portion of a parapet wall gently sloping outward to provide a convenient surface on which riflemen would lean to shoot.

MERLON: Upright portions of a parapet wall between gun ports or embrasure openings.

MOAT: Synonymous with the Ditch and usually referring to a water-filled Ditch, or a water-filled channel within the Ditch.

MAGAZINE: A protected storage area for gunpowder and ammunition.

PARADE GROUND: An open area of a fortification or camp used for the regular assembly of soldiers.

PARADE WALLS: The walls of a fortification fronting the Parade Ground.

PARAPET: A raised area of earth or masonry above the level of a rampart which shields soldiers from enemy gunfire.

PINTLE: An upright iron shaft which provides the pivot point for a cannon carriage. The pintle is securely mounted in a timber bolster or stone block and protrudes through a metal pintle plate which helps carry the weight of a cannon.

POSTERN: A vaulted secondary passage through the walls of the ramparts which allows communication with the outer defenses of a fortification.

RAMPART: A general term referring to the raised body of a fortification formed of masonry or earth which provides defenders with the firing platform to give them command of the area and approaches which surround the fortification.

REVETMENT: A facing made of fascines, timber, sods, sand bags or masonry which composes the interior slope of a parapet wall and serves as a support or retaining wall for the embankment of the parapet.

SALLY PORT: An opening or gateway out of a fortification, usually the main gate, extending through the covertway and glacis to permit troops to "sally forth", particularly on sorties or outside operations beyond the fort's walls.

SCARP WALL: The main exterior rampart wall of a fortification.

TERREPLEIN: A horizontal surface on top of the rampart and behind the parapet which provides the firing platform for artillery in a fortification.

TRAVERSE: A high mound of earth or sand bags placed at right angles to the parapet between cannons or groups of cannons to provide cover against enfilade fire and localize the effects of enemy gunfire hitting within a fortification.

TRAVERSE CIRCLE: Part of a cannon mount consisting of a wood, stone, or masonry support for a curved iron rail on which a cannon rolls when "traversed", or swung laterally for aiming.

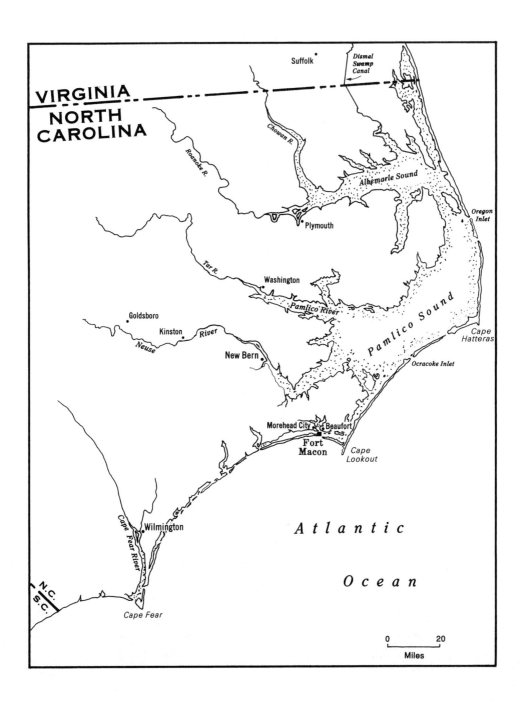

VIRGINIA
NORTH
CAROLINA

Suffolk

Dismal
Swamp
Canal

Chowan R.

Roanoke R.

Albemarle Sound

Oregon
Inlet

Plymouth

Tar R.

Washington

Pamlico River

Pamlico Sound

Goldsboro

Kinston   River

Neuse

New Bern

Cape
Hatteras

Ocracoke Inlet

Morehead City   Beaufort

Fort
Macon

Cape
Lookout

Cape Fear River

Wilmington

N.C.
S.C.

Cape Fear

Atlantic

Ocean

0   20
Miles

1
EARLY PROBLEMS OF DEFENSE

The State of North Carolina is situated in the middle of the Eastern Seaboard with its coastline jutting out into the Atlantic Ocean like an elbow. Geographically, the state would seem in an excellent location for development into a major center of ocean trade and commerce were it not for a series of offshore sea islands and sand banks that run most of the length of the state's 330-mile coastline. These sand banks run at varying distances from the mainland and are separated from it by a series of shallow inland sounds and waterways. The upper two-thirds of this chain of offshore banks have become known simply as the Outer Banks and stretch for over 200 miles from the Virginia border to Bogue Banks.

From the earliest Colonial times, these sand banks and islands have been both a curse and a blessing. On the one hand, they severely retarded the development of trade and commerce by limiting the access of ships to the sea through only a handful of inlets which interrupt the island chain. As a result, only two ports, Wilmington on the Cape Fear River and Beaufort Harbor, have sustained themselves successfully on a coast of over 300 miles in length.

In addition, treacherous shallows and the extensive shoals associated with the island chain, particularly those surrounding its three capes (Cape

1

Hatteras, Cape Lookout and Cape Fear), have destroyed hundreds of ships over the centuries and caused mariners to give the state's coast the unfortunate sobriquet "Graveyard of the Atlantic." On the other hand, the island chain has shielded the mainland from the full wrath of the stormy Atlantic and, to a great extent, has aided the task of defending the state's coast against enemy nations over the centuries. Whoever commanded the inlets commanded the shipping which tried to enter them, thereby preventing enemy vessels from reaching the vulnerable towns and settlements of the mainland. Such was the reasoning behind the defense of the North Carolina coast from the earliest times, and the basis for the establishment of forts like Fort Macon.

THE ESTABLISHMENT OF PORT BEAUFORT

Beaufort Harbor is one of North Carolina's two seaports. It is situated at the midpoint of the state's coast and at the lower end of the island chain known as the Outer Banks. It is 135 miles southeast of Raleigh, the state capital, and about 80 miles northeast of Wilmington, the other major port in the state. Beaufort Harbor is the only port which opens directly to the ocean, since the port of Wilmington is situated up the Cape Fear River. Access to Beaufort Harbor is gained from the ocean through Beaufort Inlet (formerly Old Topsail Inlet), which passes between Shackleford Banks on its east side and Bogue Banks on its west. From Colonial times, the inlet and harbor were blessed with deep water of at least fifteen to eighteen feet, as shown by maps of the period. The harbor itself is a small but sheltered road formed by the intersection of Bogue Sound with the mouth of the Newport River. Situated on the east side of the harbor is the town of Beaufort. Laid out in 1713, it is the third oldest in the state behind Bath (1704), and New Bern (1710). Beaufort developed to the extent that in April, 1722, it became the seat of newly established Carteret County, and a formally designated port of entry. In November, 1723, it was formally incorporated. The growth of the town itself was slow, however, chiefly because the Newport River did not extend into the state's interior as did the Cape Fear,

Neuse, and Roanoke Rivers, to tap into the resources of the tidewater and Piedmont areas. Nevertheless, in the years which followed, Port Beaufort enjoyed a comfortable existence with a lively trade centered in the "naval stores," lumber, livestock, fishing, and whaling industries.[1]

Prior to 1740 the defense of Port Beaufort was not a serious concern. The local Indians had been defeated and driven off during the Tuscarora Wars of 1711–13 and posed no threat. In Europe, Great Britain was enjoying a period of brief peace following the end of the Wars of Spanish Succession in 1713. The 1723 Act of the General Assembly in which Beaufort was formally incorporated contained a provision that of the thirty shillings charged for the purchase of each lot in the town, "Ten Shillings shall be for the purchasing of Great Guns, and for Fortifying the said Town; and shall be paid, by the Treasurer . . . into such Hands as the Governor or Commander in Chief for the Time being shall appoint to oversee the said work." However, nothing was done toward defense since the colonists themselves "declare very much against Fortifications," as Governor George Burrington wrote to the Lords of Trade in 1731. They were unwilling to be burdened with the expense for something they felt Great Britain should provide for their safety. Burrington pointed out, however, "as we have three harbours capable of receiving large ships (Cape Fear, Ocracoke, and Beaufort) there will be a necessity of erecting [fortifications] at each of the Said harbours. . . ." The following year, Governor Burrington again recommended that the harbors of Cape Fear and Port Beaufort be fortified but agreed with the local feeling that "the cost might prove more than the country is able at present to discharge." Thus the prospect of defense for Beaufort, as well as the rest of the colony, was not taken seriously for many years. However, events in Europe soon dictated otherwise, and the inhabitants of Beaufort would get a hard-learned lesson of the value of seacoast defense.[2]

THE SPANISH ALARMS

At the end of the 1730s the European powers erupted into a series of wars that would last for a decade. In 1739, Great Britain went to war against

Spain in the War of Jenkins' Ear (1739–1743). This war soon merged into a larger conflict, as part of the Wars of Austrian Succession known as King George's War (1744–48), in which Britain battled both France and Spain. The fighting soon spread to include conflicts between the British colonies in America, those of Spain in Florida, and of France in Canada. In short order, Spanish privateers appeared off the North Carolina coast to disrupt the shipping trade.

In April and May of 1741, two Spanish privateers operated off the Outer Banks, capturing six ships within a ten day period. During that summer, the Spanish took over Ocracoke Inlet, forty-five miles northeast of Beaufort, and made it into a base of operations. From here they captured unsuspecting ships entering the inlet or passing along the coast offshore. They sent raiding expeditions into Pamlico Sound and to the mainland, taking livestock and devastating the countryside. Eventually, the Spanish were forced to leave Ocracoke and the Province spent £10,000 providing vessels of provisions to relieve the colonists of the area. On 17 October of that year, a Spanish privateer with a crew of eighty men boldly captured a Boston schooner off Bogue Inlet, only twenty-five miles southwest of Beaufort. In January, 1742, two more vessels were reportedly taken off Ocracoke. Such depredations continued irregularly over the following years. British efforts to curb the Spanish raiders proved ineffective because on the rare occasions when a British warship actually patrolled the coast, the raiders had little trouble avoiding it to strike somewhere else. As a result, commerce among the colonies was greatly affected. Apart from the ships captured, many others remained in port or took their trade to unthreatened areas. The Charleston *South Carolina Gazette* bemoaned the fact that during the five year period ending in 1748, only twenty-one ships cleared port between Charleston and North Carolina ports. Thus seaport towns, including Beaufort, suffered great hardship.[3]

In the latter stages of the war the enemy grew even bolder and pressed ever closer to Beaufort. Spanish and French privateers discovered the sheltered bight formed on the west side of Cape Lookout and at times operated from within sight of Beaufort. It was reported that "here they lay, got fresh Provisions from the Banks, and great plenty of the best fish and good water with wood for firing, and from their masthead could see every Vessel that passed along the Coast and could in an hour's time be at sea after them." It was inevitable that the raiders would eventually realize the weakness of Beaufort and its vulnerability to plunder.[4]

In 1747, a Spanish force from St. Augustine described as consisting of "several small Sloops and Barcalanjos . . . full of armed men, mostly Mulattoes and Negroes" made several raids along the North Carolina coast. On 14 June they entered the harbor at Beaufort unopposed and captured several vessels. Thirteen men of Colonel Thomas Lovick's regiment of Carteret County militia were on duty at Beaufort but could only watch helplessly as the Spanish remained out in the harbor and did not attempt to land. The raiders soon departed with their prizes. The ease with which this was accomplished encouraged bolder action and on 26 August 1747, the Spanish returned to Beaufort, landed, and captured the town itself. Major Enoch Ward of Lovick's regiment assembled fifty-eight militiamen against the Spaniards and eventually recaptured the plundered town. Details of the action do not exist but a number of Spaniards were captured, with the rest apparently driven back to their ships. Again the Spanish ships departed with their booty.[5]

The boldness of the Spanish raid shocked the colony and finally awoke the inhabitants to the need for fortifications to protect the coast. When the General Assembly met again in 1748, an Act was passed whereby the province would issue £6000 of scrip for the construction of four forts for the defense of the coast. Of these, the two largest forts at Ocracoke and Cape Fear, would cost £2000 each. A small fort costing £500 would be erected at Bear Inlet and one of medium size, costing £1500, at Old Topsail (Beaufort) Inlet. Groups of citizens were named as commissioners in each case to arrange for the construction of the forts. The Act marked the first formal public appropriation toward fortifications on the North Carolina coast.[6]

Before any results could come from this new Act, Spanish raids on the North Carolina coast came to an abrupt climax. In September, 1748, a Spanish attack on Brunswick, on the Cape Fear River, resulted in a bitter repulse for the raiders with heavy loss. The following month, Britain, Spain, and France, all weary of the conflict, signed the Treaty of Aix-la-Chapell on 18 October 1748, ending the war. With the declaration of peace, North Carolina colonists lost interest in fortifications once again. The money appropriated for the four coastal forts remained largely unspent. A fortification on the Cape Fear River known as Fort Johnston was the only one even started.

FORT DOBBS

During the shaky peace in Europe following the Treaty of Aix-la-Chapell, the inhabitants of North Carolina returned to normal life over the next few years. In 1754, however, the French and Indian War began in North America, pitting British colonists against French colonists and their Indian allies. With it came the likelihood of French warships operating off the coast. It was at this time that Arthur Dobbs arrived in North Carolina as its new governor and found the inhabitants still unprepared for war. No public gunpowder magazines or storehouses existed. The militia was poorly armed and had no gunpowder available for its use. A gunpowder tax established in 1743 to fund the purchase of powder and shot and maintain the magazines and fortifications had lapsed. Finally, other than work on Fort Johnston on the Cape Fear, none of the other three forts authorized in 1748 had been erected. Dobbs set out to correct these problems at once and prepare the province for war. After bringing the issue before the General Assembly for action, he embarked upon an inspection tour late in the spring of 1755 to visit the sites where the fortifications had been authorized in 1748.[7]

In mid-May, 1755, Governor Dobbs arrived at Beaufort to see what plans had been made to establish a fort to protect the town and harbor. Four local men had been named as commissioners in 1748 to build a fort with the £1500 appropriated for that purpose. Dobbs found the commissioners had done no more than agree upon a site for a battery at a point about 200 to 300 yards from the town. Dobbs disapproved of this site because it "could only secure such Vessels as lay near the town, but any Vessels might come over the Bar, and lye in a safe Harbour . . . without being hurt, it being two miles at least from the battery . . . ." Enemy vessels could pass through Old Topsail (Beaufort) Inlet unopposed and freely take any vessels in the harbor without ever engaging the proposed battery nearly two miles away. This is precisely what the Spanish had done in their first raid on Beaufort in June, 1747. The battery would only become effective if invaders elected to close on the town itself.[8]

Governor Dobbs knew a more favorable site for the proposed battery was required. Having served previously as an officer in the British Army, he knew what was necessary to secure the harbor against invasion. His thoughts fell upon the inlet itself where a battery established on one side or the other would prevent hostile vessels from gaining entrance and secure both the harbor and the town. Dobbs later wrote:

> "I went therefore to the S.W. point of the Inlet where I found the Channel coming in from the Bar, was within 1/2 a mile from the point, and a fine sandy Point well fixed, above high water 5 or 6 feet, where the Roots of Trees in the sand made a sure foundation for a Battery, where they would have good water, and wood for firing, and fixed with the Commissioners to raise a fascine Battery with two faces, containing 6 guns each, one of 9-pounders to command the passage at the Bar and the other of 6-pounders to command and secure the shipping in the Channel within the point, where the Channel to the Shoal is not a mile over, and the deepest of the Channel near the Battery."[9]

The place Dobbs was referring to was the eastern end of Bogue Banks on the west side of Old Topsail (Beaufort) Inlet, at what is now known as Bogue Point. The wisdom of his choice is demonstrated by the fact that over the next two centuries successive engineers have confirmed this spot as the best place from which to defend Beaufort Inlet.

The battery which Dobbs and the commissioners planned to build on Bogue Point was simple. It was little more than a redan of two faces in an inverted 'V' or right angle made of sand and revetted with tightly bound bundles of saplings or wood called fascines. To quarter the garrison and to provide a stronghold from which to resist assault, a garrison house was built within the battery. The intended garrison was to consist of a gunner and about thirty soldiers. The armament plan was later modified so that the side of the battery facing the inlet and bar would have a heavier armament of eight 12-pounders. Work on the battery began later that year with two of the commissioners, Colonel Thomas Lovick and Colonel Joseph Bell, both militia officers, named to superintend the construction. The fortification was soon named Fort Dobbs in honor of the Governor.[10]

Work on Fort Dobbs as well as the other coastal fortifications in the province moved along quickly over the next couple of years.[11] When Governor Dobbs returned to Beaufort to inspect the progress on the fort in July, 1756, he found the garrison house "already up and covering" and felt the fort could be finished soon. The garrison house was afterward described as being "well built and of the dimensions following (to wit) forty feet in length, Thirty feet wide and twelve feet pitch, it has three floors, On the lower of which there are four rooms and a fireplace in each room." Despite this optimistic view, the following year a group of three commissioners appointed by the General Assembly to inspect the coastal forts, reported to the Assembly on 5 December, 1757, that Fort Dobbs "is built agreeable to the plan annexed to the same and that the said Fort is in no condition of defence, being built in so slight a manner and having no guns, powder and ball . . . ." The commissioners went on to fix a value of the work done on the fort at just over £435.[12]

This report was particularly disturbing to the Assembly, not only because Fort Dobbs was found to be incapable of defense, but because the value of the works estimated by the commissioners was more than £1000 less than the amount of funds issued by the Treasurer of the Southern Colonies for its construction. The Assembly therefore called Colonels Lovick and Bell, the superintendents, to account for the total of £1485 issued to them for the construction of the fort. Accordingly, Colonel Lovick appeared before an investigating committee of the Assembly and produced vouchers for the disbursements of the funds issued to him, most of which went to a single contractor named George Gibbens. Gibbens, however, did not render any account of how he spent those funds. Similarly, Colonel Bell could account for only part of the funds received from the Treasurer. The Assembly decided the accounts of Gibbens and Bell had to be better explained before they would be allowed. Gibbens later gave a satisfactory account under oath of the expenses incurred with the funds drawn upon Colonel Lovick, but Colonel Bell could not. The Assembly found Bell's "accounts are so confused that they have not time to examine and Report the same." It is not clear from the records if Bell's account was ever cleared up, or if the discrepancy between the funds spent on Fort Dobbs and the small value placed upon it by the commissioners was ever explained.[13]

It does not appear any further effort was made to complete Fort Dobbs with either armament or a garrison, as was done with both Fort Johnston on the Cape Fear and Fort Granville at Ocracoke. The success of British forces against the French in the remaining years of the war and the lack of attacks on the coast by French ships produced a reluctance on the part of the Assembly and the colonists to continue sinking large sums of money into the maintenance and occupation of the forts. After the war ended in 1764 only Fort Johnston remained in use, while both Forts Dobbs and Granville were forgotten and left to decay. Six years later, a map drawn up in August, 1770, by C. J. Sauthier entitled "Plan of the Town and Port of Beaufort in Carteret County, North Carolina" shows "Fort Dobbs in ruin." Presumably the fort collapsed and decayed away completely in the harsh, stormy elements of the coast not long thereafter, because during the Revolutionary War (1775-1782) there was no further mention of Fort Dobbs, even when the subject of defense was raised again. The first formal government effort to secure Beaufort Harbor with fortifications had ended in failure.

THE REVOLUTIONARY WAR

The opening of the Revolutionary War against Great Britain in 1775 found the coast of North Carolina not much improved from a defensive standpoint than it had been thirty-five years earlier in the war against Spain.

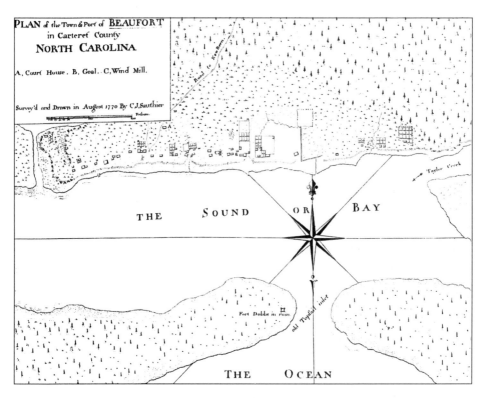

C. J. Sauthier map of Beaufort, N.C., 1770, showing "Fort Dobbs in ruin."
North Carollina State Archives.

Beaufort and Ocracoke, two of the province's three largest ports, were entirely without defense. Their chief reliance was a return to the belief that the tricky and treacherous nature of North Carolina's coastline would of itself limit the potential of attack by British ships. Even though the shoals and shallow inlets of the Outer Banks served to deter larger British warships operating along the coast of the colony, smaller draft British warships and privateers still posed a serious threat to trade and livelihood by being able to operate freely in the inlets and sounds. The seriousness of this was first demonstrated on 14 April 1776, when the British privateer *Lilly* sailed into Ocracoke Inlet and boldly capture a loaded schooner. Afterward, the Ocracoke pilots boarded the *Lilly* and her prize and recaptured them both. Although this particular incident ended favorably for the colonists it was just a taste of the type of warfare and trouble to come, and a sign that the treacherous natural features of the coast did not offer complete protection.[14]

Early defensive measures by the North Carolina colonists to protect the coast in the first years of the war did not involve the construction of fortifications. Instead a number of shallow draft vessels and row galleys fitted out with guns were used to patrol the sounds and rivers behind the Outer Banks. In April, 1776, the North Carolina Provincial Congress authorized five independent companies of soldiers to be raised for the defense of the coast and stationed at various points between Currituck and Cape Fear. These companies would be available not only to repel British raiding and foraging parties which landed on the coast, but were also provided with their own boats to board and seize British ships with the promise of prize money for whatever enemy ships and cargoes they took. One of these five companies commanded by Captain Enoch Ward was stationed at Beaufort. For more than a year these defensive measures seemed to meet the immediate needs.[15]

Meanwhile, Beaufort and Ocracoke were both enjoying a flourishing trade. The capture or blockade of the large ports of the northern colonies by the British caused a diversion of shipping to smaller ports such as Beaufort and Ocracoke. Valuable cargoes of salt, foodstuffs, and military supplies were brought in from the West Indies, France, and other countries and then sent on via sounds and inland waters to South Carolina and Virginia. Military supplies were forwarded on even to Washington's army in the north so that North Carolina ports became a vital part of the lifeline of the Continental Armies. Also, North Carolina privateers operated quite successfully from these ports against British merchant shipping and frequently returned with prizes. All in all, it was only a matter of time before the British took notice of all this activity. While the very volume of the activ-

ity and length of the coastline precluded the British from effectively stop-
ping it without the commitment of a large fleet, smaller draft British warships, tenders, and privateers came to have a degree of effectiveness with
nuisance raids and harassing operations.[16]

In September, 1777, two British brigs and a sloop spent some weeks
cruising between Capes Hatteras and Lookout. Their crews made raiding
expeditions to the Banks to take livestock and water, frightening and annoying the residents. They were also successful in harassing shipping and
blockading Ocracoke Inlet. Once a number of vessels had accumulated in
Ocracoke waiting for a chance to escape to sea, the British would sail into
the inlet and cause havoc among the ships. This was the first of many such
raids of this type to take place on the coast during the remaining years of
the war, and the inhabitants of nearby Beaufort became painfully aware of
their exposed and defenseless condition. On 20 September 1777, a number of prominent men in Beaufort sent a petition to North Carolina Governor Richard Caswell for help:

> "We beg leave to lay before your Excellency the critical situation
> of this place and the damages that may accrue to this State, as
> well as the Cause in general, for want of a few pieces of Ordnance
> placed at this Inlet. We presume with three or four 6- and 4-pound-
> ers, we would secure the inlet from the attempts of any Tender . .
> . We every day expect a visit from the enemy, as they have already
> done considerable damage at [Ocracoke] by taking away a Brig,
> and running ashore a Sloop loaded with salt."[17]

Late in the year a similar petition was drawn up by the citizens of Beaufort for presentation to the North Carolina Assembly. In this the inhabitants pointed out

> "how liable the whole [trade] is to be interrupted by the Enemy
> whenever they are apprized thereof, as there is not less than three
> Fathom Water on the Bar and the Channel is so very plain, that a
> Pilot of ordinary Judgement (tho' a stranger to the place) might
> without any great risque bring in an armed Vessel of sufficient

force not only entirely to put a stop to the said trade, but also greatly to annoy the Inhabitants of Beaufort Town in their present defenseless situation. Therefore we Your Petitioners thinking it highly necessary that a place which is become the Key of so valuable a part of our Trade should, for the good of the Public, be fortified in such a manner as to prevent the whole from being ruined by a single Ship, and considering the disadvantageous situation [to the enemy] of Bogue Point, in commanding the harbor . . . we recommend it to your honourable House, as guardians of the Public, not doubting but when you have duly considered the matter you will order some suitable Fortifications to be speedily erected, with some pieces of Cannon and Stores and a small Garrison well appointed with strict orders to give constant attendance, for the protection and encouragement of Navigation and Commerce and security of the Inhabitants."[18]

Unfortunately, nothing was done. The following month what little protection had been afforded the coast was reduced by the expiration of the one-year enlistment terms of the five Independent Companies defending the coast. Because of the expense of quartering and maintaining them, the Assembly chose to disband them.

British coastal raids resumed in the spring of 1778. In May of that year the fears of Beaufort residents were realized when two British sloops and a brig came into Beaufort Harbor after fooling the pilots into believing they were friendly vessels. Once in the harbor the British quickly seized a brig which had just been condemned and sold as a prize of the Continental frigate *Raleigh,* and another vessel from Charleston. With no harbor defenses, the inhabitants of Beaufort were just as helpless to prevent these actions as they had been in June, 1747, when Spanish privateers had done the same thing. The British attempted to leave with their prize but found themselves unable to get the brig out of the harbor. Instead they burned it and then left with the other prize. Thus the worst prediction of Beaufort residents to the General Assembly had come true. But other than reliance upon the local militia, no specific measures were taken afterward to defend Beaufort Harbor.[19]

FORT HANCOCK

Part of the failure of the General Assembly to make an effort to defend Beaufort Harbor can be explained by its preoccupation at the time of defending the nearby harbor at Cape Lookout. The bight at Cape Lookout formed a deep landlocked (at that time) bay, long regarded as one of the best sheltered harbors on the entire east coast. Only its lack of water communication with the inland sounds prevented it from eclipsing both Ocracoke and Beaufort as a port for trade. Utilized by enemy privateers in the war with Spain, Governor Arthur Dobbs later tried unsuccessfully to fortify it during the French and Indian War. Even in the present conflict efforts to fortify the harbor had been unsuccessful until March, 1778, when the French frigate *Ferdinand* sought shelter there to escape two pursuing British warships. The *Ferdinand*, commanded by Captain Denis N. de Cottineau de Kerloguen, was carrying a valuable military cargo from France for the Continental Army and had been unsuccessful in getting through the British blockade of Chesapeake Bay. Pursued by the British, Captain de Cottineau headed down the coast and sought refuge in Cape Lookout Harbor. The British apparently thought the harbor was fortified and did not follow. This was quite fortunate for Captain de Cottineau because he found much to his surprise that the fine harbor was not defended in any way. As he decided to remain at Lookout for a while, he sent ashore part of his crew under an artillery officer, the Chevalier de Cambray, to construct a temporary fort to guard the bay and aid in defending the *Ferdinand* during her stay.

As they worked on their fort at Cape Lookout, the French soon realized a wiser course would be to make contact with officials of the state to obtain assistance and funds to construct a suitable permanent fort for the harbor which would mutually benefit the state, the French, and any other friendly vessels which might use the harbor. Accordingly, de Cottineau and his artillery officer, Captain de Cambray, carrying plans of the proposed fortifications, went to New Bern, then the state capital, and met with Governor Richard Caswell for this purpose. The Governor was shown the plans and told the estimated construction cost was £5000. While Caswell was receptive to the idea of fortifying Cape Lookout, he could do little until the General Assembly met in April and heard the offer. Caswell did order the local militia to help protect the French in the meantime and helped secure £1200 in private subscription to contribute toward the work the French were already doing on the fort.[20]

When the Assembly met in April, 1778, de Cottineau and de Cambray sucessfully petitioned for the establishment of a fort at Cape Lookout. An Act of 23 April 1778, appointed commissioners to establish a fort at Cape Lookout, with the assistance of the French, for a sum of not more than £5000. The Act also provided for one company of fifty-six officers and men to be raised to serve as its garrison. For his part, Captain de Cottineau offered to furnish eighty men and boats to help with construction. He even offered to arm the fort with six 4-pounders and a couple of swivel guns from the *Ferdinand* until the Assembly could furnish heavier armament, preferably 18-pounders as recommended by Captain de Cambray. In return, de Cottineau and de Cambray asked for suitable letters of introduction to the Continental Congress and General George Washington to gain service in the Continental forces. Thus a fort at Cape Lookout, the only one built on the North Carolina coast during the Revolutionary War, came into existence.[21]

The fort came to be called Fort Hancock after Enoch Hancock, who owned the land where it was built. It was located in the sand dunes on Shackleford Banks near a whaling village and looked out over the approach and entrance to Cape Lookout bight. The plan for it drawn up by Captain de Cambray was for a trapezoidal earthwork structure protected by a ditch on its landward sides and containing a garrison house, powder house, and well. Much of the heavy work on the fort was completed in May with the help of Captain de Cottineau's crew. Even after the fort was finished that summer and garrisoned by Captain John Tillman's North Carolina company, the French stayed at Cape Lookout for most of the rest of the year. While Captain de Cottineau was busy disposing of the *Ferdinand's* cargo and trying to obtain commissions for himself and the *Ferdinand* into Continental service, part of his crew was helping to train Tillman's company with the guns the French had supplied to the fort from the *Ferdinand*. Later, Fort Hancock's armament was finally increased with the addition of heavier guns, as the French had recommended earlier in the year. A shipment of heavy cannons purchased by North Carolina from France had arrived at Edenton and in December 1778, North Carolina Governor Richard Caswell ordered eight of these guns (all 18-pounders) to be sent to Fort Hancock. Shortly afterward, Captain de Cottineau and the *Ferdinand* sailed from Cape Lookout at last, bound for other adventures and leaving behind the sand fort they had helped provide for North Carolina.[22]

Fort Hancock now became the sole defense of Cape Lookout. Captain Tillman and his company remained as the garrison for this lonely station for about two years, during which time British warships and privateers operating off the North Carolina coast made no attempt to attack it. In 1780, the demands of the war on other fronts, particularly the Southern Campaign against Lord Charles Cornwallis' British Army, caused the General Assembly to pass an Act on 4 May 1780, which disbanded the Fort Hancock garrison and ordered all its equipment and stores turned in. The fort was abandoned and played no further part in the war.[23]

THE BATTLE OF BEAUFORT

The presence of Fort Hancock about nine miles east of Old Topsail (Beaufort) Inlet may have indirectly benefitted Beaufort by causing the British to generally avoid the area in favor of other portions of the North Carolina coast where little defense would be encountered. But with the abandonment of the fort in June, 1780, Beaufort had no defense for the last two years of the war, other than a small battery mounting four 6-pounders which townspeople had erected to defend the town proper. The inlet continued to be undefended and the harbor was open to any ship which could pass through the inlet.[24]

During 1780-81 Lord Cornwallis' British Army marched from Wilmington, North Carolina to Yorktown, Virginia, surrendering on 19 October 1781 after becoming entrapped by the forces of General George Washington. The surrender of Cornwallis essentially ended the active campaigning of the war and sealed the ultimate victory of American forces. It forced a war-weary Great Britain to take steps toward recognizing American independence and ending the war. Throughout the thirteen former colonies there was jubilation that the war was essentially won and the feeling that life could now return to normal. But leaders reminded their people that the British still held Savannah, Charleston, and New York, and that no cessation of hostilities was in effect. Until the Continental Government and Great Britain negotiated some kind of settlement, the war was still in progress. So it was that early in April, 1782, North Carolina Governor Thomas Burke received information that a "force of four vessels mounting the whole of forty guns and manned with two hundred and fifty seamen is preparing in Charlestown and will sail in a few days. Their object is Beaufort in North Carolina in which they are informed is a large quantity of public and private stores. Should they be repulsed they will proceed to Ocracoke with the same view." The warning did not arrive in time.[25]

On 4 April 1782, the British privateer *Peacock,* commanded by Commodore D. McLean, and two other vessels appeared off Old Topsail Inlet. Posing as friendly ships, they forced the local pilots to guide them into the harbor. The inhabitants of Beaufort became curious when neither the pilots nor any of the men on the ships came ashore. A number of townspeople went out to the ships and did not return, including one who had gone out with a flag of truce. The realization came at last that the strangers were British. Colonel John Easton, the militia commander, gathered up a handful of men and posted them along the shore to watch for landing parties during the night.

At about 2:00 A.M. on 5 April, a landing force commanded by Major Isaac Stuart attempted to sneak ashore but was repulsed by gunfire from the militia. Undaunted, the British came ashore at another location about dawn and drove the militia back to the town battery. Soon Easton was forced to abandon the battery and retired from the town. Beaufort was in British hands as Colonel Easton took up position outside town to await the arrival of more militia troops summoned from the various communities in the area. For the next five days the British plundered Beaufort and skirmished with the militia, which continued to grow in numbers as men from other communities arrived to help contain the invaders. Colonel Easton refrained from attacking to drive them out because he feared the prisoners on the ships might be harmed, and because the British commander threatened to burn the town if he did. A couple of attempts by the British to sent boats to raid other settlements along the adjacent waterways, however, were repulsed with the loss of a few men wounded and a number captured. During this time the rest of the British fleet had joined those in the harbor. On 10 April, the British retired back to their ships with their plunder after spiking the cannons in the town battery. An exchange of prisoners was made that day, although the British refused to release the pilots whom they would need to get out of the harbor.

The militia occupied Beaufort and by morning of the 11th had two of the 6-pounders in the town battery in serviceable condition again. When the British tried to get a prize sloop close to the town underway, the battery opened fire. The British fleet bombarded the town until the battery was silenced. There were no casualties but the incident convinced the British they could not move the sloop and that night they burned her. The British ships remained in the harbor for five more days and during this time two attempts were made to land troops on Shackleford and Bogue Banks to obtain water for the fleet. Each was foiled by the militia sent to the banks to stop them. However, they had the good fortune to capture an American sloop which blundered unknowingly into the occupied harbor and thus made up for the loss of the sloop they had burned. On the night of 15 April, the militia and townspeople tried a different approach to get rid of the invaders. They set two firerafts adrift on the outgoing tide in the hope they would drift into the British fleet. The British were greatly alarmed, but the plan failed because the wind shifted. Still, the incident produced some effect because the next day the British made preparations to put to sea. At 10:00 A.M. on 17 April the fleet passed out of the harbor and through the inlet under a few parting shots fired by the miltia. Once out in the ocean, the remaining prisoners were released and the fleet departed with their prizes and plunder. Thus ended the battle of Beaufort, styled as the last land battle of the Revolutionary War.[26]

The attack on Beaufort awakened the state to the fact the war was indeed still going on. Governor Thomas Burke was afraid the ease of taking Beaufort would encourage the British to attack the more important towns of New Bern and Edenton.[27] However, no such attack took place over the months which followed. It was not until 30 November 1782, that a preliminary peace agreement was signed between America and Britain ending hostilities. Even then, the war did not officially cease until the formal signing of the Treaty of Paris on 3 September 1783, almost two years after the surrender of Cornwallis' army at Yorktown.

2
FORT HAMPTON

The years following the Treaty of Paris witnessed a general trend on the part of the fledgling United States to turn away from the concerns of war and defense toward such important concerns as reorganizing the federal government and restoring of the peacetime economy. The Continental Army was disbanded, the dozens of privateers which had so ably served America as a surrogate navy returned to peacetime trade, and what fortifications had been built were allowed to decay with neglect. Yet this general feeling of apathy toward all things military did not last long. Distant political events and disturbances caused American leaders to reexamine the pitiful state of the new country's defenses in the face of further potential clashes with European powers. The result was the first step toward a national commitment to the defense of the country's coastline against foreign aggression which continued into the Twentieth Century.

THE FIRST SYSTEM

Scarcely a decade had passed since the Treaty of Paris when the United States found itself about to go to war with Great Britain once again. Britain was involved in yet another war with France following the overthrow of the

French monarchy, and followed a policy of seizing all ships trading with France or her colonies. This included American ships, even though the United States proclaimed neutrality and the right to trade equally with both belligerents. Angered by such high-handed British tactics, many Americans demanded a declaration of war. However, memories of the power of the British Navy during the Revolutionary War prompted Congress to proceed cautiously and in January, 1794, a committee was named to examine the state of the country's seacoast defenses. The committee's report two months later showed few of the fortifications existing from the Revolutionary War were still suitable for defense. At least sixteen (later twenty-one) major ports and harbors of the country required the construction of new fortifications. On 20 March 1794, a Congressional Act was passed which provided the funds and means to establish the fortifications system recommended by the committee—the country's first major effort toward national defense. This fortifications system became known simply enough as the First System.[1]

Compared to later efforts, the First System was only a band- aid cure to the problem of national security. In the interest of saving time and expense, few of the forts authorized would be made of permanent materials such as brick and stone. Most were little more than earthen batteries. Lacking a formal military corps of engineers, the Government had to entrust the fulfillment of the program to a number of foreign-born military engineers, mostly Frenchmen. Hardly had the program begun before problems with Britain were largely settled by the signing of the Jay Treaty that same year (1794). Interest in the fortifications might now have languished once the threat was gone had not another international problem developed several years later, this time with France. Irritated by American overtures to its enemy, Britain, and a resumption of cordial trade to that country, France began to carry out a similar campaign of harassing American ships trading with British-controlled ports. The resulting "Quasi-War" with France (1798–1800) escalated to the point of open hostilities, although no formal declaration of war was ever made. As a result, a larger Congressional appropriation of funds was made in 1798 to carry on the work of the First System fortifications.[2]

In North Carolina, two fortifications were authorized under the First

System, one to rebuild old Fort Johnston on the Cape Fear which had been ruined during the Revolutionary War, and the other to erect a new structure to guard Ocracoke Inlet. Some work was done on Fort Johnston but the earthen fort at Ocracoke never progressed beyond the elementary stages before being abandoned as impractical for defense. Beaufort Harbor, meanwhile, was not named as one of the harbors to receive fortifications under the First System. However, only a few years elapsed before this situation changed.[3]

THE SECOND SYSTEM

The beginning of the Napoleonic Wars in 1803 brought great turmoil to Europe and, in turn, to the United States which continued the lucrative practice of trading with both belligerents. As a result, the French and British resumed their harassment of ships trading with each other's ports, regardless of neutrality. The British, who soon gained virtually uncontested control of the seas, were particularly heavy-handed in the seizures of American cargoes. They also impressed men from the crews of American ships into the British Navy, accusing them of being British nationals or deserters. The impressment situation reached a grave level when on 22 June 1807 the British frigate HMS *Leopard* bombarded into surrender the United States frigate USS *Chesapeake* after the latter's commander refused to turn over to the British four of his crewmen accused of being deserters from the British Navy. The American public was outraged and talked of war, but President Thomas Jefferson managed to overt a second war with Britain. Despite this, however, one concrete result of the war talk was renewed consideration of the state of the country's seacoast fortifications.

It was clear that many more harbors and ports than just the few protected under the First System required fortifications in order to provide a more suitable defense system for the nation's seacoast. Some fortifications created under the First System were no longer useable after only thirteen years by virtue of their temporary nature or lack of funds for maintenance. In short, a new and more comprehensive defensive system was needed to secure the maritime frontier of the United States. Plans for such a system were drafted and approved by Congress on 8 January 1808, with the incredible appropriation of one million dollars. The completion, repair or new construction of over fifty fortifications at thirty-six different ports and harbors on the Atlantic and Gulf coasts was ambitiously called for in what became known as the Second System. It was notable that the engineers called upon to design and work on the fortifications were all native-born members of the newly-established Army Corps of Engineers. Also notable was the fact that this system focused on longevity since most of the new fortifications would be constructed of some form of durable masonry instead of the temporary earthen batteries so prevalent in the First System.[4]

As far as North Carolina was concerned, Ocracoke and the Cape Fear River were once again named to receive fortifications. But this time Beaufort was also included, having officially become a United States port of entry in 1803. With the talk of declaring war against Britain following the *Leopard-Chesapeake* Incident in June, 1807, the North Carolina General Assembly took steps to prod the Federal Government into establishing a fort to protect Beaufort even before the Second System was approved by Congress. Later that year, the General Assembly passed a law ceding five acres of land on the west side of Old Topsail (Beaufort) Inlet on Bogue Point to the United States, provided that a fort be built on this parcel for the defense of the inlet within three years. The law also named three commissioners to survey the boundaries of the parcel and forward a plan of it to the office of the Secretary of State. The land was surveyed on 17 December 1807.

The cession of the land expedited the process of establishing a fort. Being a small harbor Beaufort was of secondary importance in the scope of the Second System, but was still entitled to a battery and garrison house for its protection.[5]

THE CONSTRUCTION OF FORT HAMPTON

Early in 1808, the tiny Corps of Engineers assigned its engineers to the various sections of the coast to begin work on the Second System fortifica-

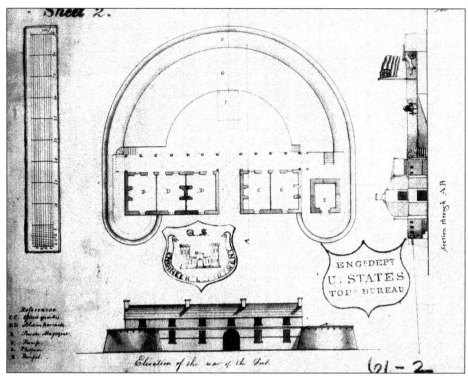

Plan and profiles of Fort Hampton by Major Alexander Macomb, 1808.
National Archives.

tions. Major Alexander Macomb was the engineer officer assigned with several assistants to the coasts of Georgia and the Carolinas. Of the three associates working with him, Captain Charles Gratiot was to superintend work on fortifications in North Carolina. During that summer, Major Macomb and Captain Gratiot arrived at Beaufort and inspected the plot of land on Bogue Point. Here Macomb drafted plans for a small semi-circular battery with a barracks for fifty men and a gunpowder magazine. The barracks and magazine would be brick buildings while the parapet and ramparts of the battery would be made of oyster shell cement called "tapia" or "tabby." In this manner it was possible to rapidly create a simple and cheap fortification. Gratiot was given instructions to purchase his materials in Beaufort and begin work on the fort. In time, this little fortification took the name Fort Hampton in honor of Colonel Andrew Hampton, a North Carolina militia officer, hero of the 8 October 1780 battle of King's Mountain, South Carolina, who had died in 1805.[6]

Captain Gratiot began construction of Fort Hampton in the summer of 1808. His principal civilian contractor was Jechonias Pigott and his work force consisted of local laborers and hired slaves. Materials for the brick buildings were purchased locally. The tapia mixture was made from burned oyster shells, sand, and water poured into wooden forms to create the ramparts.[7] The fort was a horseshoe shape with the barracks building connecting the prongs of the horseshoe to enclose the work from the rear. The fort measured about 122 feet in width and about 93 feet from the rounded crest of the salient to the rear, or outer wall of the barracks building. The tapia parapet was about eight feet high, about twelve feet thick at the bottom, tapering to a thickness of eight feet at the top. Behind the parapet, the gun platform was twenty-three feet wide. The brick gunpowder magazine was about fifteen feet long by fourteen feet wide and was situated in the right prong of the horseshoe. The barracks building was a two-story structure approximately eighty feet long by twenty feet wide with a wide porch and veranda running the length of the building's front. Each story contained three rooms for enlisted mens' quarters and two for officers' quarters.[8]

Fort Hampton was completed some time after June, 1809. In a Congressional report on the various Second System forts of 19 December 1809, it is listed as finished with five cannons (18-pounders) mounted. A Congressional report dated 5 February 1810 lists the cost of construction at $8,863.82. A short time later, the United States purchased an additional six acres and 118 square perches of land from two adjacent landowners, Jonas Small and Joseph Davis, for $200 to enlarge the United States reservation on Bogue Point. The land was conveyed 1 May 1810. Little is known of Fort Hampton's garrisons over the next two years since no post returns are known to exist, but it was occupied by U.S. Regular troops at times prior to the War of 1812. A detachment of the U.S. Rifle Corps under 1st Lieutenant Thomas A. Pateson was known to have been there in 1810.[9]

THE WAR OF 1812

The long-simmering problems between the United States and Great Britain finally erupted into war on 18 June 1812. The people of North Carolina expected immediate attacks from the British Navy. At the beginning of the war, Major General Thomas Pinckney, commanding the Sixth Military District, ordered Forts Johnston and Hampton to each be occupied by four militia companies of infantry or artillery until they could be relieved by troops of the U.S. Regular Army. Major Nathan Tisdale, commanding four militia companies from Lenoir, Craven, Onslow, and Beaufort Counties, arrived at Beaufort at the beginning of August, 1812. This force occupied Beaufort and Fort Hampton. Two coastal gunboats were also placed on duty temporarily. However, by September, the failure of any British threat to the coast prompted General Pinckney to order two of Major Tisdale's militia companies to be disbanded and the gunboats reassigned. In November, the company of Captain Joseph Bryant, 10th U.S. Infantry, arrived to relieve Major Tisdale's militia at Fort Hampton and afterward the militia was disbanded.[10]

In the meantime, the British established a naval blockade against Charleston and Chesapeake Bay, causing the diversion of shipping to the North Carolina ports. Just as in the Revolutionary War, Beaufort flourished under this busy maritime commerce. Cargoes brought into the port were transported by inland water routes through the sounds and the Dismal Swamp Canal to Norfolk, or southward to Charleston. Privateers also brought many prizes into the port. All the while, the guns of Fort Hampton provided a security Beaufort had never known during a time of war.[11]

It was almost a year before the British Navy posed any serious threat to the North Carolina coast. But as more American ships utilized North Carolina ports British attention was drawn there as well. During the early part of

1813, British warships and privateers appeared with increasing frequency off the North Carolina coast, attacking shipping and occasionally landing on the Outer Banks to take provisions. By May, 1813, they were frequently appearing off Beaufort, harassing the shipping but never attempting to provoke an engagement with Fort Hampton. Still, fearing the British might somehow force their way through Ocracoke or Old Topsail (Beaufort) Inlet, North Carolina congressmen pressed the Secretary of the Navy for gunboats to defend those inlets. On 14 June 1813, the Secretary of the Navy promised one gunboat for Beaufort, two for Ocracoke, and an additional two for Wilmington, although in actuality, they did not appear until the following year.[12] As it turned out, there was little available for defense when the largest British effort of the war against the North Carolina coast took place only one month later, echoing the worst fears of North Carolina congressmen.

On the night of 11 July 1813, a British squadron of one 74-gun ship of the line, four frigates, two brigs, two schooners, some smaller vessels, and sixty to seventy troop barges arrived off Ocracoke Inlet. Under Admiral Sir George Cockburn, it numbered about 2,500 infantry, sailors, and marines. At daybreak on the 12th, nineteen barges from the fleet, each carrying an 18-pounder carronade and about forty men, crossed the swash of Ocracoke Inlet into the harbor and sound. Firing carronades and Congreve rockets, they quickly attacked and captured two American privateers anchored in the channel. A revenue cutter narrowly escaped up the Neuse River to give the alarm. With the harbor secured, the British occupied Ocracoke and Portsmouth, setting up an encampment for 700 to 1,400 men, supported in the sound by two brigs and two schooners. For the next few days they raided the adjacent area, taking large amounts of livestock and supplies.[13]

The size of the British squadron, the large number of soldiers camped on the banks, and the large number of shallow draft vessels available to make expeditions into the adjacent sounds and rivers, all gave indications of a lengthy British stay. From Ocracoke they could easily reach out to threaten the towns along Pamlico and Albemarle Sounds, and would certainly proceed up the Neuse River to New Bern. Beaufort could easily be threatened and operations could also be conducted against Wilmington. The magnitude of the threat was such that North Carolina Governor William Hawkins called out the state militia on 17 July and ordered its units to converge on the various coastal towns to defend them. Orders were given to buy up and forward all available supplies of powder, lead, and flints for use in repelling the expected invasion. He and his entourage then personally accompanied a militia unit from Raleigh on a march to New Bern to view the situation firsthand.[14]

Meanwhile at Beaufort, preparations were made for what was considered an inevitable attack. Important papers and various stores and valued items were sent away for safety, some of the noncombatants fled to the interior, several thousand small arms cartridges were made, breastworks were thrown up, and cannons to defend them were brought ashore from vessels in the harbor. Over at Fort Hampton, Captain Joseph Bryant, commanding the small detachment of U.S. Infantry stationed there, felt very uneasy and isolated. Perhaps knowing too well the limitations of the fort, he apparently did not believe it would stand up to a British attack. So disheartened was he that he had steels made up for spiking the fort's guns should it appear the British would take the fort. He expected support from the local militia but no orders were given to this effect. The militia did not go over to the fort to help defend it, although forty men from a local militia company finally volunteered to provide assistance. At the same time, while still in the midst of the crisis, Bryant and his company received orders directing them elsewhere. They evacuated the fort before being relieved, leaving behind a few men to look after the property in the fort. Fortunately, as the various state militia units called up by Governor Hawkins began to arrive to take station at the coast, the militia artillery company of Captain Abner Pasteur was sent to man Fort Hampton. This company, along with an infantry company stationed in Beaufort, both of which were commanded by Major Nathan Tisdale, secured against any movement of the British toward the area.[15]

Fortunately for the state, the British reembarked their men and departed from Ocracoke on 16 July without attempting any further forays into the interior of the coastal area. Taking their provisions and prizes with them, they were actually at sea before Governor Hawkins even learned of their raid and called out the militia. Some of the militia companies, including Major Tisdale's two at Beaufort and Fort Hampton, were retained in the event the British squadron attempted to attack at some other point along the coast.[16]

In the meantime, Governor Hawkins left New Bern on 30 July to see for himself the condition of the State's coast defenses. The situation he found at Beaufort Harbor was not to his liking. He described Fort Hampton as "nothing more than a parapet composed of shells and lime badly cemented, each end of which is connected with the barracks, in the rear by a wall about two feet thick." Concerning the armament, Hawkins described a serious situation:

> "There are only six long 18's (18-pounders) mounted on a platform at the parapet to fire *en barbette*. Those guns were mounted on very low carriages, and in order that they might fire over the parapet, the platform had been raised within two feet of its top: consequently the men when managing them were exposed from about their knees up. Their situation would have been much more dangerous in an action than if they had been in an open plain, as much destruction might have been produced by the shells which the enemy's fire might scale from the top of the parapet. Conceiving that no time should be lost in making the necessary alterations, I instructed Captain Pasteur to have the carriages of the guns raised and the platform lowered, in such a manner as that but few of the men in an engagement should be exposed."

Nor was this the only problem encountered. Hawkins wrote further:

> "This place with an inconsiderable sum compared to that already expended upon it might be made a strong fortification. In its present situation it might be easily reduced. A number of men not much larger than that stationed in the fort by landing below out of the reach of the guns of the parapet might march round, attack and carry it in the rear without much difficulty."[17]

In addition, he found that enemy barges could pass close to Shackleford Point on the opposite side of the inlet out of range of Hampton's guns and still enter the harbor. Works on Shackleford Banks would be needed to prevent this.

Over the months following the July "invasion", Governor Hawkins wrote a number of letters criticizing the lack of effort put forward by the U.S. Government to fulfill its obligation to adequately defend the North Carolina coast. The Federal Government had lagged in providing for the state's militia forces, in providing suitable quantities of weapons and munitions, in providing the gunboats for coastal defense promised early in the summer, and in not keeping its forts adequately manned and in proper condition to offer maximum resistance.[18] Conditions improved slowly. The gunboats promised by the Secretary of the Navy in June, 1813, did not become operational at their stations until 1814. Governor Hawkins' complaints about the conditions of the coastal fortifications finally resulted in an inspection of them by Lieutenant Colonel W. K. Armistead of the Corps of Engineers in January, 1814. Armistead's recommendations for Fort Hampton echoed those of Hawkins. He reported the need for more substantial gun carriages for the armament, enlarging the fort to provide more defense in front and rear, and erecting a strong stockade in the rear. The alterations would cost $4,000–5,000, about half the fort's original cost, and they were never done.[19] Meanwhile, the militia company defending Fort Hampton since July, 1813, was finally relieved by the arrival of regular U.S. troops in April of 1814, at which time 180 men commanded by Lieutenant John S. Smallwood, 43rd U.S. Infantry, became the fort's garrison.[20]

For the remainder of 1814, British warships continued to operate off the North Carolina coast, occasionally capturing American shipping and conducting small raids ashore. Other than harassing American shipping off Beaufort and Cape Lookout, they avoided contact in this area with one exception. On 16 July 1814, the British sloop *Peacock* appeared off Cape Lookout and then off Beaufort, capturing pilots at both places by tricking them into thinking she was a friendly vessel. The British surveyed Fort Hampton and inquired about the size of the forces stationed there and at Beaufort. The warship's captain then stated his intention to return with a large fleet at a later date and attack. On the following day, a landing party was sent ashore to take provisions at Cape Lookout. News of this quickly reached Beaufort and the militia was sent over to the cape. The militiamen lay in wait as a landing party again put out from the *Peacock* on the morning of 8 July. However, the British detected the militia waiting to ambush them as they come ashore. An exchange of gunfire resulted in no loss to either side and the British narrowly made their escape back to the *Peacock,* which then departed. Contrary to the threat made by the *Peacock's* captain, the British never returned to attack Fort Hampton and Beaufort.[21] Not long afterward the War of 1812 came to an end. In February, 1815, word was received that back on 14 December 1814, the United States and Great Britain had signed the Treaty of Ghent, ending the war.

THE END OF FORT HAMPTON

Following the end of the War of 1812, the U.S. Army went through a period of readjustment. It was not feasible to keep every fort and military post fully occupied by troops and Fort Hampton was one of the forts to have its garrison reduced. In the reduction of the Army in 1815, one company of the Corps of Artillery was assigned to garrison both Forts Johnston and Hampton.[22] This was subsequently reduced further. During 1818 and 1819, only a ten-man detachment of the Second Battalion , Corps of Artillery, commanded by Lieutenant N. G. Wilkinson looked after both forts[23]. Thereafter, Fort Hampton was totally abandoned. In 1820, two engineer officers, Brig. Gen. Simon Bernard and Captain William T. Poussin, visited Bogue Point and the old fort with a view toward planning future defenses for Beaufort Inlet. Poussin drafted a plan and profile of the fort showing its condition but it was clear that Fort Hampton's role in any future defenses for Beaufort Harbor would be minor at best[24]. As with many of the fortifications of the Second System, the hurried nature of its construction and the cheap materials used made it not worth the effort and expense necessary to upgrade and modify it into a more effective fortification. It was more economically feasible to erect a completely new structure and that is what the engineers intended to do.

Although never attacked by British warships, Fort Hampton faced a battle with an enemy of a different nature. Since the fort had been built, Beaufort Inlet had been gradually widening with the sea creeping ever closer to its walls. Poussin's map of 1820 showed the high tide mark by that year had reached to the very foot of the rampart. Two other maps of Beaufort Harbor drafted the following year showed the fort occupying a small peninsula of land jutting precariously out into the inlet.[25] The fort was on the verge of being taken by the sea. Over the next several years the sea advanced even closer and in 1825, Fort Hampton was washed away at last. Local tradition claims it disappeared overnight in a summer storm. What is known is that on 3-4 June 1825, an early-season hurricane ravaged the North Carolina coast and was most likely the storm responsible for the end of Fort Hampton. By February, 1826, the high tide mark at Bogue Point stood more than 200 feet inland of where the little fort had once stood.[26] The fort had disappeared completely and no identifiable part of it has ever been found other than the occasional pieces of well-worn brick that wash up on the beach around Fort Macon which may have once been part of Fort Hampton's walls.

3

CONSTRUCTION OF FORT MACON

    The United States had learned a number of hard lessons in the War of 1812, among them was the continued inadequacy of her seacoast fortifications. In some instances American forts had given a good account of themselves, such as the repulse of British warships by Fort McHenry in Baltimore, Fort Bowyer at Mobile Bay, and Fort St. Philip on the Mississippi River. In other instances they had not, such as the failure of Fort Washington to prevent the British from ascending the Potomac River to capture and plunder Alexandria, Virginia. In still other instances, the lack of defenses at certain points left important areas exposed and open to exploitation by an enemy for operational and staging purposes. The British Navy gained control of Chesapeake Bay, for instance, which gave it a foothold from which to mount expeditions against other points. Vast changes were necessary in the national system of seacoast defense. A well-planned and comprehensive system of strong permanent fortifications was needed which would 1) protect *all* important ports, cities, and military bases on the coast; 2) supplement the Navy and at the same time free it for offensive purposes; and 3) provide a mutually supporting chain of coastal defense to deny an enemy the establishment of a foothold or base on the coast from which to conduct operations. In contrast to the hastily prepared, cheaply built forts prevalent with the previous systems, what was needed was a new system of well-constructed, permanent fortifications. They should incorporate the latest principles of fortification design and be able to sustain themselves in battle or under siege for specific periods of time. It was recognized that such a system of permanent fortifications would be costly and require many years to complete, but the European powers had been engaged in building similar defensive systems for decades. It was also recognized that the United States should begin such a program now, in a period of peace, rather than in the hurried anticipation of war.

THE THIRD SYSTEM

The "Third System" of fortifications began soon after the close of the War of 1812. Instead of beginning as the last two systems had by sending individual Army engineers out to far-flung sections of the coast to design and build forts themselves with only general principals to guide them, the Third System started on 16 November 1816 with the creation of a Board of Fortifications. This board's purpose was to reconnoiter and evaluate defensive sites on the coast, plan and design the fortifications to defend them, coordinate the system of forts with the operational framework of the Army and Navy, and determine a plan for their mutual support, with the establishment of lines of communication in the interior for the movement of troops, supplies, and commerce. To find a head for this board the United States turned to France, the country most innovative in the art of fortifications. Here they obtained the services of a French engineer of great reputation in Europe, Simon Bernard. Bernard, a former aide-de-camp to Napoleon I, was brought to the United States in 1816 and given a brigadier general's commission to head the new Board of Fortifications.[1] Between 1817 and 1821 reconnaissances of the coast were made to evaluate and choose sites and plan the forts which would occupy them. Many of the reconnaissance surveys and fort designs were done by General Bernard himself, assisted by a fellow French-born officer of the Topographical Engineers, Captain William Tell Poussin, who served as cartographer and draftsman.

The forts which were the product of Bernard's Board of Fortifications, though possessing their own individuality, all had certain basic principals. They would be constructed of durable brick and stone, possess heavy armament, utilize vaulted bombproof casemates to shelter their garrisons, magazines and supplies, be sufficiently strong to resist a fleet of enemy warships or an open assault by enemy land forces, and be capable of resisting a siege for between ten and fifty days, sufficient time for friendly outside forces to be massed to break the siege. As for the size and number of guns used with individual forts, these tended to increase proportionately with the size and importance of harbors they were to defend. The ranking of forts in importance and a determination of which forts were to be built first was done by a priority rating system that consisted of three classes. First Class forts constituted those which would protect the primary ports or areas which were considered as requiring immediate defense. Second Class forts would defend ports of secondary importance or places which already had some measure of protection. These were judged to be less pressing and were to wait until First Class forts were completed. Third Class forts constituted all other forts and defenses necessary to complete the comprehensive defense system.

As construction of the various forts of the new system got underway and continued over the years which followed, two distinct influences manifested themselves in the designs of the various forts. The first forts, planned and built up to the late 1820s tended to be one story structures, relying heavily on the surrounding ground to shield their walls from the direct fire of siege guns. They also utilized large bastions, covertways, and similar elaborate measures to provide flanking defense against assault. Armament tended to be mounted as a barbette tier or a combination of barbette and single casemate tiers. From the late 1820s onward, however, "perpendicular" fortifications became the chief reliance of the Third System. They were heavily influenced by the theories of French engineer Marc-René Marquis de Montalembert, which gained widespread acceptance in America. Perpendicular fortifications used multi-story forts built above ground level with multiple tiers of cannons firing through the embrasures of their casemates in addition to the barbette tier on the top. Such forts could generate enormous amounts of firepower from their massed tiers. Both types of forts had their advantages and disadvantages, but collectively they constituted an awesome defensive system and stood as masterpieces of the military art of their day. Work began on the first forts of the Third System in 1818 and continued past the end of the Civil War almost fifty years later. Thirty-eight new-construction forts would be built or begun on all three coasts, along with a number of forts from the earlier systems which were modified and upgraded for inclusion into the system. One of the new-construction forts was slated for Beaufort Inlet to replace Fort Hampton. It was considered a Second Class fort to be built after the First Class forts had been completed. Initially known as the "Fort on Bogue Point", in time it became known as Fort Macon.

THE FORT ON BOGUE POINT

In 1820, Brigadier General Simon Bernard and his cartographer, Captain William T. Poussin, made a reconnaissance of Beaufort Harbor. They took notes, measurements, and surveys of the area to determine a site and design for the new fort to replace Fort Hampton. With information from the survey, Bernard designed a fort which Poussin drafted into two maps in 1821, one being a plan and the other showing profiles and sections.[2] The fort would be an irregular pentagon shape with a perimeter of 271 yards, measured on the scarp wall of its main work, or citadel. As was typical of early Third System forts, it would have one story and be constructed low in the ground with a wide earth glacis and covertway protecting its walls from direct fire. Not typical was the fact the covertway completely encircled the main work, which was more in keeping with classical European fortifications. The main armament would fire from both the citadel and covertway and be mounted *en barbette* since the presence of the covertway masked any guns firing though casemate embrasures in the scarp. The perimeter of the covertway was 440.3 yards. Of the five fronts, the first three formed the main battery. Front I faced ships coming over the bar into Old Topsail (Beau-

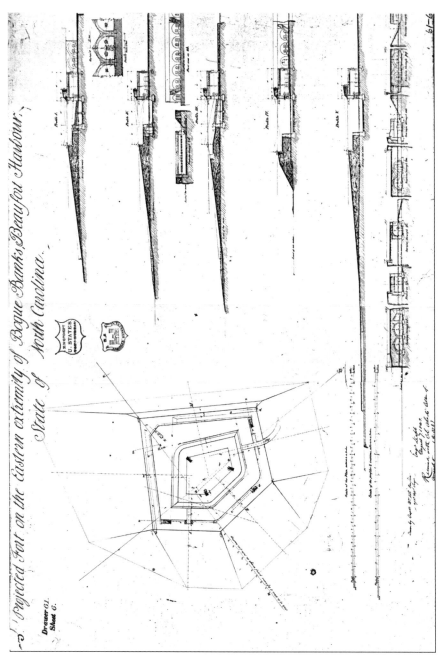

Original Bernard survey map showing plans and profiles of the "Projected Fort on the eastern extremity of Bogue Banks, Beaufort Harbour, State of North Carolina."

National Archives.

fort) Inlet. Front II faced not only the main channel passing through the inlet, but also the intersections of channels from the sound between Shackleford Banks and Beaufort with the main channel. Front III commanded Beaufort Harbor and the entrance into Bogue Sound. The two remaining fronts, IV and V, simply formed a right angle to enclose the work on its landward side.

With the fort built low in the ground, defense against assault was critical since the glacis provided a ready-made ramp for storming parties to rush up to the covertway. Accordingly, the covertway and citadel would be separated by a floodable ditch thirty-six feet wide to pose an obstacle to the enemy. Flanking defense for the ditch would be accomplished by defensive galleries under the covertway for reverse, or counter, fire through the counterscarp wall. Normally, the use of bastions was the usual way of providing flanking defense for a fort, but in this case they were not practical. Bastions required a great deal of land area, which was simply not available on narrow Bogue Point. Also, they were expensive to build, and such an expense could not be justified for a small fort guarding only a secondary port. Instead, four sets of counterfire galleries, loopholed for musketry, would be sufficient to sweep the avenues of the fort's ditch in conjunction with fire from carronades and musketry from the casemates of the citadel. For the two avenues of the fort's landward faces, the ones most likely to be assaulted, double counterfire galleries would generate additional firepower at the angle where they met. To accommodate the double galleries in the counterscarp wall, the ditch was widened out to sixty-two feet at this angle.

Entrance to the citadel was via a single roadway which cut through the glacis and counterscarp on the fort's least vulnerable side, Front III, facing Beaufort Harbor. A draw bridge would be used to provide access over the ditch to the sally port of the citadel. To prevent the roadway from funneling enemy cannonballs directly into the gate of the sally port, the roadway curved as it passed through the glacis. A postern with a second draw bridge was located on Front I of the citadel to provide additional access to the seaward guns on the covertway. Inside the citadel would be twenty-six bombproof casemates, with three magazines and five smaller storage rooms located at angles of the scarp and parade walls. The magazines and water cisterns would be shielded from enemy fire by three massive stone stairways which provided access from the parade to the terreplein above.

As Third System forts went, Fort Macon was considered small when judged by its intended armament of thirty-eight guns and howitzers, four mortars, and eight carronades firing from the casemates. Its intended garrison was to be 20 soldiers in time of peace, 150 in time of war, and 280 to resist assault.[3]

After completion, the plans were filed away for future use. Under the ranking established by the Board of Engineers the fort on Bogue Point was considered as a Second Class fort, since Beaufort was considered a secondary port. Because it was the policy of the Board to finish the forts with First Class ranking before commencing any Second Class forts, it seemed likely that many years would pass before work would commence on Bogue Point. At least that was how the Board's priority system was supposed to work. However, even in those days, politics sometimes tended to change the way procedures really worked.

EARLY PROBLEMS

By 1824, construction on nine of the First Class forts was underway. With growing impatience, however, North Carolina political leaders noted that nothing had been said by the Army concerning the two Third System forts intended for the North Carolina coast, the Bogue Point fort and a second fort intended for Oak Island to guard the mouth of the Cape Fear River. When the Secretary of War submitted to Congress his funding estimates needed for fortifications for the year 1825, there was still no mention of the two proposed North Carolina forts. North Carolina's eminent elder statesman, Senator Nathaniel Macon, became concerned that North Carolina was once again being ignored by the Federal Government. Although both forts had been rated Second Class by the Board of Fortifications, Macon and other North Carolina Congressmen felt otherwise and desired some kind of commitment toward their construction in the near

Nathaniel Macon (1758–1837)
North Carolina State Archives

future. On 20 January 1825, Senator Macon wrote Secretary of War John C. Calhoun requesting that cost estimates for these two forts be submitted to Congress for the fortifications appropriations bill for 1825. Secretary Calhoun replied the following day that when the appropriations bill had been submitted to Congress the cost estimates for the two North Carolina forts had not yet been worked up by the Engineer Department. Since that time, however, the estimates had been received and amounted to $175,000 for the fort on Bogue Point and $251,000 for the fort on Oak Island. It was now too late for the War Department to add these estimates in on the appropriations bill since it had already been reported to the House of Representatives by the Way and Means Committee. However, as Secretary Calhoun suggested, Senator Macon was free to submit separate legislation or amendments on this subject to have these forts included for appropriations. He recommended an initial appropriation of $30,000 for the Bogue Point fort and $50,000 for the Oak Island fort. He also pointed out, though, that even if Macon succeeded in this, all of the handful of officers comprising the Corps of Engineers were already assigned to other forts or projects and could not be taken from their present duties to commence two new forts.[4]

Regardless of whether engineers were available, Macon knew that obtaining the appropriations was the first step toward constructing these forts. He had North Carolina Congressman Romulus Saunders propose an amendment to the fortifications bill when it came up in the House of Representatives on 8 February 1825, that the recommended sums of money be included for forts on Bogue Point and Oak Island. After some discussion, however, the opponents of the amendment argued against starting new forts when the ones already under construction were not finished. They saw nothing so pressing and vital to defend on the North Carolina coast at this time as to warrant beginning these new forts. Consequently, the amendment was voted down. On 21 February, the appropriations bill came up in the Senate, where Senator Macon and others supporting him argued convincingly for an amendment to the bill to grant the sums of $30,000 to the fort on Bogue Point and $50,000 to the fort on Oak Island. Their arguments were successful and the measure passed by a margin of twenty-nine to eleven. On 23 February, the bill was sent to the House for approval. This time North Carolina Congressmen and their supporters eloquently overcame the opposition as to the need for the two forts. Particularly persuasive was the view of the Chairman of the Commerce Committee that all coasting trade of the Union, whether using the coastwise trade routes or inland trade routes through the sounds and canals, had to pass the North Carolina coast where it might easily be disrupted by an enemy in time of war if not properly defended. As a result, the amendment was approved by a margin of eighty-two to thirty-three. Thus, contrary to the policy that all First Class forts must be completed before any Second Class forts were begun, North Carolina secured the money to begin her two Third System forts. All that remained was the purchase of the land at each fort site and to obtain an Army engineer to begin these projects.[5]

Five months passed where nothing could be done on the North Carolina forts because all the officers of the Corps of Engineers were busy with other projects. During the summer, however, the slowing of construction activities on forts in the Gulf of Mexico due to heat freed Engineer Lieutenant Stephen Tuttle for transfer to North Carolina. In July, 1825, Tuttle arrived in North Carolina and had land purchased on Oak Island where the fort to guard the mouth of the Cape Fear River would be constructed. After completing preliminary site work, Tuttle continued on to Beaufort in September to similarly purchase land on Bogue Point for the new fort adjacent to the existing Government reservation. Here he ran into trouble. The owners of the more than 400 acres comprising the eastern end of Bogue Banks which the Government deemed necessary as a suitable reservation for the new fort refused to come to terms to sell. Tuttle did what preliminary surveys he could and returned to Oak Island to proceed with the construction of that fort.[6]

In the meantime, the Engineer Department realized the need for separate engineer officers to oversee the Oak Island and Bogue Point projects. As a result, Lieutenant Tuttle remained at Oak Island while another engineer was found for Bogue Point. The choice for the latter site was Lieutenant William A. Eliason, who had served for three years as the assistant engineer at Fort Monroe, Virginia. Eliason arrived at Beaufort on 2 November 1825 to begin his new duties. On the following day he wrote a letter to the Chief of Engineers reporting his arrival and at the end gave what appears to be the first mention in official correspondence of the name which the Army had chosen for the fort on Bogue Point: "It is respectfully suggested that my address be at Fort Macon, Beaufort Harbour, NC." The new fort was named after Senator Macon, he man whose influence in Congress had been instrumental in obtaining the appropriations necessary to begin construction of the two North Carolina forts many years ahead of the War Department's schedule.[7]

Lieutenant Eliason faced several problems immediately upon his arrival. First, his initial attempts to settle with the local landowners for the tract of land comprising the eastern end of Bogue Banks where Fort Macon and its reservation were to be established met with no more success than had those of Lieutenant Tuttle some weeks earlier. At least two of the owners seemed determined to inflate the price of their parcels beyond what was deemed fair market value. Fortunately for Eliason, the issue was quickly taken up by higher authority. The failure of the local landowners on Bogue Point to cooperate with the Government over the purchase of the several parcels prompted the War Department to request that North Carolina Governor H. C. Burton act to condemn the land and cede it to the U.S. Government. Accordingly, late in November of 1825, the North Carolina General Assembly began the necessary legislation and on 4 January 1826, passed an act ceding 405.59 acres of land on Bogue Point to the United States. The landowners were now obligated to sell. They would be offered a fair price as well as retain fishing rights to the land. Thus for the time being, yet another problem had been put to rest.[8]

Another problem was Eliason's illness which kept him confined to bed for much of the month of December and consumed valuable time needed to advertise contracts and other preliminary work. Just before the New Year he was finally able to put together advertisements for contracts to supply three million bricks, 14,000 perches of building stone, and other materials which he placed with the local New Bern newspaper as well as newspapers in Washington, DC, Baltimore, Philadelphia, New York, Norfolk, Richmond, and Boston. He also advertised in the New Bern paper, appealing to the owners of slaves to hire them out to work during the year, as 100 to 150 laborers would be needed to work on the fort on Bogue Point. He offered the owners a wage of forty cents per day worked for each slave. Meanwhile, proposals for materials were received and opened on 16 March 1826. Of those received, Eliason chose the bid of Andrew Way of Washington, DC, to provide the stone at $3.98 per perch. He also chose for his brick bid the proposal of Thomas Crown, also of Washington, DC, to provide three million bricks at $9.00 per thousand. Crown already held a brick contract for the fort at Oak Island.[9]

Yet another problem of which Eliason may or may not have been aware was the effort in the U.S. House of Representatives of a Pennsylvania Congressman to delete in the annual fortifications appropriations bill a sum of $25,000 appropriated for Fort Macon for the year 1826. The same old opposition arguments of the previous year resurfaced as to why Beaufort Harbor needed a fort and why should Second or Third Class forts be started before First Class forts were finished. North Carolina Congressman John H. Bryan led the successful rebuttal which reiterated the importance of a fort at Beaufort, and the folly of halting further funding when an engineer was waiting on site for construction to commence. The opposition argument collapsed and the appropriation of $25,000 for Fort Macon for the year 1826 remained intact.[10]

By and large the most serious problem affecting the construction of Fort Macon was the severe erosion of Bogue Point which, in addition to Fort Hampton, had claimed much of the site on which General Bernard and the Board of Fortifications had chosen to build the new fort. The fort originally would have been only about 100 feet southwest of Fort Hampton, but most of the chosen site had already eroded. In fact, local residents told Eliason that Bogue Point had eroded as much as one-quarter of a mile in the past ten years. Indeed it was clear an entirely new site project would have to be commenced. Eliason was delayed from making the necessary surveys of other possible sites until his instruments arrived early in February, 1826. Further delays were encountered due to bad weather and a revised evaluation of the site was not available until late March. What he found was that the site for the new fort had to be moved about 600 feet west of the site chosen as a result of General Bernard's original survey.[11]

Eliason also began the task of working up a comprehensive "memoir" which analyzed every material and cost which would be associated with constructing the fort. Costs were figured into fractions of cents. For instance, he calculated a common laborer could excavate and throw into a wheelbarrow fifteen cubic yards of earth during a ten-hour work day at a wage of one dollar a day. Thus fifteen cubic yards of earth could be said to cost one dollar and a single cubic yard 6.7 cents. A second laborer at the same wage would be able to transport the fifteen cubic yards of earth in a ten-hour work day for the same cost. Thus the combined cost of one man to excavate and another to haul each cubic yard of earth would be 13.4 cents. Similarly, he calculated a brick mason would lay about three cubic yards of masonry (about 1,200 bricks) in a ten-hour work day at a daily wage of $2.50, thus making the cost of a cubic yard of masonry 83.3 cents. Wear and tear on such tools as laborers' spades and rammers were even figured at 2.388 cents per cubic yard.

The cost of creating each physical feature of the fort was likewise calculated in exacting detail. A square yard of heart yellow pine flooring two inches thick with joists he figured as costing $1.557, including dressing and framing. The cost of making each window for casemate quarters, complete with painting, weights, and hardware would be $25.145. A pair of shutters for each window, complete with painting and hardware, would cost $8.50 to make. A six-panel door for the casemate quarters would be made for $16, including hinges, lock, and painting. Twenty-eight cannon embrasures were needed in the casemates at a cost of $50 each. Twenty fireplaces and chimneys were needed at a cost of $80 each. Two bridges would cost $215 each, while three hot shot furnaces would cost $300 each. Such were a few of the individual expenses Eliason could expect to encounter in constructing the fort.[12]

Even though Fort Macon was considered a small fort, the amount of materials and work necessary for its construction were staggering. Eliason calculated the amount of earth necessary to form the fill above the casemates, in the parade ground, on the terrepleins, and on the surrounding glacis would be 115,688.252 cubic yards, of which the glacis alone would require 100,576 cubic yards. Part of this fill, 17,313 cubic yards, would be supplied when the laborers dug the excavations for the five ditches and the pits for the foundations of all the walls and casemates. The dirt from the foundations could be thrown outward onto the glacis. The rest would have to be supplied from the neighboring marshes and excavation sites. The foundations would require 11,979.011 cubic yards of stone masonry. The number of bricks required for the walls and arches was 9,180,927. Also, 290 tons of brownstone, known as Connecticut Freestone, was required for steps, cordon, and coping. The amount of yellow pine plank to form the flooring of the casemates was 2,040 square yards. All in all, Eliason's total figures for the projected fort on Bogue Point broke down as follows:

Cost of masonry $173,281.905
Cost of carpentry $4,835.180
Cost of embankments and fill $43,394.05
Other expenses (embrasures,
furnaces, fireplaces, loopholes, etc.) $3,961.500
Unforeseen expenses $4,527.365

$230,000.000[13]

This was the projected cost of the fort as it was originally planned by the Board of Fortifications. Almost immediately, however, changes were proposed to the original plan. After some consideration and correspondence, the Board of Fortifications decided against incurring the expense of a stone foundation for the fort, opting for a timber foundation instead. The footings of the walls would rest on a timber crib work consisting of a double layer of two-inch plank. Eliason also found it necessary to adjust the amount of cubic yardage of earth excavation and fill. Without using a stone foundation, less excavation would be necessary for foundation pits (a total of 12,011 cubic yards). However, he found it necessary to alter the glacis profiles so that more fill and turf (a total of 149,891 cubic yards) were needed. In all, the amount of excavations for the work was increased to 167,652 cubic yards. These changes likewise changed the cost estimates for the fort as follows:

Cost of embankments and fill $70,224.064
Cost of masonry $135,357.820
Cost of carpentry $3,699.000

Other expenses $6,800.000

Unforeseen expenses and contingencies $3,919.116

$220,000.000[14]

Meanwhile, in Washington, DC, the news of the heavy erosion at Bogue Point caused great concern with the Chief of Engineers, Major General Alexander Macomb, and the members of the Board of Fortifications. Obviously, there was little point in starting construction on a new fort as long as

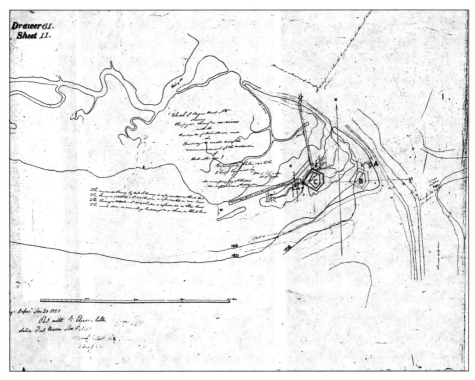

Engineer drawing showing shoreline changes to Bogue Point, 1821–28. Fort Hampton is marked A; original site of Fort Macon is marked B; final site of Fort Macon is marked C.
National Archives

the figure of Bogue Point was undergoing rapid change from encroachment of the sea. There was so much concern that in May, 1826, Lieutenant
Eliason was ordered to come to Washington and personally describe the
extent of the erosion problem. He did so and stayed for a few weeks to
confer on the problem and its potential effect on the construction of Fort
Macon. On 1 July, he was finally given instructions to return and commence
work on the fort but to do so according to instructions from General Bernard, with which he was furnished. In the instructions, Eliason was allowed
to proceed with the construction but only with extreme caution, taking
time to observe the encroachment of the sea toward the new site. Should
the encroachment continue, he was to report whatever steps might be necessary to counteract the erosion and preserve the site. Thus it might become necessary for the Engineer Department to take on the preservation
of the site of Fort Macon as a second and completely different project,
entirely separate from the construction of the fort itself.[15]

For Eliason, the prospect of proceeding cautiously was a limiting factor in the construction of the fort. He could not enter into long-term contracts for materials knowing that at any moment he might have to stop the
project. As a result he was forced to disengage from the contract arrangements for materials he had made in March as a result of his newspaper ads.
His plans for commencing Fort Macon now centered on first using laborers to dig a canal connecting the sound with the construction site, and
then to commence the embankments forming the glacis around the fort.
At the same time, the carpentry force could be engaged in constructing
buildings and equipment. This would consume most of the year 1826 and
provide time to continue studying the erosion problem. Before returning
to North Carolina, he journeyed to Baltimore later in July, where he purchased implements and provisions, and arranged for their shipment to
Beaufort. On 26 July Eliason returned to Beaufort.[16]

In August, 1826, work on Fort Macon formally commenced. Carpenters built accommodations for the workmen, storage sheds, wheelbarrows,
and lighters for an estimated 150 laborers. The supplies and implements

ordered from Baltimore by Eliason arrived at Beaufort by ship and were brought over to the site. Laborers were enrolled beginning on 21 August and were put to work digging a canal from Bogue Sound to the fort site. Earth removed from the canal was used either to form a towing road alongside or to begin the embankments of the glacis. Work continued in this way over the next few weeks, during which time Eliason also commenced a suitable wharf on Bogue Sound equipped with a cargo crane so that vessels carrying supplies and materials could easily be unloaded.[17]

In addition to the construction and concerns for the stability of Bogue Point, one additional concern claimed part of Eliason's attention during the fall of 1826. In the beginning of that year the North Carolina General Assembly had condemned a total of 405.59 acres on Bogue Point by Legislative Act to provide the U.S. military reservation for Fort Macon with the stipulation that the owners of this land would be fairly compensated. Unfortunately, the landowners and the U.S. Government were still unable to reach an agreement as to what constituted a "fair price". The Act which ceded the land to the U.S. Government, however, contained a provision to deal with such a deadlock. The U.S. Attorney for the North Carolina district was to requisition the land from the Governor, who would in turn request a writ of *venire facias* be issued from the North Carolina Supreme Court of Law and Equity to the sheriff of Carteret County, in which the land was situated. The sheriff would have to summon twenty-four freeholders of the county and select eighteen of them by lot to form a jury to value the land. Their valuation would be final and would serve as the amount awarded to the landowners.[18]

This procedure was carried out to settle the claims and during September, the jury of freeholders valued the land at a total of $1,287. Eliason then submitted this judgement to the Engineer Department for approval and payment. Afterward the 1826 North Carolina General Assembly appointed a committee to distribute to each landowner his proper share of the judgement. The land dispute was thus settled at last.[19]

CONSTRUCTION PROCEEDS

During the winter of 1826–27 and spring of 1827, construction on the fort proceeded smoothly. Workers dug the canal from the sound, formed some of the embankments of the glacis, and excavated the ditches of the work. Also during 1827, work began on a large, two-story house about one-third of a mile from the fort. This was intended to be the quarters of the superintending engineer and afterward came to be known as the Eliason House, since Eliason lived there during his tenure at Fort Macon. Once the fort was finished, this house became the quarters of the commanding officer of the post. Eliason busied himself with studying the means to control erosion on Bogue Point along with a number of other concerns. He experienced difficulty in keeping a sufficient force of slaves to perform the labor duties and continued to run ads in local newspapers to attract more workers. In December, 1826, he was forced to up his pay for first class laborers to fifty cents per day. The force working on Fort Macon grew from 17 mechanics (carpenters), 56 laborers and one overseer in August, 1826, to 24 mechanics, 184 laborers and five overseers/supervisors in January, 1827.[20]

Eliason hoped to commence the masonry of the work during 1827 and began to advertise for bricks before the end of 1826. The caution with which he was ordered to proceed in regard to construction prevented his engaging in any long term contracts for large numbers of bricks at a time. Consequently, his ads for bricks stated he would "contract for small quantities at a time, with any individual." Unfortunately, he did not see any bricks produced in the immediate area which impressed him as being suitable for the fort. He saw clay in the area from which better bricks might be made but felt the brick manufacturing practices and capability of the region were lacking. However, at some point during this time he encountered at least two prominent local businessmen willing to venture into the brickmaking business to supply the fort. Moreover, they were willing to adopt the manufacturing processes of northern brickyards and make their bricks according to whatever specifications Eliason needed.[21]

One of the men was Otway Burns, a wealthy businessman and a hero

of the War of 1812 who had commanded the privateer *Snap Dragon* in numerous attacks against British shipping. Burns became the first to decide
to make the venture and even went so far as to act on a suggestion of Eliason
to hire a foreman from a brickyard at Alexandria, Virginia, to come serve
as the superintendent of his brickyard. The other man was Doctor James
Manney, a former North Carolina legislator who was under contract as the
doctor for Eliason's work force. Manney also went to the expense of hiring
men experienced in the industry to set up and superintend his yard. Eliason
realized there was still a great potential for problems and ill feelings on the
part of the brickmakers because he would have to make rigid inspections
of all brick shipments before they were accepted. The bricks would have to
meet the required standards for size and texture or they would be refused.
Given the indifferent nature of the clay found in the area and the
brickmakers' lack of manufacturing experience, the necessary degree of
quality control might be difficult for them to achieve. In his yearly report
for 1826, Eliason predicted "there is great reason to fear much difficulty
encountered and discontent engendered in the course of execution of a
[brick] contract if the necessary degree of regard in inspections be executed." The market for bricks offered by Eliason was a price of $8 per
thousand bricks delivered at the Fort Macon wharf. For every hundred hard
bricks there were to be five soft bricks and five bats. At first, Manney and
Burns were the primary brickmakers but in time a number of other men
likewise began to supply bricks.[22]

The spring of 1827 was a busy one. The fort site was excavated to a
level where foundation pits for the masonry would be opened. The wharf
on the sound was completed so that materials could be floated up by barges
and lighters directly to the work site. In addition to superintending these
operations and making his studies of the shore erosion problem, Eliason
helped oversee the setup and initial operations of the brickyards of Burns
and Manney. The first bricks from these yards were received in the latter
part of May and early June. By the middle of June, Eliason reported 250,000
bricks on site and another 400,000 nearing completion in the brickyards.
He had the laborers dig the first foundation pit for the scarp wall at the

angle of Fronts I and V in preparation to commence the masonry of the work at last. On 21 June 1827, the cornerstone of Fort Macon was formally laid. The event was attended by U.S. Congressman John H. Bryan, who had blocked the attempt in Congress to halt funding for the work the previous year, members of the bar attending court, and a number of other visitors from Beaufort, New Bern, and the local area. The most significant part of the work—the masonry—had now begun.[23]

Eliason quickly found two problems facing him as he attempted to continue with the masonry. First, the percolation of ground water into the foundation pits was so great that it was not practicable to reach the required foundation depths of three feet below low water mark using the pump then available to keep water out of the excavation. He could only excavate as close to the required depth as possible and allow the bottom of the timber foundation to attain proper depth by settling naturally under the weight of the masonry. Of even greater concern, however, was Eliason's growing dissatisfaction with the quality of workmanship of the local masons he had employed. After about a week he finally stopped the work and dismissed them. He then sent to Philadelphia to hire ten good master masons. Since it would be about a month before they would arrive, Eliason used the time to receive bricks and build another pump to help control ground water in the foundation pits when work resumed.[24]

At this time, Eliason received notice he was to be superceded at Fort Macon by a higher ranking engineer, Captain John Lind Smith, and would continue as Smith's assistant engineer. Captain Smith arrived at Beaufort on 26 July and formally took charge of the Fort Macon project the next day. Eliason served as Smith's assistant through the summer of 1827 and then departed in September on a leave of absence. Meanwhile, the ten masons hired earlier by Eliason in Philadelphia also arrived and it seemed that work could continue unhindered.[25]

Captain Smith's tenure as chief engineer at Fort Macon was to be brief and tumultuous as he faced a number of problems. He called into question Eliason's changes to the foundation depth, much to the latter's ire, and determined to see for himself if the ground water could be controlled enough to reach the required foundation depth of three feet. He quickly found the same problem Eliason had encountered and that even two pumps were insufficient. A third and fourth pump were ordered to be built. Masonry work progressed chiefly on the scarp and counterscarp walls of Front V and the counterfire galleries adjacent to each end of that front. In October, Smith made changes in the inspection and type of bricks to be received from the local brickmakers, accepting only hard bricks and excluding the bats and soft bricks previously accepted. Smith felt only the hard bricks were suitable for the fort's masonry. The brickmakers were angered by these changes, particularly Doctor Manney, whose large inventory of bricks was most affected. Heated words and threats passed between Manney and Smith, resulting in Manney being temporarily relieved as the project surgeon. A duel was threatened. Smith refused to do any further business with Manney and the entire situation with the brickmakers remained tense for some time. In November, Smith notified the Engineer Department he intended to arrest and bring charges against Lieutenant Eliason when the latter returned from leave. Smith charged that Eliason had aligned himself with Doctor Manney and others in opposing Smith's methods of construction and had publically injured Smith's reputation. The charges proved to be false and were subsequently withdrawn by Smith.[26]

There were two even greater problems over which Smith had no control. A month after his arrival, what work had been done suffered great damage when a hurricane swept the coast on 25 August 1827. Seawater inundated the site to a higher degree than any previous storms and with ruinous effect. When the storm had passed, the *Raleigh Register* noted: "Fort Macon has become a victim to the *war of elements*, it is literally in ruins and the progress they had made will now avail them nothing–the canals made on the island for the transportation of their materials are all filled up, together with the foundation . . . A beautiful instance of the sublime occurred there, whilst the storm was raging in all its majesty, an enormous quantity of lime had been collected for the use of the Fort, this took fire, and presented the appearance of a burning volcano amidst the roar and fury of the angry ocean."[27]

After this setback, another labor shortage occurred just at the time workers were most needed to repair hurricane damage to the site and perform the excavations for foundation pits and the embankments of the glacis. Smith advertised for more laborers for immediate use, first for fifty on 31 August, and then for one hundred on 26 September. He also required that the owners of those slaves who were working furnish them with their own blankets and suitable warm clothing to enable them to work through the inclement weather of the approaching winter. Still, the labor situation remained critical and greatly retarded any hope of repairing the hurricane damage or progressing on with the work[28].

As a result of all these problems and setbacks, the Engineer Department chose to remove Smith to other duty in December, 1827, and to reinstate Lieutenant William A. Eliason as superintending engineer at Fort Macon upon his return from leave. Eliason resumed command of the Fort Macon project in January, 1828.[29]

Eliason now inherited all the problems left by Smith: a great amount of storm damage yet to be repaired, a shortage of laborers, unhappy brickmakers, and the need to go forward with construction to make up lost time. He continued advertisements for laborers and procured what numbers he could. Much of the Congressional appropriation of $15,000 for that year had to be used to effect repairs of the storm damage. Eliason also spent $1,000 to construct a whole new set of construction buildings and quarters for his work force. Despite these concerns, work went forward on the two most important construction phases of the fort, the masonry and the excavations of earth to form the embankments of the glacis. During the months leading up to October, 1828, the masonry around the perimeter of the scarp wall and the parade wall of the casemates was raised to a level of four feet above low water mark. The perimeter of the counterscarp wall was raised to eight feet above low water, including two of the counterfire galleries. Of the other two galleries which were not as far along, the gallery in the fort's north angle was purposely left unfinished. This allowed the canal to pass through the glacis and counterscarp to the fort's ditches so that supplies and earth could be brought directly into the site. In the fiscal year ending 30 September 1828, about 5,000 cubic yards of masonry was laid. Fort Macon was taking shape.[30]

The situation with the brickmakers was another matter, however. By this time, there were as many as thirteen different persons supplying bricks for the fort, including Doctor Manney, with whom Eliason resumed business. Of these, the largest contracts were still held by Burns and Manney. The brickmakers expected Eliason to lift the restrictions placed on the bricks by Captain Smith and resume the terms of the old agreement to receive the ten percent of soft bricks and bats as previously set up. Eliason refused to do this, however, in agreement with Smith's reasoning that the hard bricks were better for the masonry of the work. A large supply of bricks was already on hand at the fort so he felt himself now in a position to reduce the price per thousand bricks to $7 for some of the large stockpiles of bricks the brickmakers currently had on hand. But the brickmakers felt Eliason was trying to take advantage of the large inventories they had accumulated to lower the price and threatened to stop deliveries. They also appealed to the Engineer Department on 19 June 1828, for the price offered per thousand bricks to be raised. The Department instructed Eliason to bring the price back up to $8 per thousand for good hard bricks of proper size. A shaky peace was restored between Eliason and the brickmakers which would last just over a year.[31]

During the fiscal year ending 30 September 1829, the masons at Fort Macon laid 3,000 cubic yards of masonry, which was less than the 5,000 cubic yards laid the previous year. However, much of the masonry in 1829 was involved with forming the embrasures and loopholes of the various casemates. This was far more exacting, tedious, and time consuming than just laying plain masonry. Once past this level it remained to bring all the walls to their full height and begin to turn the arches of the casemates. In the meantime, laborers still continued on the embankment of the glacis while carpenters worked on windows and sashes.[32]

Unfortunately, by October, 1829, trouble with the two principal brickmakers, Burns and Manney, erupted again. Eliason had begun to notice many of the bricks being delivered were of poor quality or were falling short of the size requirements. He warned the brickmakers to correct the problems or the bricks would not be accepted. He felt the clay being used by the brickmakers was of a better quality than that used previously and therefore any size or quality variation must be a result of improper manufacturing. To Burns it was suggested that new brick molds might be a remedy. Eliason noted Manney's problem was having too many bricks "wholly unfit for masonry and principally if not wholly on account of the quality have his bricks been rejected and they are really so bad that I have broken many bricks on my knee . . . ." On 8 October, Eliason issued an order establishing a rigid inspection of brick size and quality with the provisions that bricks not meeting these standards would not be accepted at the full price of $8 per thousand. Most brickmakers had stocks of bricks which were unacceptable under this order, but Eliason expressed a willingness to buy up any stocks of usable rejects if the brickmakers would accept a reduced "bargain" price. All agreed except Manney and Burns, who at once raised a storm of protest arguing that this order should have come earlier in the year instead of now when everyone had already manufactured large stocks of bricks. Burns was particularly incensed that a large load of his bricks had been rejected for full price because they fell short by only one-eighth of an inch of the size requirement. He fired off a letter to the Chief of Engineers protesting that "Lt. Eliason is a difficult man to deal with, and has had disputes and difficulties with almost everyone who has had any dealings with him." Even though he had about 100,000 bricks which were one-eighth of an inch too short, Burns demanded they be accepted at the full price of $8 per thousand because they had already been made before the new order was issued. Eliason countered that the brickmakers had always known before the order that bricks of inferior size or hardness would not be accepted at full price. While the rejection of bricks only one-eighth of an inch short of the standard might seem excessively harsh, the ever-meticulous Eliason supplied figures which showed the use of such bricks increased the number of bricks required to make a cubic yard of masonry from 403 to 473-1/2 with a corresponding increase in the mortar and labor to lay them. The price to lay one cubic yard of masonry was thus increased by

15.6 percent. To defray this added cost, Eliason's position was that it was only fair that bricks of admittedly inferior size should be purchased at less than full price. All the other brickmakers seemed content with this and were happy to sell off their stocks of inferior bricks for what they could get.[33]

Despite the whining of Manney and Burns, Eliason managed to purchase enough of a supply of bricks to ensure that work on the fort could continue for the remainder of the fiscal year. However, the continued difficulties with the brickmakers gave the Engineer Department concern that progress on the fort might become threatened. Perhaps it was time to assign another superintending engineer to the project for the benefit of all concerned. Eliason continued to serve at Fort Macon into the summer of 1830. Unfortunately, the death of one of his children and the illness of another caused Eliason to request an immediate transfer in August. Ultimately, he was transferred to Pea Patch Island, Delaware River. Replacing him once again was Captain John L. Smith. Oddly enough, just as Smith arrived he was faced by a hurricane which swept the coast during 16–17 August in much the same way as had happened when he had taken command of the fort in 1827. Fortunately, while the hurricane caused considerable erosion of the beach, its only significant damage to the fort was to ruin the dike running along beside the canal from the fort to the wharf, and to sweep away just under one foot of sand built up to form the glacis. Most of the sand was blown over into the ditch where it had to be removed.[34]

FINAL STAGES OF CONSTRUCTION

The period of 1830–33 was marked by rapid progress on Fort Macon. The disputes with the brickmakers seem to have been resolved and all phases of the work proceeded smoothly. During the fiscal year ending 30 September 1830, the walls and arches of the casemates had been finished. The scarp wall stood at different points from about fifteen feet to full height. Some work had also been done on the counterscarp wall. About half the doors, door and window frames, shutters, lathes, mantles, flooring, and other carpentry for the casemates was completed. Much work was done in forming and sodding the glacis. Smith had a plank road constructed from the canal around the top of the glacis to enable horse-drawn carts to deliver sod for the glacis. Each cart, with a small horse and a boy to drive it, carried the equivalent of ten wheelbarrow loads of sod and eliminated the need for ten laborers to push the wheelbarrows at a time when a shortage of labor persisted.[35]

During the fiscal year ending in 1831, even greater progress was made. The scarp, counterscarp, and parade walls were finished as were the roofs of the casemate arches. The latter were sheathed with lead sheeting three-sixteenths of an inch thick with the joints soldered to render the roofs waterproof. In the valleys between the casemate roofs, gutters were formed and connected to cast iron pipes laid laterally in the parade walls which would carry off the rain water funneled into the gutters. Downspouts in the parade wall conducted the water to four brick cisterns constructed under the parade ground at four of the angles of the parade wall. About half the valleys of the casemates were filled with sand during the year. Much work was done sodding the glacis. Because much of the best sod of the marsh immediately adjacent to the fort had been exhausted, it was necessary to extend the canal further into the marsh where more sod could be obtained. Work was begun on cutting and laying the blocks of Connecticut Freestone to form the copings and cordon which capped the walls. Most of the woodwork for the casemate quarters such as doors, windows, and sashes was finished.[36]

The amount of progress done on Fort Macon by 1831 led the Chief of Engineers, Brigadier General Charles Gratiot, to conclude that Fort Macon might be finished in 1832. This proved to be too optimistic, but the fiscal year ending 30 September 1832 was still marked by much progress. The rest of the casemate valleys were filled with sand, the parapet and glacis walls were completed, and the brick archwork of the three sets of stairs leading from the parade ground to the upper terreplein were finished and ready to receive their stone steps. Work was begun on heavy gates, flooring for the casemates, and bridges. Contrary to original plans, the two bridges across the ditch were simple bridges rather than drawbridges. Work also continued in dressing and laying the stonework of the cordon and coping. Laborers worked on applying a cement wash to the fort's walls. Not all of Captain Smith's attention was occupied with the fort during this period, however. Part of it was directed to finding a remedy for the erosion of the shore adjacent to the fort.[37]

Even before construction began on Fort Macon, the erosion of the shore was of great concern to the Engineer Department. Lieutenant Eliason had devoted considerable study toward its causes which fortunately had not progressed to the point of endangering the fort's construction. Following the hurricane of August, 1830, which caused considerable damage to the shoreline and encroached upon part of the fort's glacis, Captain Smith decided to make an attempt to control the erosion. During 1831–32, he had barriers of fascines and brush erected on the beach and securely (it was thought) anchored in the sand with stakes and piles, and weighted down with brick bats to form a barrier to the sea. During the summer of 1832, however, much of this was washed away. Smith then resorted to extensive pile breakwaters filled with brush and sand, and weighted down with a crib work of logs. These were made to extend out into the water and zigzag back along the beach. This effort met with success and caused an immediate accretion of sand along the structures. By this means the beach began to build itself back and with continued work it was felt possible to reverse the erosion process. For the time being, the shoreline had been stabilized. In reality, however, Smith had only initiated the first effort in what was to be a long, drawn-out process. One hundred and forty years later another generation of engineers would still be grappling with the problem of shore erosion on Bogue Point.[38]

Captain Smith was not to see the completion of the fort. In April, 1833, he was transferred to work on the forts of New York Harbor. His replacement was Lieutenant George Dutton, aged thirty. Dutton continued with the remaining work on the fort during 1833 which included the remaining stonework for the cordon, coping, and stairs; grading and sodding the glacis, terrepleins, parapet, and parade ground; making stair railings, hinges, and other metalwork; finishing gates, magazine doors, and the remaining flooring and woodwork for the casemates; and additional breakwaters on the shore opposite the fort. With this, the fort was essentially completed. On 1 November 1833, Dutton reported the fort would be ready for inspection about the middle of the following month. All that remained was police work, collection of materials and so forth. Across the harbor at Beaufort Barracks, Brevet Major R. N. Kirby's Company G, 1st U.S. Artillery, was waiting to occupy the new fort as its first garrison.[39]

But Fort Macon was not finished in 1833. It so happened Major Kirby took a dim view of his company having to occupy the fort in its present state. No barracks buildings had been built on the reservation outside the fort to house troops other than the commanding officer's house one-third of a mile west of the fort. Beyond a few ramshackled temporary buildings left by the construction crews, the only other place for troops was the fort casemates which he felt were simply uninhabitable. They had windows, doors, and flooring but otherwise just bare brick walls. As such they were damp and judged to be unhealthy. Kirby had an extremely valid point. The Engineer Department's only responsibility was to fortifications, not to the construction of military buildings. As far as the engineers were concerned, the casemates of the fort were intended only to shelter the garrison during bombardment and provide defense during assault. But where was the garrison to stay at all other times? The Quartermaster Department held responsibility for all other military buildings, including barracks, and in this case (as well as for other new forts) seems to have given no thought as to where the garrison of Fort Macon would be quartered when not directly under attack. Complaining to the Quartermaster General's Office and the Adjutant General's Office, Kirby requested the construction of barracks buildings outside the fort for his company. Included with his letters were specifications and costs for the buildings he felt were needed, and affidavits from Doctor James Manney and another local doctor stating their beliefs that the casemates were not suitable for regular quarters. The complaints were considered but the Army was unwilling to assume the added expense and effort of building an exterior barracks. However, it was agreed to take another year for the Engineer Department to fit out eighteen of the fort's casemates so that they could be made habitable as quarters. Thus Fort Macon's completion was delayed until 1834.[40]

During the year 1834, Dutton concentrated his efforts on the eighteen casemates of the fort intended for use as squarters. Each of the rooms was ribbed with furring, lathed, and then plastered to provide a finished dry wall. Doors were provided for the communication passages between each casemate and folding windows were installed to close the embrasures on the inside of the casemates. The five casemates of Front II were set up as officers' quarters. These rooms received special details such as molding and trimwork done in a more ornate Greek Revival style with folding interior shutters at the parade windows for privacy. Other work done consisted of building a new wharf, a new dike from the main entrance of the fort to the wharf, and further work on the breakwaters stabilizing the shoreline.[41]

With these items finished, Dutton reported Fort Macon as complete and ready for inspection as of December, 1834. As a result, Major Kirby's artillery company was ordered to take possession of the fort as its first garrison, which was done on 4 December 1834. After eight years of construction the fort was structurally complete. The total cost of $349,384.94 to build it had exceeded the $220,000 originally estimated by Lieutenant Eliason back in 1826, and far exceeded the $175,000 originally estimated by the Board of Engineers. It was the eighth fort of the Third System to be completed.[42]

4

THE ANTEBELLUM YEARS

After the difficulties and problems of the past years, Fort Macon now took its place as one of the completed and garrisoned forts of the Third System. Though structurally complete, the fort was found by its first garrison to be in no condition for defense and still plagued by some important problems.

THE NEW FORT

When Major R. M. Kirby's company settled into garrison duty at newly-completed Fort Macon, there were two primary concerns which Kirby felt should be corrected by the Army. The first was his continued unhappiness over the situation of quarters for his company. Even with the improvements made by the Engineer Department to render the fort's casemates habitable, he still felt they could never be suitable or healthy permanent quarters for troops, especially in hot weather. He pressed again for the construction of buildings normally prevalent at a post of this type such as exterior barracks, boathouse, storehouses, stables, hospital, and proper workshops for carpenters and blacksmiths. Unfortunately for Kirby and his men, the Quartermaster Department turned a dcaf ear to his requests.

Kirby's were only the first in a long succession of complaints which would follow from subsequent garrisons about having to be quartered in the damp casemates.[1]

The second problem was one in which the Army did take an interest. Although Fort Macon was finished structurally, it was far from complete from a defensive standpoint. No gun mounts had been built, none of the cannons of its intended armament had ever been sent, and none of the three hot shot furnaces proposed in the original plans had yet been built. The only weapons Major Kirby's company had to respond with to an attack were its muskets and the three iron 6-pounder field cannons of its regular company armament. Once Major Kirby reminded the Engineer Department of this defenseless state, Lieutenant George Dutton was ordered to submit a plan for arming the fort. Dutton complied and submitted a plan on 17 April 1835, in which he stated that 32-pounders would be the maximum caliber needed in view of the fact only sloops of war, corvettes, and similar-sized ships could cross the sixteen to twenty foot bar to enter Beaufort Inlet. The arrangement of guns was proposed as follows:

Front I:	Covertway	9 32-pounders
	Citadel	3 18-pounders
Front II:	Covertway	10 24-pounders
	Citadel	2 18-pounders, 3 8-inch howitzers
Front III:	Covertway	2 32-pounders, 7 24-pounders
	Citadel	3 18-pounders
Land Side Defenses		4 10-inch mortars
In the Casemates		8 18-pounder carronades
Total pieces		51 Guns [2]

Before anything further could be done toward arming the fort, however, Lieutenant Dutton was transferred to another station in the summer of 1835. It was not until November that another engineer officer, Lieutenant Alexander J. Swift, became available for duty at Fort Macon. At the same time, the Ordnance Department ordered ten 24-pounder cannons (but no gun carriages) to be issued to Fort Macon from the Fort Monroe Arsenal in Virginia. With this limited armament on hand, Swift was authorized to procure materials and build cannon emplacements, which he did during the winter of 1835–36. In January of 1836, he also was authorized to build one hot shot furnace, which was completed in the parade ground by March, 1836. During February, seven more 24-pounders, ten barbette gun carriages, ammunition, a gin and sling cart arrived from the Fort Monroe Arsenal.[3]

Unfortunately, Major Kirby and the men of Company G would never see Fort Macon's new guns mounted. With the outbreak of the Seminole War in Florida at the end of 1835, Kirby's company was hurriedly ordered to Florida by the War Department. So rapid was its departure by steamer on 2 February 1836, that Kirby was not even authorized to bring the company's three 6-pounders, which were left at Fort Macon. With the garrison gone, Lieutenant Swift finished his work on the hot shot furnace and fourteen gun mounts on the upper terreplein. These latter consisted of wooden pintle platforms with wooden traverse circles laid on brick foundations. The cannons themselves remained unmounted, however.[4]

Following the departure of Kirby's company, Fort Macon remained ungarrisoned for the next six years. The small standing army of the United States in this period had its hands full with the Seminole Wars and other such conflicts. Excepting the forts of the most important harbors of the United States, which usually kept permanent garrisons, Congressional economizing and the shifting of available troops to trouble spots meant that many of the forts guarding secondary harbors of lesser importance such as Fort Macon went ungarrisoned for extended periods of time. Rather than leave such forts totally abandoned, however, the Army would station a caretaker at each of them to look after the public property and report any problems or needs. The caretaker usually was an ordnance sergeant whose primary duty was to look after the weaponry of the fort, but whose unofficial duties usually ranged from minor maintenance around the post to providing security for the public buildings and stores on hand.

During the six years between 1836 and 1842, Fort Macon was in the charge of an ordnance sergeant who was often assisted by one or two civilian laborers hired as extra-duty men as funding allowed. At times there were projects and duties to be taken care of around the post such as digging a new well, building a new boatshed, or repairing damages done by the various storms which swept the coast. At other times it must have been a solitary, almost boring existence at the post since there was no habitation on the entire length of Bogue Banks other than a handful of fishermen living here and there along the island. A boat provided the only communication with Beaufort for mail, occasional supplies, and incidentals. On a couple of occasions the engineer assigned to this particular section of the coast arrived to make an inspection of the fort.[5]

In June, 1839, an inspection of the fort by Engineer Captain Alexander J. Swift revealed some disturbing problems at the fort which required attention. As with any newly-completed structure of this type, a certain amount of settlement and subsidence was to be expected. Swift found all the casemates had cracks in their arches emanating from the communication passage through each wall into the adjoining casemate, which was naturally a weak point in the masonry. The cracks had not widened for the last few years and were therefore not viewed with alarm. However, the casemates leaked, which indicated a serious problem involving the casemate roofs and the system by which water was drained from them into the cisterns. Also of concern was the fact the magazines were damp, and the wooden gun mounts built in 1836 were decaying. Finally, and perhaps most serious of all, the sea had begun to encroach upon the fort site again. The old brush jetties put out during the last years of the fort's construction had held the sea in check for a while but were now largely gone. Permanent measures were needed to halt the advance of the sea. The Engineer Department realized more work was needed to repair the fort and preserve its site. As a result, an appropriation of $15,000 for the fort was requested from Congress for the fiscal year of 1840–41. As Captain Swift was soon assigned other duty, a temporarily unattached engineer, Captain Robert E. Lee, was sent late in 1840 to make a thorough report on the condition of the fort and its site and to determine what specific measures and costs were necessary for repairs.[6]

Captain Lee made his inspection of Fort Macon during November and December, 1840. Concerning the erosion of the shoreline, Lee concluded as had Captain Swift the previous year, that permanent jetties made of stone built perpendicularly to the shore to force the accretion of sand were the only remedies. Such jetties had been tried by the Engineer Department for the first time at Fort Monroe, Virginia, and Fort Moultrie, South Carolina, with great success. Lee estimated a cost of $25,000 to construct two stone jetties anchored in a grillage of palmetto logs. One would be situated at Bogue Point to prevent further loss of the point and to force the accumulation of sand in front of the fort. The second would be built opposite the southwest angle of the fort to continued the accumulation of sand westward.[7]

As for the fort itself, Lee found numerous problems in need of correction. The serious problem of leaking was caused by obstructions in the pipes conducting water from the valleys between each casemate roof to the cisterns. The water backed up in the soil in the casemate valleys and found its way into the masonry through places where the lead sheathing of the casemate roofs had been lapped at joints or against the parade and scarp walls. Lee chose to dispense with the lateral pipe in the parade wall and called for gutter chases with downspout pipes to be cut into the parade wall at each of the casemate valleys as a more effective way to drain the water out of the soil above the casemates. The downspout pipes would all tie in to a brick gutter under the parade running at the foot of the parade wall which would conduct the water to the cisterns. Excavations would be necessary to give access to the casemate roofs to repair the gutters, lead sheathing, and cracks in the casemate arches, which Lee called to be filled with grout from above and repointed. Dampness in the magazines was a ventilation problem to be cured by rebuilding the wooden inner lining of each magazine with ample spacing between it and the brickwork for air circulation. Further improvement of the ventilation system would be caused by installing new magazine doors with ventilation grating, and by cutting a ventilation opening through one wall of each magazine to increase air draft. Other needed repairs included painting the casemate quarters, a sluice gate to control sea water flooding into the ditch, and repairs to the wharf, glacis and parapet. To place the fort in a proper state for defense, permanent brick and stone gun mounts and traverse circles were needed for the full intended armament, which was changed to forty-eight barbette guns. A second hot shot furnace was needed to serve the guns on the covertway. To better secure the fort against assault, more firepower was needed for interior defense. Emplacements for six carronade cannons were to installed in the counterfire galleries under the covertway so that the ditch could be swept with cannonfire. The total cost for all these repairs was estimated by Lee to be $17,674.[8]

ALTERATIONS AND MODIFICATIONS

Captain Lee's report sparked a second phase of construction at Fort Macon that lasted for the next five years. Only a few months after Lee's reports were submitted, the Engineer Department was ready to initiate dual projects for the repairs at the fort and the preservation of its site with the construction of stone jetties. Superintending the projects again was George Dutton, now a captain. Dutton found a great deal of preparatory work was necessary before any of the actual repairs or construction could commence. First, the old decayed and worm-eaten wharf had to be repaired for the reception of materials. Next, quarters and shops for the workmen had to be repaired and made habitable. These consisted of mechanics', overseers', and laborers' quarters, blacksmiths' and carpenters' shops, all located southwest of the fort. They were the same ones built during the fort's construction and were in poor shape after fourteen years of exposure to the elements. Finally, Dutton had a small railroad built about three-quarters of a mile from the wharf to the proposed locations of the two jetties on the beach so that the stone and other materials for them could be pulled by horse-drawn flatcars directly to their sites.[9]

With the preliminaries completed, Dutton began repairwork in June, 1841. His workmen excavated the earth from the upper terreplein adjacent to the parade wall of the citadel to gain access to the gutters lying in the bottom of the casemate valleys. In accordance with Lee's recommendations, drainage openings were cut through the parade wall at each valley which were then tied in to vertical downspout pipes in gutter chases cut into the parade wall. The downspout pipes were tapped in to a covered gutter laid at the foot of the parade wall to the four cisterns under the parade. Repairs were also made to the cisterns because the water in them was brackish and unfit for drinking. When Dutton's workmen excavated the parapet adjacent to the scarp wall to repair the cracks in the casemate arches, a chilling discovery was made. The weight and pressure of the earth parapet was found to be forcing the scarp wall to lean outward and separate itself from the casemate arches. Gaps as much as three inches wide were found, which allowed water to seep into the masonry.[10]

The movement of the scarp wall was a major unforseen structural problem which had to be remedied at once. Dutton knew the only certain solution to this was reconstruction of the fort walls, which there was no intention of doing. Instead, masonry counterforts would have to be built up as an extension of the casemate walls to tie in to and buttress the scarp wall. Masonry fill would be placed in the valleys between both sides of each counterfort and the adjacent casemate roofs which would displace large amounts of heavy earth of the parapet and thus produce less pressure and weight acting to push against the scarp wall. This new work was directed initially to Fronts I, II, and III.[11]

In addition to these concerns, other work on the fort included rebuilding the wood liners of the magazines with ample ventilation space between them and the brick walls, cutting ventilation passages in one wall of each magazine, building grated doors for the magazines, lowering the breastheight wall of the covertway one and one-half feet on Fronts I, II, and III, and constructing twenty-six permanent stone gun mounts on those three fronts. Unfortunately, the unexpected expense of the counterforts ate heavily into the $15,000 appropriation for the year by Congress for fort repairs. On 1 April 1842, the appropriation was exhausted and repair work came to a stop.[12]

As for the jetty project, Dutton obtained palmetto logs from the Cape

Fear area to fashion the timber grillage which would serve to anchor each of the jetties on the ocean bottom. The granite stone, in pieces weighing from 100 to 3,000 pounds, was obtained from the Hudson River and Staten Island, New York. The jetty west of the fort, Number Two, was completed with a total of 1,875 tons of granite. The jetty east of the fort, Number One, was completed for part of its length with a total of 740 tons of stone before the appropriation of $25,000 for this project was likewise exhausted. Some 3,800 feet of sand fence was erected along the beach to catch drifting sand.[13]

Further complicating Dutton's work, the end of the Seminole Wars in Florida in 1842 meant many of the Army's units would now be reassigned to various posts and stations, of which Fort Macon would be one. The casemates and commanding officer's house would have to be fixed up for the reception of troops, construction materials would have to be moved and stored out of the way, and the fort cleaned up. With no money left, it was necessary to extend to Dutton some funds from the Engineer Department's Contingencies of Fortifications appropriation for this purpose. On 1 June 1842, however, Dutton was transferred to other duty and Lieutenant J. H. Trapier was assigned to complete the work. Toward the end of the month, even these contingency funds were exhausted and Trapier was forced to stop work. On 28 July 1842, when Company F, 3rd U.S. Artillery arrived to garrison the fort, the work on the casemates was not completed.[14]

Unfortunately, Congressional appropriations requested to continue the engineer work on the fort and its site were not released until early 1843. As a result, when work stopped in June, 1842, Lieutenant Trapier was unable to do anything else for the next eight months. When the appropriations were finally released in February, 1843, Trapier could at last resume his work. Of first concern was to finish counterforting operations on Fronts IV and V. This was done during the fiscal year ending on 30 September 1843. Also done were a number of other tasks which included increasing the thickness of the rear walls of two of the magazines; building fourteen granite traverse circles on the upper terreplein; excavating the soil over the four counterfire galleries and making repairs to cracks and the lead sheathing on their roofs; raising the floors of the counterfire galleries to

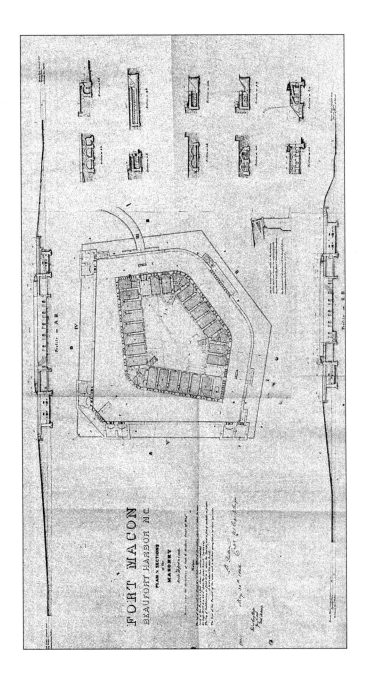

Engineer drawing of Fort Macon following completion of alterations and modifications of 1841–46.
National Archives

facilitate the installation of carronades; grading and sodding of portions of the terrepleins, glacis, and banquettes; raising the level of the ditch; installing a shingled revetment along the top of the breastheights of the citadel and covertway; and numerous smaller repairs. In addition, the Engineer Department on 10 May 1843 ordered the modification of all entrances to the citadel and counterfire galleries for greater defense. The main gate at the sally port was to be modified by the addition of multiple sets of defensive gates and partitions. The eight-foot wide entrances to the two posterns of the citadel and the entrances to all four counterfire galleries were to be reduced to just three feet in width by bricking them in and providing them with new gates. Portions of this work were completed during the year.[15]

As for the project for the preservation of the site of Fort Macon, the two jetties worked on the previous year were completed and strengthened. In addition, the Engineer Department decided to expand the program by authorizing the construction of four additional jetties, two more at the point and two others westward of Jetty Number Two to prevent storm tides from cutting across between the fort and the commanding officer's quarters. Contracts for 3,000 tons of granite stones and 17,000 linear feet of Palmetto logs were made for this new phase of work. A railroad was constructed 900 yards to the site of the farthest jetty, Number Four, which was then commenced and mostly completed.[16]

Lieutenant Trapier continued in charge of repairs to the fort until 2 June 1844, when he was replaced by Lieutenant Daniel P. Woodbury. During the fiscal year ending 30 September 1844, a great part of the major repairs to the fort and work on the jetties was finished. Inside the fort, the alterations to the sally port, posterns, and counterfire gallery entrances were completed, including new gates. The faces of three counterfire galleries were altered to make a total of six carronade embrasures. The mounts and traverse circles for the carronades were also installed. The remaining sets of traverse circles for the barbette guns were laid. The stair wells leading to the north and south counterfire galleries were altered to receive communication passages into the ditch. Most of the rifle loopholes in the casemates received sashes. Extensive grading and sodding of the glacis, terrepleins, and banquette continued. A second hot shot furnace to serve the guns of the covertway apparently was built at this time. There was also another unforeseen expense. During target practice by the garrison, several of the pintle blocks of the finished gun mounts loosened. It became necessary to strengthen all the existing pintle blocks by building brick beds around them. The twenty-two remaining sets of pintle blocks were drilled and made ready to lay, also with brick beds. On the beach, two more jetties, Numbers Three and Five, were built, along with most of a small jetty, Number Six, before funds were exhausted.[17]

For the year 1845, Lieutenant Woodbury completed all the major repairs and alterations to the fort. These included the installation of the remaining pintle blocks and beds for the barbette guns, adjustment of some of the traverse circles, increasing the thickness of the rear wall of the last magazine, the installation of the remaining loophole sashes, and further adjustment of the banquettes, ditch, and glacis. A self-acting sluice gate was installed to control water in the ditch. On the beach, Jetty Number Six was rebuilt and extended, as well as other work being done on the existing jetties and the beach. In June, 1846, Woodbury returned to Fort Macon to make some additional repairs. These included more work to adjust the grade of the glacis, terrepleins, parapet, and parade; the repair of leaks; whitewashing the casemates and galleries; color-washing the exterior masonry; and fitting out four casemates on Front IV which had never been finished.[18]

With the completion of these last repairs in 1846, Fort Macon was at the pinnacle of readiness for defense. It had permanent mounts for forty-eight barbette guns and six for carronades. The alterations made to the counterfire galleries and entrances made it formidable against direct assault. The casemate quarters were in their best condition ever. The structural problems with the masonry of the arches and walls had been arrested. The set of six permanent jetties had resulted almost immediately in restoring the beach and stabilizing the encroachment of the sea. As such, Fort Macon was in its peak condition as a fort of the Third System. The cost of these alterations and repairs, and the work for the preservation of the site,

when added to the cost of previous repairs and the original cost of construction, brought the total cost of Fort Macon to $463,790.[19]

PROBLEMS OF THE GARRISON

When Company F, 3rd U.S. Artillery, arrived at Fort Macon on 28 July
1842, it found a situation of great confusion. The casemates were only partially ready for the men. The engineer work being done on the fort was
stopped in a state of only partial completion due to exhaustion of funds.
Materials and construction debris lay scattered about. The buildings outside the fort, including the Eliason House (commanding officer's quarters), were occupied by the engineers. No cannons were mounted for the
fort's defense. There was little to do but clear away as much of the debris as
was possible and make the best of a poor situation. During the weeks which
followed, 900 pounds of straw was ordered for the bedsacks of the soldiers'
bunks, arrangements were made to purchase a supply of firewood for the
winter, and further arrangements were completed to procure fresh water
in Beaufort. Funds were also acquired on account of the Quartermaster
Department for minor repairs to the quarters which included building partitions in the five officers' casemates of Front II and equipping them with
wood stoves. While engineer work was stopped, the soldiers used a horse
belonging to the Engineer Department to pull the flat cars from the wharf
to the fort when supplies were landed.[20]

In February, 1843, the work of the engineers on Fort Macon began in
earnest, necessitating great care so that the soldiers and the workmen did
not interfere with each other's duties. Because the railroad to the wharf
was heavily used by the engineers to transport the stone and materials for
their project and the horse previously used was back in the engineer's hands,
the soldiers found it difficult to transport their own supplies and provisions
to the fort from the wharf. A letter on the subject was sent to the Quartermaster Department and in May of 1843, the latter relented in allowing the
garrison to acquire a horse of its own for the post as well as a new boat to
replace three old, dilapidated boats which had been at the post for years.

While this request was successful, another was not. In April, 1843, the acting commander of Company F, Lieutenant E. O. C. Ord, sent a request to the Adjutant General's office requesting that a chaplain be assigned to the post. The local preachers, he said, were too poor to preach for nothing and the Post Fund was not large enough to have them paid. The War Department was unable to fill this request and the garrison's religious needs were filled by lay readings by the officers.[21]

In August, 1843, Engineer Lieutenant Trapier wrote to the Engineer Department that repairs of the casemate quarters were necessary and suggested that if approved, the garrison should be moved elsewhere until the repairs were completed. Lieutenant Christopher Q. Tompkins, now acting commander of Company F, took this opportunity to recommend to Brigadier General W. K. Armistead, commander of the Eighth Military District, that the garrison be moved to Beaufort or New Bern while this was going on. He also took occasion to report an existing condition of considerable concern to the garrison: the need for a post hospital outside the fort. Currently, one of the casemates was used for a post hospital and was felt to be totally unsuited for this purpose because of the dampness and inadequate ventilation of the casemates.[22]

As it turned out, the Chief of Engineers did not approve Lieutenant Trapier's proposal to repair the casemates. These repairs were felt to be a concern of the Quartermaster Department and were not regarded as part of the fort's defenses, which was an Engineer concern. However, as Lieutenant Trapier's letter made its way through the chain of command, all bureau heads of the War Department agreed on the necessity of establishing a hospital building outside the fort so that any sick men at the post would have a healthier environment in which to convalesce than the damp casemates. Accordingly, when Captain William Wall arrived at Fort Macon on 3 October 1843 to take over as Company F's new commander, he had been given authority to build a one-story frame hospital outside the fort. Unfortunately, Wall found prices for lumber and materials so high he suggested postponing construction of the hospital until the spring of 1844. Even then, the hospital would not be built as other concerns took precedence.[23]

On 8 February 1844, the garrison of Fort Macon was increased by the arrival of one half of Company B, 3rd U.S. Artillery, and the company's commander, Captain John R. Vinton, who as senior officer assumed command of the post. At first, considerable concern was expressed as to where room for this additional unit could be found in a fort already crowded with Company F and the engineer workmen. Captain Vinton did manage to squeeze his men into the fort. However the enlisted men of both companies were now quartered in four casemates. Of the officers, Engineer Lieutenant Trapier shared the large Eliason House with Lieutenant Christopher Q. Tompkins and his wife. In actuality, Captain Vinton, as senior officer, was entitled to take the Eliason House for himself since it was acknowledged to be used as quarters for the commanding officer. However, he declined at first so long as Lieutenant Tompkins' wife was present and instead took quarters in a small, two-room house about 250 yards from the fort which had originally been erected as overseer's quarters during the fort's construction. Later, when Tompkins' wife returned home for the summer, Vinton and his son did take over the Eliason House while Tompkins moved into the overseers' house. Of the other officers, Captain Wall and the remaining junior officers each took one of the casemates of Front II in the fort. The remaining casemates of the fort were used as quarters for noncommissioned officers; laundresses and ordnance sergeant; hospital; offices; storage; mess rooms; kitchens; bakery; guard room; and library.[24]

Despite the confusion with the engineer repairs going on at the fort, Captain Vinton was content at Fort Macon. A man of considerable intelligence and refinement, he was quite satisfied with his small command and the simple pleasures it afforded. He enjoyed fishing, swimming, and mixing with the gentry who always came to Beaufort during the summer months to enjoy its waters and sea breezes. He brought a piano which not only provided hours of personal enjoyment but also ensured the success of two parties he held in the Eliason House for the local society set. He arranged for a minister to come over from Beaufort each Sunday to deliver a sermon to the garrison, and for a time took upon himself the tutoring of two music boys of the garrison. During the summer, he brought his nine-year old son to live with him and spent much time personally attending to the boy's education. In his brief stay, Vinton seems to have enjoyed his tenure at Fort Macon perhaps more than any other of its commanders.[25]

Vinton's enthusiasm was apparently not shared by all. Both the junior officers and enlisted men grumbled over what Fort Macon had to offer. Their quarters in the fort casemates were damp, poorly ventilated, and in need of repair. The fort itself was in a state of only partial completion with all the engineer activities in progress. The completion of the permanent gun mounts on the covertway was cause to mount some of the fort's guns which had been lying around for years so that the men could at least do what they were supposed to do as artillerymen. Even this turned into frustration, however, when target practice loosened several of the stone pintle blocks, necessitating the engineers having to come back to make repairs and alterations to all the gun mounts. Many of the men of the garrison missed the diversions and activities of the larger military posts near major cities. As for the local area, the men generally seem to have found Beaufort lacking in books, diversions and society. Although the town's residents were regarded with kindness and respect, it was noted that there was not one family in the town where the officers would visit socially. Many of the men were bachelors who seem to have felt themselves stifled for lack of eligible females in this small, poor fishing town. But such was the lot of many soldiers in isolated military posts all across the country who would all certainly sympathize with those stationed at Fort Macon.[26]

As it turned out, neither of the two companies at Fort Macon had much longer to be worried about being stationed there. On 28 October 1844, Captain Wall's Company F boarded a steamer under orders to report to Fort McHenry, Maryland, for a school of instruction in light artillery. Captain Vinton was left with only his half of Company B at Fort Macon, which was insufficient by itself to properly man the fort and perform the requisite duties. Orders were soon given for Vinton to reunite with the other half of his company, which was stationed at the August Arsenal, Georgia. On 25 November 1844, his half company departed from Fort Macon by steamer. [27]

The departure of the garrison left the engineers free to complete the repairs of the fort unhindered, which they did in 1846. Other than the engineers, the only military personnel left at the fort were Ordnance Sergeant Peter D. Stewart and a civilian fort keeper. Little further thought was given to Fort Macon over the next two years because of the Army's involvement with the Mexican War. When the war ended in 1848, however, the Army began to bring most of its units back home where they were assigned to various posts and stations. In this manner, Company H, 2nd U.S. Artillery, was assigned to Fort Macon as its third garrison.

On 12 October 1848, Captain Henry Swartwout, commander of Company H, arrived at Fort Macon in advance of his troops to inspect his new station. Unlike Captain Vinton, he did not find things entirely to his liking. There were many repairs necessary to the fort for the reception of troops. Locks, hinges, and other ironwork was rusted, requiring attention or replacement. The casemates and the two outside houses used for officer's quarters needed repairs and painting. The boats needed paint and repairs, and the wharf was almost entirely gone. He estimated at least $1,000 in repairs were needed and sent a report of the matter to the Quartermaster General. At the end of the letter he remarked coldly: "I hope, General, it may meet your views to order the necessary repairs. When it becomes necessary that an officer should be located on a sandbank the Government should at least be willing to give him comfortable quarters."[28]

In the meantime, Company H arrived at Fort Macon on 28 October 1848, where it was to spend almost a year. The men made the best of their situation. In September, 1849, however, the company received orders directing it to Florida where further troubles with the Seminole Indians had broken out. On 2 October 1849, the company departed by steamer, leaving Fort Macon again unoccupied. This was the last time the fort was garrisoned prior to the outbreak of the Civil War. Only ordnance sergeants would be on hand to look after the fort in the intervening years: Thomas Dailey replacing Peter D. Stewart in 1851, and William Alexander replacing Dailey in 1859.[29]

DECLINING YEARS

Fort Macon in the 1840s was in the best condition and readiness it would ever achieve as a Third System fort. During the decade of the 1850s its condition went gradually downhill because of having no garrison and for want of timely repairs due to Congressional economizing. The harsh environment of the coast quickly took its toll. Unprotected ironwork quickly rusted away, wood began to rot, embankments of the parapet and glacis suffered from wind and water erosion, and leaks developed in the casemates once again. Other than completing a new wharf in 1851 and some minor repairs, little else was done to the fort or its site for several years. During 1854 and 1855, Congress at last appropriated some money to effect a few more repairs of the casemates, embankments, and jetties which helped restore the condition of the fort and its site to some extent. Also during this time, in an effort by the U.S. Lighthouse Board to improve coastal navigation along North Carolina's dangerous coast, a lighthouse and beacon were erected on the reservation to aid commerce through Beaufort Inlet. The "Bogue Banks Lighthouse" was a fifty-foot red brick tower with a fourth order Fresnel lens and was first illuminated on 20 May 1855. It stood about 200 yards northwest of the fort. The beacon was established on a thirty-foot wooden tower south of the fort.[30]

Hurricanes struck the area in August, 1856, and September, 1857, doing considerable damage to the shore and cutting away between the jetties and the beach. The jetties were left in the surf detached from the beach and accomplishing no purpose. Yet another storm in October, 1859, lopped off 60 feet of beach and brought its storm tide to within 100 feet of the crest of the covertway. Repeated requests by the Chief of Engineers for appropriations of $40,000 to repair and extend the isolated jetties back to the beach and to build two new jetties went unheeded by Congress. However, during the winter of 1859-60, Engineer Captain John G. Foster in charge of this section of the coast had some temporary brush and sandbag jetties thrown up which seemed to temporarily stop the encroachment of the sea.[31]

In the meantime, the fort's condition began to decay rapidly again from neglect, rot, storms, and the elements. In many places the masonry required repointing. Three casemates leaked and all of them required renovation inside. Ironwork was rusted and needed replacing. One of the bridges over the ditch and the shingled interior revetment of the covertway was decayed. Both hot shot furnaces needed replacement. A new bridge was needed over the canal and the embankment of the roadway to the wharf needed repairs. The wharf was being undermined by currents and also suffered from decay. Captain Foster estimated $17,000 in repairs were needed to recondition the fort. Still, an economy-minded Congress failed to supply any appropriations to meet these problems. Thus on the eve of America's greatest crisis, Fort Macon stood in a woeful, neglected state.[32]

5

CONFEDERATE OCCUPATION

The fateful year of 1861 began in turmoil. The election of Republican Abraham Lincoln to the Presidency in November, 1860, was quickly followed a month later by South Carolina's secession from the Union. The disenchantment and discontent felt by other Southern states prompted them to follow suit beginning in January, 1861. Within the first week of January, most of the U.S. forts and arsenals of the states of the Lower South were seized and occupied by state troops. The formation of the Confederacy followed soon thereafter.

The State of North Carolina did not immediately join the seceded states, but large segments of the population sided with the Confederacy. Pro-secessionist factions loudly called for the state to join her sister Southern states in defiance of the Federal Government. Even though the state made no formal move in that direction, fears remained high that the U.S. Government would react to all these incredible events by sending troops into the South to reoccupy the forts and arsenals and restore order with force. In January, a rumor was received that a U.S. revenue cutter loaded with troops was on its way to occupy Forts Caswell and Johnston on the Cape Fear River to keep order in North Carolina. In the frenzy of the times, local pro-secession militia forces marched on the two forts to seize them before

Federal troops arrived. Both forts were taken from the ordnance sergeants in charge of them during 9–10 January without the sanction of the state. When it turned out the rumor about the revenue cutter was untrue and the state obviously had no intention of joining the secession frenzy, the militia sheepishly relinquished possession of the forts, restoring the ordnance sergeants to duty. A greatly embarrassed Governor John W. Ellis sent his regrets to Washington.

Fortunately, at Fort Macon, Ordnance Sergeant William Alexander had no such trouble from the local population. Beaufort was quiet and so were Morehead City and Carolina City, two new towns which had developed on the west side of Beaufort Harbor in the late 1850s when the Atlantic and North Carolina Railroad was completed between the harbor and Goldsboro in 1858. Alexander had over thirty years in the Army and would be retiring soon. All he could do is hope the furor over secession might somehow pass him by as he went on about his duties over the weeks which followed.

SEIZURE OF FORT MACON

By April, 1861, Sergeant Alexander had begun to feel a definite uneasiness over the rapidly deteriorating situation between the United States and the Confederacy. What direction would North Carolina take? As caretaker of a U.S. fort which was sure to be one of the first places for trouble to break out, he felt a growing concern for his personal safety and that of his wife. In a letter to the Chief of Ordnance, he requested a revolver for his personal use. He was told, however, that none were on hand. On 12 April, armed hostilities formally began with the bombardment of Fort Sumter in Charleston Harbor by South Carolina forces. The electrifying news of war spread rapidly throughout the South, and it was only a matter of time before Fort Macon was involved, one way or the other.[1]

On 14 April, only two days after the bombardment of Fort Sumter and one day after its surrender to South Carolina forces, Alexander's worst fears were realized when he was informed that plans were being made to seize Fort Macon that very day. He at once sent a letter of his predicament to the

Chief of Ordnance: "I learn from a reliable source that a company of Secessionists commanded by Josiah S. Pender of Beaufort are today going to
seize this Fort and property, and am at a loss how to act, in premises, what
to do, or where to go. I have served in the U.S. Army for the last thirty years,
and am now no longer fit for any active service, have my family at the Post,
and all my property; the latter I expect to lose, having no where to move it,
and cannot at this time convert anything into money."[2]

The secessionists Alexander was referring to was a group calling themselves the "Beaufort Harbor Guards" led by Captain Josiah S. Pender, a
Mexican War veteran, local entrepreneur, and ardent secessionist. As soon
as Pender received word of the attack on Fort Sumter he knew that war had
begun and that the time to act was now. Fort Macon must be taken at once
before Federal troops could occupy it. On the afternoon of 14 April, he
formed his company of seventeen men, along with a number of citizens
from Beaufort and Morehead City, and cadets from the A.M. Institute at
Carolina City—fifty-four men in all. The group boarded the steamer *Cora*
and arrived at the rickety wharf at Fort Macon at 3:00 P.M. that afternoon.
Pender's command then went up to the fort where Sergeant Alexander was
found. The takeover was conducted in a most gentlemanly and respectful
manner as Alexander was in no position to resist and under the circumstances could not stop Pender's men. He could only express his regret over
the necessity that Pender and his men felt themselves under. The entire
incident was over in thirty minutes. Pender had the fort. Alexander and his
family remained on hand for the next two days, during which time he tried
unsuccessfully to get Pender to sign receipts for the fort and its property.
On 17 April, Alexander and his family were carried to Beaufort where they
took up residence under orders from the Ordnance Department to remain
there.[3]

Captain Pender triumphantly telegraphed South Carolina Governor
Francis W. Pickens of his actions and closed with the line: "We intend that
North Carolina shall occupy a true instead of a false position, though it be
done by revolution." Curiously, he did not notify North Carolina Governor
John W. Ellis, perhaps in fear of disapproval for his actions since Ellis was

not particularly sympathetic to the secessionist movement. However confident he may have been in his actions, Pender quickly found that the fort he had taken was far from being in a state of defense. Of the seventeen 24-pounders which constituted the fort's chief armament, only four were mounted on Front I of the covertway on carriages weakened from years of exposure and decay. These were the only ones remounted after the engineers had repaired the gun mounts in 1844. The other thirteen lay on skids at the wharf where they had been stored for years. The woodwork of the casemates, revetments, and bridges was decayed. Much of the ironwork around the fort was rusted and in poor shape. It would take weeks of hard work to place the fort in condition for defense.[4]

Meanwhile, in Raleigh, North Carolina Governor John W. Ellis was moved to the same course of action as Pender, although by a different set of circumstances. On the day after Fort Macon was seized, 15 April, President Lincoln issued a call for 75,000 troops to quell the Southern insurrection. On that day, Governor Ellis received a telegram from the Secretary of War which asked North Carolina to furnish two regiments as its quota of these troops. Ellis was shocked by Lincoln's decision to use force against the Southern states and flatly refused to be a part of it. Instead, North Carolina would join her sister Southern states in resisting the Federal Government's use of force. He immediately ordered state troops to seize all Federal arsenals and forts within the state, including Fort Macon. Unaware that Captain Pender had already seized Fort Macon he gave the following order to Captain Marshall D. Craton and his company of state troops known as the Goldsboro Rifles: "You will proceed with your Company to Fort Macon and take possession of the same in the name of the State of North Carolina. This measure being one of self defense and protection merely, you will observe strictly peaceful policy and act only on the defense." By 3:00 P.M. that afternoon, Captain Craton's company and a second company known as the Goldsboro Volunteers, under Captain Junius B. Whitaker, which had formed only a few hours earlier, were on a train of the Atlantic and North Carolina Railroad leaving Goldsboro for Morehead City. As the train reached New Bern early that evening, it was greeted at the depot by hundreds of cheering civilians. Passing on, the train reached Morehead City at 9:00 P.M. The men spent the night in Beaufort and on the following morning relieved Captain Pender's company upon their arrival at Fort Macon. On 17 April, Captain Craton received instructions from Raleigh to take all active measures for the defense of the fort and to hold it against all comers. The note also contained the following: "Convey to Captain Pender the assurances of Governor Ellis' high appreciation and entire approval of the patriotic course pursued by the Company under his command."[5]

On 17 April, the schooner *George Handy* arrived at Fort Macon with a work force of sixty-one free negro volunteers and twenty-one slaves under the command of Captain Henry T. Guion. This work force, along with a large amount of tools, materials and supplies, had been raised by the city of New Bern for the fort's defense. Captain Guion and his work force set up engineer operations at the fort under the command of Engineer Colonel W. Beverhout Thompson for the purpose of mounting guns and making all repairs necessary to put the fort in a proper condition for defense. Groups of free negro volunteers and slaves were enrolled from various eastern North Carolina counties and brought to the fort to work for periods varying from days to weeks to get it in a condition of defense. On 25 April, for instance, the work force had grown to 207, including laborers, blacksmiths, carpenters, cooks, etc. The number of workmen constantly changed as men became discharged and slaves were returned to their owners. However, others arrived to take their places.[6]

The work done by these men was backbreaking. A railroad was laid from the wharf into the fort to roll in supplies, materials, cannons, and ammunition as it arrived. The rickety wharf was repaired and strengthened. Sand bags were filled by the hundreds and carried into the fort to form breastworks on the parapet. Between 21 and 24 April, the workmen brought the thirteen 24-pounders lying at the wharf into the fort and mounted six of them on the six remaining gun carriages. Six bronze field guns were also brought into the fort at this time, and platforms constructed for them. Sand which had accumulated in the ditch was dug out. The most exhausting work was the leveling of the sanddunes and thickets westward from the fort to create a flat open plain and clear field of fire over which an assault force would have to pass fully exposed to fire during any approach on the fort. At times as many as one hundred laborers were employed on this important task. The dunes were eventually leveled to a distance of 1,000 yards from the fort. Due to the urgency of getting everything completed before an attack by Federal troops could be made, the workmen for a time were pushed from before sunrise until midnight seven days a week. Under these circumstances the sick list grew rapidly. At last, some of the urgency died away and the workers were not pushed as hard. Beginning on 28 April, Chief Engineer Thompson ordered that Sundays would be observed as a day of rest.[7]

In these early days of the war, patriotic fever took over as in every town and county men formed companies and tendered them to the Governor for the defense of the state. The State Adjutant General's Office frantically tried to keep track of them and began sending these various companies to camps and rendezvous areas after they were formed. Fort Macon was one of the points to which troops were directed. Captain Craton's Goldsboro Rifles and Goldsboro Volunteers had formally taken over the fort and relieved Captain Pender's volunteer group. On 16 April, the Elm City Rifles and Neuse Cavalry of New Bern went down by rail to join Craton. On 17 April, Colonel Charles C. Tew, aged thirty-three, commander of the Hillsboro Military Academy, was appointed to take command of Fort Macon and the troops gathering there. He was sent down the railroad that night by a special train to Morehead City and took over command of the fort from Captain Craton on the morning of the 18th. On 18 April, the Wilson Light Infantry and Edgecombe Guards passed down the railroad to the fort, arriving the next day. On 21 April, the Guilford Grays and Orange Guards arrived at the fort, followed on the 22nd by the Warren Guards.[8]

At this point Colonel Tew found himself with more troops on hand than he actually needed or could conveniently use with all the other activity going on to get the fort ready for war. As a result, the Warren Guards were ordered back to Goldsboro to await orders on the 23rd and Tew announced by 25 April that no more troops were needed at the fort. Any other units were requested to direct themselves to other camps. However, two other companies which this order did not reach soon arrived at the fort: the Milton Blues on 26 April and the North Carolina Guards on 28 April. Both these companies were sent back. At this time one of the companies already in the fort, the Edgecombe Guards, left the fort on the 25th under orders to proceed to Raleigh to join the state's first volunteer regiment. On 4 May, the Elm City Rifles were ordered back to New Bern. In other changes during May, Captain Josiah Pender's Beaufort Harbor Guards, now recruited to a full company, was ordered to join the garrison. Late in May, another local company, the Old Topsail Rifles, was also ordered to report to Fort Macon.[9]

Despite the confusion, the overcrowding, the shifting of troops and the hard work, morale at Fort Macon was at a frenzied high as most of the young men of the several companies comprising the garrison looked upon this as the greatest adventure of their lives. Their only knowledge of war came from books and the dashing stories of their fathers and grandfathers of fighting the British, the Indians or the Mexicans. Their words of patriotism and bravado given in the enthusiasm and spirit of the moment in letters home betrayed the fact that they had little understanding of the seriousness and desperation of the struggles which would soon befall them. In one letter quoted in a Raleigh newspaper, a soldier wrote on 19 April: "We are not prepared for our enemy yet. We have but five guns mounted on the outside and only four mounted inside before the porthole (Beaufort Inlet); if Lincoln will only give us a week or ten days, and he will send us down a lot of Yankees, we will treat them to bloody graves." Almost a week later, though, an account of the fort stated a "dozen or more guns have been mounted and the boys feel perfectly confident that Lincoln has no fleet that can enter that harbor. If it is attempted they say that they will blow the last piece of timber out of the water." Another wrote: "We are able of contending with any fleet the Abe may send along, and the *sooner* he sends it the better the whole garrison will be satisfied. They are all anxious for a brush . . . . " In another letter: "But let them come and we will teach them a lesson that will cause them to rue the day they attempt to subjugate the people of North Carolina or any other state." In still another letter: "All are actively engaged in drilling in infantry and artillery tactics. We are also engaged in mounting guns and setting the fort in order to receive the Republicans, and should they delay their attack for a few days, we hope to be prepared to blow them high and dry in short order."[10]

A picture of life in the fort during these first few weeks of the war gradually emerges through the lines of letters written back home. Overcrowding was a large problem since the fort contained far more men than it was ever designed to hold. One soldier wrote: "There are about forty of us in a room about thirty-five feet long and fifteen feet wide . . . The officers are in another room, but I am as well fixed as I would wish to be." Concerning food, another wrote: "Our fare is very good considering we are soldiers. We have peas, bacon, bread, and biscuits." Another observed: "The daily routing (sic) of duty is drilling, working the guns, moulding bullets, making cartridges, etc. The recreations are sea-bathing, fishing, and reading. Bibles are numerous in the Fort, and those who read the most are found to be the best soldiers." By June, when life at the fort had become more routine, James A. Graham of the Orange Guards gave this very detailed account to his mother of the soldier's typical day: "You wished to know how we spend our time. We have to get up at a quarter past 5 in the morning and have our beds made up and rolled by 6, at 6 1/2 we have to drill for an hour and then get breakfast. We then have nothing to do till 10, when we have to drill again for an hour. Drill again at 5 in the evening. Dress parade at 6 1/2 and then Supper. Answer to roll call again at 9 o'clock and have all lights out by 10. Between times we very often have some work to do. When I am not drilling I am generally sleeping, reading, or studying military tactics. On Sunday we have no drills and generally have preaching once and sometimes twice."[11]

The soldiers received many articles sent to them by their families, such as food, clothing, uniforms, and books. They also enjoyed great support from local towns in the area. The ladies of New Bern contributed bedsack mattresses, pillows, cartridges, sand bags, cartridge bags, and various items of clothing which they had sewed or made up for the men of the fort. The ladies of Beaufort were also sewing mattresses and other articles while at one point the ladies of Goldsboro made cakes to be sent down to the fort, as well as mattresses, towels, and a flag for the Goldsboro Rifles contributed by the ladies of the Wayne Female College. Bulletins were placed in the various newspapers calling for public contributions of everything from sand bags to benches and chairs to bacon, meal, flour, lard, and so forth. Two ladies from Washington, North Carolina, contributed a large "Pine Tree Flag" (the unofficial State Flag), which flew over the fort during the first couple of weeks. About 1 May, however, the ladies of Morehead City came over to the fort to present a large Confederate flag which they had made. A salute of nine guns was fired as this flag was hoisted up the flagpole. The sounding of the guns brought a number of soldiers who had been down the beach scurrying to the fort in belief an attack had begun. Their discomfiture over their mistake was a source of considerable amusement and joking among the garrison thereafter.[12]

Interestingly, the appearance of the Confederate flag over Fort Macon caused an unexpected controversy among some of the garrison. Since North Carolina had not yet seceded from the Union and joined the Confederacy, some felt the appearance of the Confederate flag was unwarranted and presumptuous. Their choice to volunteer for service was for the defense of the state against invasion and at this point had nothing to do with service to the Confederacy. Several members actually left the ranks in protest and did not return until North Carolina did finally secede from the Union to join the Confederacy on 20 May 1861. The rest of the garrison had no such problems of conscience. News of the state's secession reached the fort at 9:00 P.M. on 21 May and brought "the wildest and most enthusiastic demonstrations of joy." The garrison formed by companies on the parade ground and marched to Colonel Tew's office with the Confederate flag flying. The men called for Colonel Tew to come out, which he did and delivered a stirring address as the men shouted and cheered. At the close of the address, three cheers were given for both the state and the Confederacy, whereupon the men began singing the "Old North State Forever" and "Dixie". Eleven guns were fired at noon the next day in celebration.[13]

THE QUEST FOR ARMAMENT

By far the biggest concern at Fort Macon was the acquisition of more cannons for its defense. Once Governor Ellis learned that both Fort Macon and Fort Caswell at the mouth of the Cape Fear River had been seized by state troops, he knew they would require heavy guns for proper defense. None were available in the state but fortunately both Governor Francis W. Pickens of South Carolina and Governor John Letcher of Virginia were willing to help out in this regard. As a result, Duncan K. McRae, a noted state judge who had gone to Charleston on 16 April, was requested to act as a Special Commissioner for Ellis to procure what guns and ammunition might be spared by South Carolina for the two forts. On the same day, John D. Whitford was sent to Richmond in a similar capacity.[14]

At Charleston, Judge McRae conferred with Governor Pickens and Brigadier General P. G. T. Beauregard, commanding the Confederate Provisional Forces at Charleston, about acquiring guns and ammunition for North Carolina. As General Beauregard was dismantling and changing some of the harbor batteries following the surrender of Fort Sumter, a number of guns could be spared. An agreement was reached whereby North Carolina would be given nine heavy guns, ammunition, and 20,000 pounds of powder. Of these, one 8-inch columbiad from Fort Sumter and two 32-pounders from a battery on Sullivan's Island would be sent to Fort Macon and the rest to Fort Caswell. This plan was soon changed, however, so that Fort Macon would receive two 32-pounders and two 24-pounders from the "Enfilade Battery" on Sullivan's Island. On 18 April, these guns were loaded aboard the steamer *Chesterfield* and carried to Wilmington. From this point the guns were carried by rail to Morehead City. On 24 April, the four guns and their ammunition arrived at Fort Macon and were carried into the fort. Judge McRae personally accompanied them from Charleston to Fort Macon.[15]

In Richmond, John D. Whitford met with Governor John Letcher and Mr. Joseph R. Anderson, owner of the Tredegar Iron Works, which was the principal ordnance manufacturer for the South, to purchase ordnance for the state, including heavy columbiads for Forts Macon and Caswell. Among the large order for cannons and ammunition placed for North Carolina with the Tredegar Iron Works were two 10-inch columbiads to be divided between the two forts. Four 8-inch columbiads were also ordered but Tredegar was unable to fill the request. With the help of Governor Letcher, however, Whitford was able to purchase these from the nearby Bellona Foundry, which also made ordnance. The six columbiads were shipped to North Carolina at the end of April and in May all were ordered to Fort Macon instead of being shared with Fort Caswell. Only one gun carriage for one of the 10-inch columbiads was available and this was mounted on the fort's upper terreplein during 12-13 May. Gun carriages for the remaining columbiads had to be made from scratch at Wilmington. A shipment of 8-inch columbiad carriages from there finally arrived at Fort Macon on 31 May, which enabled two of the 8-inch columbiads to be mounted in the fort during 6–7 June. About this time, however, the remaining two 8-inch columbiads were ordered to Fort Ocracoke, on Beacon Island in Ocracoke Inlet. For heavy guns, Fort Macon thus was left with one 10-inch and two 8-inch columbiads mounted and one 10-inch columbiad unmounted.[16]

In addition to Richmond and Charleston, a greater source of ordnance in these early months of the war was the U.S. Navy's Gosport Navy Yard at Norfolk, which was seized by Virginia state troops on 20 April. Large stores of powder, ammunition, and about 1,200 of the U.S. Navy's cannons were captured with the Navy Yard, some of which were soon shared with North Carolina and other Confederate states. One of the earliest requests for guns from the Navy Yard for North Carolina was made on 29 April 1861, by Major W. H. C. Whiting, Inspector-General for North Carolina coast defenses. Whiting desired twenty old 32-pounder carronades to be distributed between Forts Macon and Caswell, and the defenses of New Bern for flanking defense and harbor protection against small craft. These stubby cannons were long obsolete as navy broadside guns but were perfect for fort defenses to fire grapeshot and canister into enemy assault forces. Fort Macon's share of seven of the twenty carronades arrived on 18 May, and were placed in the fort's four counterfire galleries under the covertway as soon as casemate carriages could be made for them.[17]

Requests for more guns from Norfolk to arm Fort Macon and other coastal batteries then under construction at Ocracoke, Hatteras, and Oregon Inlets were placed by Governor Ellis and approved. Accordingly, on 8 June a schooner loaded with 32-pounders arrived at Fort Macon from Norfolk, via the Dismal Swamp Canal. Other loads of cannons, mainly 32-pounders, arrived from Norfolk afterward during June and part of July. One barge-load of 32-pounders had the misfortune to sink at Harbor Island, about thirty miles northeast of the fort. A crew of workers from the fort was sent to the scene, retrieved the guns and brought them to the fort at last on 26 June. By mid-summer, a large number of cannons from Norfolk were on hand at the fort.[18]

The gun carriages needed to mount these cannons were not so readily available, since the Navy gun carriages for shipboard use on hand at the Norfolk Navy Yard were largely unsuitable as barbette mounts for a fort. Consequently, most of the regular barbette gun carriages needed for North Carolina's forts had to be made from scratch. Most of Fort Macon's barbette gun carriages were made in Wilmington, whose iron works and shipbuilding facilities made this possible. Still, the time required to fabricate them coupled with the high demand for them by other forts and batteries meant only slow delivery—sometimes weeks between the arrivals of gun carriage shipments. It was June before workers were even able to replace the ten old decayed 24-pounder guns carriages which had been in the fort since 1836 with new ones.[19]

THE SUMMER OF 1861

With all the hustle and bustle going on in and around Fort Macon during the first months of the war, there still remained much to do. An investigation of deficiencies at the fort dated 31 May disclosed many items which the Confederates felt were still needed, particularly more big guns: two 11-inch Dahlgrens, two 8-inch columbiads, six 32-pounders, three 10-inch seacoast mortars, two Coehorn mortars, and four 32- or 24-pounder howitzers. Other needs included 200 rifles, accoutrements for 400 men, gun carriages, ammunition, columbiad elevating mechanisms, and a host of smaller items such as fuses, sabots, sights, and implements. Meanwhile, on 27 May, Brigadier General Walter Gwynn, commander of the state's newly-formed Northern Department, inspected the fort and wrote to Governor Ellis: "I find Fort Macon much more exposed than I had supposed. But one heavy gun has yet been mounted bearing on the channel. There are no land defenses and the guns on every face of the Fort, both by land and sea, are exposed to an enfilade or flank fire. No traverses have been erected to protect them. The guns are all in Barbette without [merlons] to protect either them or the men. The work in progress, that of levelling the sand banks adjacent to the Fort is judicious, but most expensively conducted, the earth being removed by handbarrows . . . The complete defense of the Fort will be expensive and a work of time . . . ." Gwynn felt the present garrison of the fort was insufficient and not less than 2,000 men were required to completely and effectually protect Beaufort Harbor. He felt advanced posts should be maintained along both Bogue and Shackleford Banks with lines of videttes established along the sea fronts of these islands to rapidly communicate any attempted landing of the enemy. Field batteries were also needed at different points of these islands to repel landing attempts, and troop reserves were needed at Morehead City and New Bern.[20]

For the time being the establishment of outpost forces and field batteries adjacent to Fort Macon and Beaufort Harbor did not materialize. Indeed, in the rush now to organize regiments for immediate field service some of the troops were actually *taken* from Fort Macon. The Old Topsail Rifles left the fort on 3 June to join the Second North Carolina Regiment. On 17 June, the Wilson Light Infantry and Goldsboro Volunteers left the fort to form yet another regiment. This left as the fort's garrison the Goldsboro Rifles, Orange Guards, and Guilford Grays, all three of which were infantry, and the Beaufort Harbor Guards, which was artillery. Fortunately, on 1 July a newly-organized company of artillery and engineers from Craven County joined the garrison. It was commanded by Captain Henry T. Guion, the fort's acting chief engineer officer since 1 June.[21]

Even the fort's commander was effected by the lure of field duty. Colonel Charles C. Tew accepted the position of colonel of the newly-formed Second North Carolina Regiment and would soon leave Fort Macon to take command of it. His replacement, Major William L. DeRossett, was assigned to the fort from the defenses of the Cape Fear just before Colonel Tew departed. DeRossett, however, was at Fort Macon only a short time before he too took the field as major of the newly-formed Third North Carolina Regiment even before Colonel Tew's departure. Tew finally left the fort by 5 June and for most of the summer command of the fort devolved upon senior Captain Pride Jones of the Orange Guards. Jones was likewise involved with trying to organize his company and others into a field regiment designated the Ninth North Carolina, although this regiment failed to materialize. In the meantime, Governor Henry T. Clark, who had succeeded the ailing Governor John W. Ellis upon the latter's death on 7 July, assigned his friend Lieutenant Colonel John L. Bridgers, aged forty-one, of Edgecombe County, to command the fort on 24 August. Bridgers had been the captain of the Edgecombe Guards when it came to Fort Macon back in April, but had found the rigors of field command too strenuous for his poor health. A garrison command at Fort Macon was felt to be more suitable for him.[22]

The changing of troops and commanders at the fort was not the only problem encountered during the summer. The effort to arm the fort and improve its defenses was hampered temporarily from an unexpected direction. On 27 June, the State of North Carolina formally ceded her military to the Confederacy with the actual transfer of authority set to take place on 20 August. On 28 June, orders were issued by the North Carolina Military Board to incur no new expense to the state for the coast defenses since the Confederacy would soon be assuming responsibility for them. As a result, in mid-July the Ordnance Officer at Fort Macon, Lieut. Thaddeus Coleman, learned that ten 32-pounder barbette gun carriages and seven casemate carriages for 32-pounder carronades, all of which he had been long awaiting, were ready at Wilmington. However, the quartermaster of the department was unable to assume the cost of transporting them to Fort Macon because of the 28 June orders. Captain Guion, the fort engineer, prevailed upon the Ordnance Department at New Bern for help while an officer from the fort was sent to Wilmington to find a way to get the gun carriages to Fort Macon. They eventually did arrive, but some of them came only after 20 August, when the Confederacy formally assumed responsibility for the state's defenses. However, several other shipments of gun carriages from Wilmington to Fort Macon, which had probably already been paid for, arrived at Fort Macon during the last half of July and first part of August, including a long-awaited gun carriage for the fort's second 10-inch columbiad.[23]

The arrival of the 10-inch columbiad carriage on 27 July meant that this gun, which had been lying unmounted in the fort since May, could at last be installed for defense. However, it was not to benefit Fort Macon. Orders received from Raleigh directed the transfer of the gun and its carriage to Hatteras Inlet for the two forts being erected there. Brigadier General Walter Gwynn protested the transfer of the gun since it was so badly needed at Fort Macon but was overruled. The gun was moved back to the wharf and on 19 August was loaded aboard the schooner *George Handy* to be sent to Hatteras.[24]

During the summer, work on the fort's defenses continued with the engineer work force of free negroes and slaves headed by Colonel W. Beverhout Thompson and, after 1 June, by Captain Henry T. Guion. The most labor-intensive task remained the levelling of sand hills and removal of brush and undergrowth outward from the fort. This continued until 6 July. Other tasks involved unloading cannons, gun carriages, lumber, coal, and materials from vessels and transporting them into the fort. Cannons were mounted and five new brick and stone gun mounts were added on the landward sides of the citadel. Sand bags were filled and placed on the parapets, a new flagstaff was erected, and one of the old buildings outside the fort was made into a hospital. A battery was constructed to cover the approaches between the fort and the lighthouse. Various other smaller duties were completed in and around the fort. By 20 August 1861, the date the Confederacy formally assumed responsibility for all North Carolina defenses, Fort Macon was in an excellent condition for defense. The work performed by the work force of free negroes and slaves to transform this neglected, deteriorated fort into a proper condition for war was remarkable. Now, with the transfer of authority to the Confederacy, the accounts of the state were closed and the work force paid off. With their dismissal, all further work details around the fort would come from the garrison.[25]

The garrison of the fort remained as the three unattached companies of infantry (Goldsboro Rifles, Guilford Grays, and Orange Guards), and Guion's and Pender's companies of artillery, which had become designated as Companies B and G, respectively, of the 10th North Carolina Regiment (or First North Carolina Artillery). Not long after the Confederacy assumed responsibility for the fort, two additional artillery companies joined the garrison. One was the Old Topsail Rifles, Captain Stephen D. Pool, which returned to the fort from Virginia on 25 August. This company had been stationed at the fort at the end of May but had left in June for field service. After serving briefly in Virginia, the company was ordered back to Fort Macon. It eventually was designated Company H, 10th North Carolina, and served thereafter as heavy artillery. The other company was a newly-formed company of heavy artillery designated as Company F, 10th North Carolina, Lieutenant Daniel Cogdell, which arrived on 29 August.[26]

At the time the Confederacy took over the fort on 20 August 1861, the armament of the fort consisted of one 10-inch columbiad, two 8-inch columbiads, nine 32-pounders, nineteen 24-pounders, and five 6-pounder field guns. Also at the fort, but unmounted, were the following: one 42-pounder, one 42-pounder carronade, seven 32-pounder carronades, forty-five 32-pounders, and seven 24-pounders. There were far more of these guns than was ever intended to be mounted at the fort. Colonel James A. J. Bradford, North Carolina's Chief of Artillery and Engineers, inspected the fort two days before the Confederacy assumed responsibility and reported: "The fort itself is in good repair, and is in condition to resist with effect any attack that may be made upon it seaward or landward, within the range of its armament . . . I deem it indispensible that this and all the batteries on the coast should be furnished with a long rifled 32-pounder, the range of which would enable them to compete with ships having similar guns."[27]

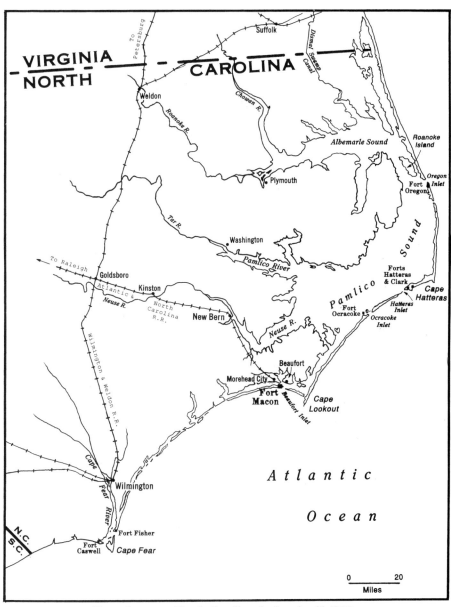

Map of eastern North Carolina during the Civil War.

Bradford's perceptive recommendation about providing rifled cannons for the various North Carolina coastal forts seems to be one of the earliest realizations of the need by the forts for the accurate long-ranged fire which the dawning age of rifled artillery could provide against the array of large caliber guns which powerful steam warships could amass. To fulfill the need for rifled cannons of large caliber for seacoast defenses, Confederate authorities at the Norfolk Navy Yard began to rifle some of the smoothbore cannons on hand there. Bradford noted in his report that some of these should be sent to the North Carolina forts. However, before any notice or action could be taken on his recommendation, the first battle on North Carolina soil took place. The result was not only a stinging endorsement of the need for rifled guns, but also a demonstration of the inadequacy of the coastal defenses as a whole in the face of an adversary whose resources had apparently been badly underestimated. The repercussions of this battle would set the tone for defensive measures for the remainder of the year.

AFTERMATH OF HATTERAS INLET

On 27 August 1861, a powerful fleet of seven Union warships, including two large steam frigates, and a number of smaller vessels, all under the command of Commodore Silas H. Stringham, anchored off Hatteras Inlet. Here stood Forts Hatteras and Clark, two of the earthen batteries built by the state during the summer which had just been transferred to Confederate authority. On the following day the Union ships attacked Fort Clark and smothered it with such a heavy fire the garrison was forced to abandon it during the afternoon. The five 32-pounders of the little fort's armament were so outranged that Union sailors on one of the frigates were heard to howl with laughter when much of the fort's return fire splashed well short of the ships. On the following day, 29 August, Fort Hatteras met the same fate and surrendered with most of the combined garrisons of both forts. Union Army troops landed on the beach to attack from the land side never even got the chance to participate.[28]

The ease with which the guns of Union warships had forced the surrender of the two forts which were thought to be so formidable was completely demoralizing to State and Confederate officials. The 32-pounders which had comprised the bulk of the armament of both forts had been completely outclassed in range and weight of metal by the larger 9-, 10-, and 11-inch guns of the warships. The need for long-ranged rifled guns of heavy caliber in all the coastal forts had thus been graphically and expensively illustrated. The only gun the Hatteras forts had which could have competed with the ships was the 10-inch columbiad which had been transferred from Fort Macon ten days earlier. Unfortunately, it was still lying on the beach where it had been unloaded because there had been no gin on hand to mount it. The folly of transferring it had resulted only in its capture by the Union along with the rest of the armament of the two forts. Confederate authorities now hurriedly tried to send some rifled guns to the North Carolina coast while Governor Henry T. Clark called for more troops to defend the coast, even at the expense of recalling some of the North Carolina regiments sent to Virginia.[29]

What was even more incredible was the demoralizing effect the battle had on other nearby Confederate installations. With confidence in the coastal forts lost, Confederate hopes for defense crumbled. Fort Oregon at Oregon Inlet and Fort Ocracoke at Ocracoke Inlet were hastily abandoned by their garrisons even though no immediate attack was threatened. In the haste to leave, most of the armament and stores were left behind and in both cases lost. The abandonment of Fort Ocracoke was particularly unnecessary since the large-class Union warships which had attacked Hatteras could not have approached close enough to attack the fort due to the shallow water surrounding it. Thus by one battle at Hatteras Inlet, a large yawning hole was opened in North Carolina's coastal defenses which completely exposed the sounds and inland rivers to Union exploitation.[30]

On the heels of these disasters came word to the War Department in Richmond on 3 September that the garrison of Fort Macon was likewise preparing to abandon the post without a fight. This in turn brought Brigadier General Richard Gatlin, newly-appointed commander of the Department of North Carolina, to the fort to investigate. Gatlin found the report to be completely untrue. In fact, the garrison of Fort Macon was ready and confidently awaiting a Union attack. They had been at work gathering provisions, filling and strapping shells, loading cartridge bags, and mounting more guns. Pickets had been extended along Bogue Banks to watch for the enemy and were equipped with signal rockets to give early warning of an enemy landing, especially at night. At midnight on 31 August, a false alarm sounded, and the garrison turned out on the parade ground and coolly went to their posts in expectation of impending attack. No attack came but the intensity of the prospect of impending attack was heightened by the sight of refugees from Hatteras and Ocracoke, and even some of the local civilians fleeing inland in anticipation of a Union attack. Captain Josiah Pender's battery, acting as light artillery, armed itself with some of the 6-pounder field guns at the fort, meanwhile, and was established on Bogue Banks on 1 September six miles west of the fort to support the pickets and resist any enemy landing attempt.[31]

General Gatlin reported back to Richmond on 4 September that "the person giving the information [that Fort Macon was about to be abandoned] is devoid of all truth. The post is commanded by Lieutenant Colonel J. L. Bridgers, North Carolina State Troops, who as a captain at Bethel was specially distinguished for gallant conduct. No doubt but that he will display the same courage whenever occasion calls for it. The garrison is made up of raw troops, unaccustomed to service at heavy guns. They know the manual of the piece, and are active in their efforts to learn their duties. With the assistance of good artillery officers they will in a short time be fit for any emergency. The fort cannot be taken unless by regular siege, and even then is capable of being defended for a long period. I have no apprehensions about it."[32]

Two days passed and then came reports an attack on the fort was imminent. A British warship which arrived off Beaufort Inlet passed along word that a large U.S. Navy squadron was preparing to attack the fort in the next several days. Ominously, on 7 September, four Union warships appeared off Beaufort Inlet looking like the vanguard of a larger approaching force. General Gatlin, in company with his newly-assigned commander of North

Carolina coast defenses Brigadier General Joseph R. Anderson, travelled down to Fort Macon on the following day from his headquarters at Goldsboro to view the situation firsthand. Even sixty-six-year old Edmund Ruffin, Virginia's famous fire-eating secessionist who had fired the first cannon against Fort Sumter, had come to the fort to see the action during this period. Fortunately, no attack came and by the 9th only one enemy steamer remained offshore.[33]

In between alarms a great deal of preparation and activity was going on in and around Fort Macon as State and Confederate authorities, now jolted out of their false sense of security, sought to prevent disaster from happening at Fort Macon as it had at Hatteras. On 2 September, the newly-mustered 26th North Carolina Regiment, Colonel Zebulon B. Vance, was ordered to the coast by rail from Raleigh. After being stationed several days at Morehead City, the regiment was moved across the sound on 7 September in anticipation of the Union attack and took position on Bogue Banks six miles west of the fort with Captain Pender's battery. On the following day, the 7th North Carolina Regiment, Colonel Reuben P. Campbell, arrived at Carolina City and crossed over to Bogue Banks to take position four miles west of the fort. It remained here for about one month before returning to Carolina City. In the fort itself, the garrison was increased by the arrival of yet another artillery company, Company F, 40th North Carolina (3rd Artillery), commanded by Captain Joseph Lawrence. In the effort to obtain rifled cannons, a 5.82-inch rifled columbiad and its gun carriage were shipped from the Tredegar Iron Works in Richmond on 5 September to New Bern and Fort Macon. The gun was mounted in place by 13 September.[34]

Another important deficit was the garrison's lack of guidance and training from a professional artillery officer. The green companies of the garrison, as General Gatlin had pointed out, eagerly stumbled through the instruction for heavy artillery as best they could but no one in the fort had been schooled in formal artillery training. At the insistence of Governor Clark, General Gatlin and others, Commodore W. F. Lynch and a party of officers and men from the Confederate Naval vessels *Beaufort* and *Winslow* at New Bern went down to Fort Macon on 6 September by train to help familiarize the garrison with the guns. As the garrison was expecting the arrival of the Union fleet as reported by a British warship, Lieutenant Colonel Bridgers was very relieved when they arrived. He confessed to them he knew nothing about heavy artillery or the defense of forts, but stated: "I only know that that flag must not come down." When told that one of Lynch's naval officers, Lieutenant William H. Parker, would be temporarily assigned as the fort's chief of ordnance, Bridgers added: "Now my mind is at rest." When Parker held a drill and practice firing, the green garrison did quite well. The other naval officers and men found their services were not needed and returned to New Bern. Parker remained at the fort about two weeks as acting chief of ordnance, training the garrison in the use of the big guns.[35]

While at Fort Macon, however, Commodore Lynch saw the need for more rifled guns and on 8 September sent one of his officers to Norfolk under orders to obtain one. Within a few days a banded, rifled 32-pounder was sent by the Confederate Navy Department from Norfolk to Fort Macon and was mounted in place by 22 September. The effectiveness of this piece was limited because with the banded breech it would not fit properly on the regular 32-pounder gun carriage which was the only thing available for it, and because it only had seven shells. Nevertheless, Fort Macon now had five cannons of long range: one 10-inch and two 8-inch columbiads, the rifled columbiad and now the rifled 32-pounder. While the fort could now offer a credible defense with those pieces, it was not realistic to expect only five guns to bear the brunt of a naval attack. More long-ranged guns and ammunition were still needed.[36]

The skill and training of the men would soon be put to the test. At 8:00 P.M. on 21 September a report was received of a Union fleet on its way to attack Fort Macon. The garrison turned out and worked until early hours on the 22nd making preparations for attack. There was no sign of the enemy until the 23rd, but by dusk of that day six Union warships had arrived and anchored off the fort. Another long night was passed in the fort but by the first light of the 24th only two of the six steamers still remained. Later in the morning two others passed in the distance heading south and in the afternoon one of the two anchored off the fort also departed. Once again, another false alarm. However, there was one casualty—Lieutenant Colonel Bridgers. The stress and exertion of commanding the fort and the repeated alarms had taxed his poor health to the point he was compelled to offer his resignation from the service. In a letter to Governor Clark on 24 September, following the departure of the Union warships, he wrote: "I leave for home Wednesday morning [the 25th] for I think now is a quiet a time as we shall have. To leave is to me a bitter pill but I regard it as a necessary one. I think I owe it to myself—to the garrison and to the State."[37]

The choice of the Confederate War Department to replace Bridgers was Colonel Moses J. White, aged twenty-seven, of Vicksburg, Mississippi. White had served briefly in the old U.S. Army after graduating second in his West Point Class of 1858 and had joined the Confederate Army after the secession of his home state. White was trained in artillery and ordnance, and had been serving in Tennessee as ordnance officer in the forces of Major General Leonidas M. Polk. Unfortunately, like his predecessor, White suffered from frail health, and had a history of epilepsy. White arrived and took command of the fort on 5 October.[38]

During September, 1861, the danger of naval attack was not the only danger facing Fort Macon. The buildup of a large Union force on Hatteras Island and the exposed nature of the inland sounds meant the fort could also expect the possibility of Union forces approaching via the sounds. A line of old vessels had been sunk across the entrance to Core Sound from Pamlico Sound but was ineffective as a barrier. Even local citizens complained of the ease with which light draft Union vessels might pass through these sounds to seize Beaufort, Morehead City, and the railroad depot to cut off Fort Macon from its supply line. As a result, on 5 October, Brigadier General D. H. Hill, in command of the Department of North Carolina's newly-created District of the Pamlico in which Fort Macon was located, ordered that batteries be erected at Harker's Island, six miles east-northeast of Fort Macon to close off the approach in the sounds from the direction of Ocracoke and Hatteras. After completing surveys of the area, a battery mounting four 24-pounders brought over from the fort was begun on the

northeast point of Harker's Island on 12 October, using work details from
Lieutenant Daniel Cogdell's Company F, 10th North Carolina, and a group
of free negro laborers furnished by the Beaufort Committee of Safety. The
battery bore on the approaches through the sound and closed off the deep
strait between the island and the mainland. On 22 October, a second battery mounting two 24-pounders from the fort was begun on Shell Point on
the southeast end of Harker's Island situated in a large midden of oyster
shells thrown in the water by the local Indians in ancient times. This battery would cover the channel passing around the island between it and
Shackleford Banks. Both the two batteries operated as satellite fortifications of Fort Macon. They were manned by Lieutenant Cogdell's Company
F, 10th North Carolina; Captain Joseph Lawrence's Company F, 40th North
Carolina; and Captain Benjamin Leecraft's newly-formed Company G, 36th
North Carolina (2nd Artillery) from Carteret County.[39]

During this time there had been no relaxation in the effort to get more
rifled guns for Fort Macon. At least four more were needed in addition to
the two which had arrived in September. Both General Gatlin, the Department commander, and General Hill, the district commander, sent a number of requests for more rifled guns from the Norfolk Navy Yard but were
turned down by the Navy Department. The Secretary of the Navy responded
that up to 2 October, 242 guns including six rifled 32-pounders had been
sent to the North Carolina defenses and no more could be spared. Hill
even went to Norfolk in person on 18 October to plead his case, but was
unsuccessful in acquiring more guns. In desperation, a different approach
was tried. In Charleston, South Carolina, the firm of J. M. Eason and Brother
had developed a portable rifling machine which could rifle smoothbore
cannons in the field. With the assistance of North Carolina Governor Henry
T. Clark, General Gatlin arranged for the Easons to bring this machine to
North Carolina in October to rifle some of the old 32-pounders at both
Fort Macon and New Bern.[40]

There was a great sense of urgency in getting the Easons and their
machine to North Carolina because of increased enemy activity. During
most of October, parties sent out from Union warships off Beaufort Inlet

were busy taking soundings of approaches to Bogue and Shackleford Banks and also questioning loyal fishermen about the Confederate defenses of the area. These were seen as indicators that an attack was forthcoming. On 21 October reports were received of a large Union expedition of ships and transports with 15,000 troops about to put to sea from New York and Hampton Roads to attack Fort Macon and New Bern. When this expedition finally put to sea from Hampton Roads one week later, the need for rifled guns became critical. Fortunately, the Eason Brothers finally arrived at New Bern with their rifling machine and rifled five 32-pounders in the river batteries below New Bern. Following this, the Easons brought the machine to Fort Macon and rifled in place four of the fort's 32-pounders.[41]

As it turned out, the impending attack was another false alarm. The powerful Union expedition was real enough, but its destination turned out to be Port Royal, South Carolina, not the North Carolina coast. Had the expedition actually attacked Fort Macon, the performance of the fort's four new rifled guns probably would not have matched that of the other rifled 32-pounder received the previous month. There was no way to band the four new rifled guns in the field to reinforce the breech against the strain of shooting the heavier rifled projectiles as the Norfolk rifled 32-pounder had been. It is questionable whether these guns were safe enough to shoot with full charges without the risk of bursting the barrel.

Apart from rifled cannons, more columbiads were obtained for Fort Macon, although in one instance not without a disagreement over possession. Back in June, two of the four 8-inch columbiads the fort had received from Richmond in the first weeks of the war had been transferred to Fort Ocracoke on Beacon Island in Ocracoke Inlet. After Hatteras Inlet was captured on 28-29 August, the garrison of Fort Ocracoke abandoned the post, leaving behind its armament of two 8-inch columbiads, four 8-inch Navy guns, and fourteen 32-pounders. Union warships did not immediately take possession of the fort and the fort sat unattended for two weeks before it finally dawned upon someone that maybe there was still time to save some of the guns and equipment. On 15 September, the steamer *Albemarle* and part of the 27th North Carolina Regiment went down to the fort from New

Bern and saved the two 8-inch columbiads, which were carried back to New Bern and mounted in one of the river batteries. Before anything else could be saved, however, a Union force destroyed both the fort and the remaining guns on the 16th.[42]

The presence of the two salvaged columbiads at the New Bern defenses sparked hopes at Fort Macon that one or both of them would be returned to the fort, particularly since the need for long-ranged heavy guns was now so great. The fort's officers felt that the potential of these valuable guns was being wasted in the river batteries where the smoothbore 32-pounders that constituted the bulk of the armament of the New Bern defenses were more than sufficient against Union gunboats coming up the Neuse River. At New Bern, however, the officers charged with the Neuse River batteries and the district ordnance officer, John D. Whitford, had no intention of giving up any of the columbiads. Great reliance was placed upon these two guns for the defense of the city, Whitford argued, and Fort Macon would be better served with having more rifled guns instead, which used less gunpowder. Whitford even wrote to Governor Henry T. Clark to block any attempt to take the columbiads back to Fort Macon. The issue as to where the columbiads would stay was not resolved until General Hill, the district commander, visited Fort Macon on 25 October as tension mounted over the impending departure of the Union expedition supposedly set to attack the fort. He saw how deficient the fort was in heavy guns and gave orders that one of the two 8-inch columbiads be sent to Fort Macon at once. Ordnance Officer Whitford protested to General Gatlin but the latter refused to go against Hill's decision. Fort Macon once again had three of the four 8-inch columbiads it had originally received from Richmond five months earlier. The fourth columbiad remained where it was at Fort Ellis in the Neuse River below New Bern.[43]

At the same time the Union expedition was putting to sea, General Gatlin was anxiously awaiting the arrival of yet another 8-inch columbiad from Richmond which he hoped would reach Fort Macon in time to be of service against the expected Union attack. After repeated requests for guns to the Ordnance Department in Richmond, he had finally been promised an 8-inch columbiad for Fort Macon but with an attack imminent, delays were experienced with the railroad in shipping it between Richmond and Goldsboro. Finally the gun reached Goldsboro and was sent down the railroad to Fort Macon on 27 October.[44]

Even though the Union expedition passed on by to Port Royal, South Carolina, without making any attacks along the North Carolina coast, the eleventh-hour attempts to add to the fort's armament had resulted in upgrading the armament to a very formidable array of heavy and long-ranged guns which included one 10-inch and four 8-inch columbiads, one rifled columbiad and five rifled 32-pounders. At some point later in the fall, however, the banded rifled 32-pounder was transferred elsewhere, leaving Fort Macon with only the four unbanded guns rifled by the Eason Brothers.

THE UNION NAVY AND FORT MACON

Despite Confederate fears of an impending attack on the fort by a Union Navy force similar to the one which had attacked Hatteras, the Union Navy had early on declined to attack Fort Macon because of its recognized strength. The fort was far stronger and more defensible than the simple earthwork forts at Hatteras, and consequently the chance of success against it were regarded as being unfavorable. The Union Navy's views regarding Fort Macon were aptly summed up in the words of Commander S. C. Rowan, commanding the USS *Pawnee*, one of the ships which had participated in the Hatteras attack. In a letter to the commander of the Atlantic Blockading Squadron on 20 September 1861, Rowan advised: "Fort Macon can not be taken by the ships. I am told it is a casemated fort, and, should you succeed in driving them from the barbette guns, they can retire to the casemates and allow you to empty your shell lockers with impunity."[45]

All the preparations in and around Fort Macon during September and October of 1861 had not gone unnoticed by the Union Navy warships on station off Beaufort Inlet. The Confederates could plainly be seen mounting their new cannons and improving the fort's defenses. One naval commander estimated as many as seventy-five guns in position. Also, rumors were received that the fort had been covered with railroad iron as a further protection. It was recognized that with these preparations and the large number of Confederate soldiers stationed on the Banks for its defense, the only way to capture Fort Macon was with a large-scale combined operation by both land and sea. Commander Rowan, for example, felt such an effort would require a "well-commanded land force, in two divisions, one to be transferred to the nearest point on the Neuse River and take Beaufort in the rear, while the other division passed down the sound. The [fort] could then be taken by approaches in the rear, which is its weak point."[46]

A similar view was expressed by Captain George A. Prentiss, commanding the Union steamer *Albatross*, stationed off Beaufort Inlet. Prentiss also noted Confederate preparations for the fort's defense and the large number of Confederate infantry stationed near the fort on Bogue Banks. He reported: "The place can be carried, but it will require 10,000 men to cooperate with the fleet." Prentiss believed the Union ground forces could land on both Shackleford and Bogue Banks, secure themselves from attack, and establish positions from which to bombard the fort. He felt that under fire from these two points, as well as from a Union fleet offshore, the fort would be overwhelmed and taken.[47]

The Union Army also recognized the need for such a plan. In the fall of 1861 as Union authorities formulated the prospect for another attack on the North Carolina coast, including Fort Macon, their plans centered on a large combined operation involving the participation of both the Army and Navy. During the fall and winter of 1861, these plans were rapidly carried forward in the form of yet another amphibious expedition.

INCIDENTS OF THE FALL AND WINTER

In between alarms was the inevitable boredom and frustration of garrison duty for the men stationed in Fort Macon and on Bogue Banks. Many had signed into service believing the war would consist of only a couple of quick battles after which everyone could return home. Few would have dreamed they would still be here more than one-half of a year after the war had started. Many felt the frustration of being trapped in a seemingly dead end garrison situation while so many battles and exciting events were taking place on other fronts, especially in Virginia. Every day they saw the enemy in the form of warships hovering on patrol and blockade just a few miles off the banks and inlet. However, they were not normally disposed to offer any excitement of coming in to exchange shots with the fort. During the first part of November, this situation changed and at last the men had the satisfaction of an actual encounter with enemy sailors.

As the Union fleet of the Port Royal Expedition passed the North Carolina coast on 1 November, it was battered by a terrific gale which caused the loss of several ships. One of these was the 1,124-ton Army sidewheel steam transport *Star of the Union,* which came ashore in a damaged, leaking condition on the night of the 2nd on Bogue Banks at a point about sixteen miles west of Fort Macon. The vessel was carrying sixty-four horses, provisions, and a large amount of quartermaster stores, much of which was lost. The eighty crewmen aboard saved themselves by rigging a line to shore and pulling a boat along it back and forth between the wreck and shore until everyone had gotten off. The crewmen marched unarmed down the beach toward Fort Macon to surrender. The captain of the vessel, John J. Garvin, mounted one of the horses which had survived and went ahead to the camp of Colonel Zebulon B. Vance's 26th North Carolina, now situated two miles west of the fort. Here he surrendered himself and his men. The sight of so many live enemy sailors was quite exciting to the Confederates but their stay was very brief. On 4 November, the prisoners were put aboard a train under guard at Morehead City and transported to Raleigh for detainment.[48]

As far as the wreck of the *Union,* Colonel Vance sent a portion of his regiment and one field gun of Pender's battery under Lieutenant J. P. Robinson up the beach to take possession of it and salvage what they could. The beach was strewn with hay, barrels, wreckage, and dead horses. The Confederates rounded up fifteen horses which had survived and removed various articles such as blankets, Sharps rifles and cartridges, two small engines, and other items. Many other valuable articles were lost as the vessel soon broke in half and settled. On 6 November, the Union gunboat *Alba-*

tross passed close to investigate the wreck but did not attack the Confederates. The next day the *Albatross* returned but again showed no hostile disposition. Under a flag of truce, a party from the warship approached the Confederates, inquiring of the name of the wreck and the fate of the crew. Meanwhile, the salvage continued under difficult conditions. The Confederates worked in the cold water by day and slept in the cold, damp air at night nestled in the sand dunes without tents. The Union warships in the area fortunately did not attempt to interfere for some time. On 12 November, however, two Union gunboats passing at different times, the *Gemsbok* and the *Monticello,* moved in close and fired a total of twenty-two shells at the Confederates, who took cover behind the dunes. No one was hurt. Salvage was concluded in December and wreck was ultimately burned on 18–19 December.[49]

During the fall and winter of 1861, the Confederates in and near Fort Macon were under a far greater threat from disease than from the enemy. Large numbers of soldiers packed together in damp casemates, or exposed windswept camps along the island created ideal conditions for sickness. Epidemics of fever, measles, and mumps swept through the ranks of almost every company. Captain Stephen D. Pool's Company H, 10th North Carolina, from the fort garrison, which maintained outside picket posts on the banks, was much affected by sickness, as was Colonel Vance's 26th North Carolina, which maintained station on the exposed banks until almost the end of November. Vance's men had a particularly difficult time during their stay on the banks because many of them were from the mountain counties and unaccustomed to the heavy, damp atmosphere of the coast. A number of men died during this time, including nine from one of Vance's companies in a period of one week. Over at Carolina City, a hospital was established in the town hotel and remained almost constantly filled with at least one hundred sufferers each week. Fortunately, local ladies' aid societies helped with the sick and contributed supplies.[50]

Colonel Vance's men were allowed to move back over to the mainland from the banks at the end of November and establish winter quarters at Carolina City. As for the other Confederate regiment stationed in the area,

Colonel Reuben P. Campbell's 7th North Carolina Regiment had been stationed on the banks only about a month during September and consequently had suffered far less sickness in its camps at Carolina City. Campbell's regiment later established winter quarters at Newport in December. Captain Pool's Company H from the fort garrison, however, continued to maintain the line of outside pickets on Bogue Banks. On Shackleford Banks on the opposite side of Beaufort Inlet, a detachment of twelve men was also stationed, with headquarters at the Cape Lookout Lighthouse. They watched the movements of the blockading Union gunboats offshore and transmitted valuable information back to the fort. Several times boats from the Union vessels were landed ashore to buy fish from local fishermen, many of whom were loyal to the Union, and obtain information. Each time some of the men of this detachment were present, posing as fishermen themselves and mingling with the unsuspecting Union sailors. The fishermen never gave away the identity of the soldiers and no useable information was given out to the enemy sailors.[51]

At the end of 1861, command changes took place in two of the fort's companies. On 30 November, Captain Joseph Lawrence, commanding Company F, 40th North Carolina, at the Harker's Island batteries, resigned from service. Captain Richard H. Blount took command of the company in his place. The second command change was far more serious, however. It was found that Captain Josiah S. Pender, of Company G, 10th North Carolina, had been engaging in wrongful conduct. Colonel White, the fort commandant, brought charges against him for absence from command between 3 and 20 November, falsely claiming General D. H. Hill as authority for his absence, and improperly appropriating a number of articles from the wreck of the *Union* by a falsified requisition of General Hill. Pender was court martialled and found guilty of four out of five charges against him. He was dismissed from the service on 19 December. Captain James L. Manney, son of Doctor Manney who had been a brick contractor during the fort's construction, assumed command of Company G upon Pender's dismissal.[52]

During November and December, supplies of projectiles for the fort's rifled 32-pounders were finally received. One shipment was received from the Norfolk Navy Yard and others were supplied by the Ordnance Department at New Bern, which had been casting projectiles. Because these shells had been so hard to come by, and because the powder supply in the fort was also at a premium, no attempt was made to try out or practice with these shells. However, early in December, Brigadier General Lawrence O'Brien Branch, who had recently replaced General D. H. Hill as commander of the District of the Pamlico, visited Fort Macon and ordered three or four of the projectiles made at New Bern to be test fired. Unfortunately, one of the shells became wedged in one of the rifled 32-pounders and another was forced into the gun only with great difficulty. Branch had all the New Bern projectiles set aside until they could be checked with a ring gauge. It was found afterward that many of these projectiles had protuberances which would cause them to jam in the bore. All were checked and filed down until they would pass with proper tolerances through the ring gauge. It was certainly fortunate to have discovered this now rather than in the heat of battle.[53]

The year 1861 ended with the following disposition of forces for the defense of Beaufort Harbor: the infantry companies Goldsboro Rifles, Guilford Grays, and Orange Guards (now designated Companies A, B, and G of the 27th North Carolina Regiment, respectively), and the artillery Companies B (Guion) and G (Manney), 10th North Carolina, constituted the fort's immediate garrison. Captain Pool's Company H, 10th North Carolina, was doing outside picket duty on the banks. At Harker's Island, Cogdell's Company F, 10th North Carolina; Blount's Company F, 40th North Carolina; and Captain Benjamin Leecraft's Company G, 36th North Carolina, manned the two batteries guarding the northeast approaches through the sounds. At Carolina City, Vance's 26th North Carolina was in winter quarters, as was Campbell's 7th North Carolina at Newport.

The new year began with a flurry of activity to improve the defenses of eastern North Carolina. Most of the activity was directed toward the erection of batteries and defenses for Roanoke Island, Washington, New Bern and Wilmington. Fort Macon was not forgotten and requisitions to the Ordnance Department in Richmond had resulted in the promise of more columbiads. Colonel White, the fort's commandant, had been concerned, meanwhile, that the fort's armament was too exposed and had requested in December that some means of erecting bombproof casemates over and around the guns be devised to reduce their exposure. In January, 1862, Engineer Captain R. K. Meade was sent to the fort to study the possibility of doing this. Unfortunately for White, the idea was abandoned due to a lack of materials and what was felt to be a want of time. The services and attentions of the Department's engineers were demanded elsewhere as another large Union amphibious force was gathering at Hampton Roads for an expedition south. All indications were that its target was the coast of North Carolina.[54]

6

THE SIEGE OF FORT MACON

By the beginning of the new year 1862 reports had been received of another powerful Union expedition being assembled at Hampton Roads to attack some point on the coast. To General Gatlin, commander of the Department of North Carolina, the fact that so many of the ships being assembled by the enemy were light draft steamers and river vessels left no doubt the expedition's intention was to operate in the sounds and rivers of the North Carolina coast. Thus the long-dreaded day had arrived in which the Union would push forward in force into the inland coastal section of the state's coast from the foothold which had been gained at Hatteras the previous August. By 5 January, it was also known that the expedition was commanded by Brigadier General Ambrose E. Burnside.[1]

THE BURNSIDE EXPEDITION

As Confederates feared, the armada which came to be known as the Burnside Expedition was indeed headed for the North Carolina coast. The expedition had its beginning only a few days after the Union success at Hatteras Inlet when in early September, 1861, Major General George B. McClellan, commanding the Army of the Potomac, proposed to the Secretary of War an idea to form a "coast division" of at least ten regiments, chiefly from New England states whose men were familiar with seafaring and the ways of the coast, as an amphibious strike force. The division, with all its supplies and equipment, was to be moved about in shallow draft transports and vessels capable of operating in shallow sounds and rivers, with the support of shallow draft gunboats. The force was intended to move rapidly to capture and secure lodgements in important areas of the coast, and penetrate inland to threaten lines of communication and supply. The original intention was for this strike force to operate in the waters of the Chesapeake Bay and Potomac River in conjunction with McClellan's army, but soon was planned as a completely independent operation for the coast of North Carolina. McClellan easily won approval of his plan and was authorized to proceed with its formation. On 12 September he ordered Brigadier General Ambrose E. Burnside, aged thirty-eight, to New England to raise troops for the expedition which Burnside would lead. Burnside was a personal friend of McClellan and a prewar business associate. There is evidence to indicate much of the plan for the creation of a coast division was Burnside's.

Burnside made arrangements with the governors of the Northeast to supply regiments for the expedition. Meanwhile, the docks, bays, and rivers of the New York area were scoured for suitable vessels. Burnside eventually ended up with a diverse collection of about eighty vessels of different types. By early January, the vessels had been assembled at Hampton Roads while the troops constituting the Coast Division were assembled at Annapolis, Maryland. Burnside divided the regiments of this 12,000-man force into three brigades under three of his friends and West Point colleagues: Brigadier Generals John G. Foster, Jesse L. Reno, and John G. Parke. Interestingly, General Foster had up until the commencement of the war been with the Engineer Corps and was the engineer in charge of Forts Macon and Caswell, and the harbor forts of Charleston in the years before the war began. Since the expedition was targeted at the North Carolina coast, Foster's knowledge of Fort Macon was undoubtedly of great benefit to Burnside.[2]

On 5 January the embarkation of troops on the transports began at

Annapolis. All vessels then rendezvoused off Fort Monroe with Commodore L. M. Goldsborough in charge of the Navy part of the expedition. The official orders for the expedition were issued from General McClellan on 7 January which named three primary objectives on the North Carolina coast and gave considerable latitude toward pressing into the interior of the state. The order instructed Burnside to carry his fleet through Hatteras Inlet into Pamlico Sound and specified the "first point of attack will be Roanoke Island and its dependencies. It is presumed that the Navy can reduce the batteries on the main island, by which . . . it may be hoped to capture the entire garrison of the place . . . The commodore and yourself having completed your arrangements in regard to Roanoke Island and the waters north of it you will please at once make a descent upon New Berne, having gained possession of which and the railroad passing though it you will at once throw a sufficient force upon Beaufort and take the steps necessary to reduce Fort Macon and open the port. When you seize New Berne you will endeavor to seize the railroad as far west as Goldsborough, should circumstances favor such a movement. The temper of the people, the rebel force at hand, & c., will go far toward determining the question as to how far west the railroad can be safely occupied and held."[3]

At last, on the night of 11 January, the expedition put to sea and a course was directed south to Cape Hatteras. The weather was a problem from the start. The 12th of January was foggy but on the following day the fleet managed to reach Hatteras. That evening a severe gale struck as the fleet was trying to pass through Hatteras Inlet into the sound. Bad weather then continued for almost two weeks. Several vessels were lost but with great delay and difficulty most of Burnside's fleet finally passed through Hatteras Inlet into Pamlico Sound. However, it was not until 4 February that all was in readiness to begin the movement across the sound to attack the Confederate forces on Roanoke Island. On the morning of the 5th, Burnside's forces started northward in their transports, preceded by a squadron of gunboats, sixty-five vessels in all. On 7 February the attack on Roanoke Island, the first objective, began. While Navy and Army gunboats engaged Confederate forts along the sound and a squadron of Confederate gunboats, Union troops were landed unopposed at the middle of the island. On the following day after a brief battle, Burnside's forces overran Confederate defenses on the island and captured it, along with about 2,500 prisoners. The forts so laboriously built over the fall and winter to defend the island fell with their complete armament into Burnside's hands. The first expedition objective had been met. The success at Roanoke was followed two days later by the destruction of the Confederate gunboat squadron below Elizabeth City. The northeast sound region of North Carolina had been secured. It remained now for Burnside to concentrate on the next of his two remaining objectives.[4]

CONFEDERATE REACTION

The Confederate reaction to the news of Burnside's fleet mustering in Hampton Roads early in January was much the same as during the several alarms the previous September and October: a flurry of correspondence from General Gatlin and Governor Clark to the War Department for reinforcements, frenzied efforts to push forward work on defenses, and frantic appeals for more cannons, arms and equipment. While the alarms of the previous fall had all been the result of false rumors, this huge expedition, the largest yet put together by the Union, was definitely intended to attack the North Carolina coast. As it now stood, none of the various far-flung defensive posts of the North Carolina coast from Wilmington to Roanoke had even remotely enough troops to put up an adequate defense. The shallow draft of the vessels carrying the expedition gave it the possibility of reaching anywhere into the sounds and rivers of the coast. Even with these facts, the War Department was painfully reluctant to release troops from Virginia to defend the North Carolina coast. The Secretary of War simply did not take the threat seriously despite all the reports and intelligence.[5]

At Fort Macon, news of Burnside's fleet preparing to go to sea brought an order on 10 January from General Gatlin to send all the surplus cannons lying at the fort to New Bern, where they might be put to use. All the guns which were not intended to be used in the fort were sent off. This included the large number of unmounted guns, mainly 24- and 32-pounders acquired from the Norfolk Navy Yard the previous summer, and the remaining field guns which had been used by Captain Pender's company during the fall. On 11 January, General L. O'B. Branch, the District commander, sent a message to all commanders of posts, ordering them to keep their pickets and lookouts vigilant, to transmit promptly any information on the movement or appearance of the enemy fleet, and to guard against the officers and men becoming affected by panic or given to excitement by the local residents. About this time came the welcomed news that two columbiads for Fort Macon, one 10-inch and one 8-inch, ordered weeks earlier, were ready at the Tredegar Iron Works in Richmond. They left Richmond by rail on 14 and 15 January but were delayed one week in their arrival. An irritated General Gatlin, afraid that the fleet might attack the fort before they arrived, complained to the War Department on 20 January: "I desire to draw your attention to the neglect of the railroad companies in failing to forward military supplies with dispatch. A 10-inch columbiad for Fort Macon has just reached here (Goldsboro), having left Richmond three days ago. The agent accompanying it says that no accident happened on the way. The delay occurred at Petersburg and Weldon. Unless something is done to correct the criminal neglect of these railroad people a sad misfortune may befall us. Even now I know not if the gun with reach Fort Macon in time." Of course, Burnside's fleet did not move directly to attack the fort and the garrison had time to mount the guns for the fort's defense.[6]

As the enemy concentrated at Hatteras and collected in the sound, Confederates took much satisfaction from the battering the winter storms gave the fleet. However, it was clear that the bad weather would only briefly delay the inevitable and strangely the War Department did not use the time to rush a sufficient number of troops to the North Carolina coast to strengthen its defenses. Likewise, though it was evident Burnside must make an attack on Roanoke Island first rather than leave it unattended to threaten his rear, no major efforts were taken by Major General Benjamin Huger, commanding the Department of Norfolk of which Roanoke Island was a part, to hurry down reinforcements from the thousands of troops in his department. Thus, when the blow fell at Roanoke Island on Brigadier General Henry A. Wise's force of fewer than 3,000 men it was completely overwhelming.

News of the loss of the island caused a public outcry. Newspapers demanded the heads of those responsible for the inadequate defense of the island. A committee of the Confederate Congress was formed to investigate the causes of the island's loss. To make matters worse, close on the heels of the Roanoke disaster came news of even greater disasters in Tennessee. Public spirit sank under the weight of the string of reversals in the winter of 1862.

In the weeks after the fall of Roanoke, Burnside contented himself with consolidating his gains and making a number of minor raids and expeditions into the surrounding country. Unfortunately for the Confederates now trying to anticipate his intentions, the position he occupied gave rise to a bewildering number of options as to where he might attack next. The War Department felt his next movement would be directly against Norfolk and Suffolk from the south, or to cut the railroad lines to these places from the west. However, as another option, an ascent of either the Roanoke or Pamlico/Tar Rivers would reach the Wilmington and Weldon Railroad, one of the main north-south arteries to Virginia. An ascent of the Neuse River would threaten the capture of New Bern, second largest city in the state, cut the Atlantic and North Carolina Railroad (the lifeline to the Beaufort area and Fort Macon), and provide a valuable staging area to launch further operations into the interior. A direct movement to capture Fort Macon through the sounds would give Burnside the use of Beaufort Harbor as a base for naval and logistical support before moving on to his other objectives.

General Gatlin believed Burnside would move against New Bern. He gave orders for General Branch, commanding the District of the Pamlico, to consolidate and concentrate the scattered forces throughout the district as much as possible. On 12 February, Branch wrote Colonel White, commanding Fort Macon, inquiring as to how many months of provisions could be stored in the fort for the garrison in case it was cut off from New Bern. He also told White to be thinking about how many of the nine companies of infantry and artillery he commanded at the fort and at the batteries on Harker's Island could be safely and effectively sheltered in the fort in the event of siege. As a result, the fort was sent enough provisions for a seven month supply for its garrison. As for the number of companies which could effectively be sheltered in the fort, White decided to retain the artillery companies of Guion, Cogdell, Manney, Pool, and Blount. Leecraft's artillery company and the three infantry companies would be sent to New Bern when the time came to concentrate forces.[7]

That time was rapidly approaching, however, as Branch began to consolidate his scattered forces and pull in his remote outposts. On 18 February, he ordered that the batteries at Harker's Island be withdrawn and the guns removed to New Bern. On 26 February, the three infantry companies of the 27th North Carolina which had been at the fort since the beginning of the war (the Goldsboro Rifles, Guilford Grays, and Orange Guards) left the fort to join the rest of their regiment in camp below New Bern. On the following day, Captain Blount's company left its camps on Harker's Island and crossed back over to the fort. On 2 March, Lieutenant Cogdell's company followed after the guns and property were removed from the batteries. On 5 March, the 7th North Carolina abandoned its winter quarters at Newport to join Branch's forces at New Bern. The 26th North Carolina had already been similarly withdrawn to New Bern from its winter quarters at Carolina City, leaving Colonel White and the five artillery companies with him at Fort Macon the only Confederate soldiers remaining in the area of Beaufort Harbor.[8]

In the midst of all this excitement, there took place an incident of considerable interest. Early on the morning of 28 February, the lone Union warship *State of Georgia* had been patrolling off Beaufort Inlet when it was approached by another vessel. This would not have normally attracted more than passing interest in the fort. However, the second ship put on a sudden burst of speed and dashed toward the inlet, leaving the Union ship firing angrily at her without effect. As the garrison manned the guns the approach-

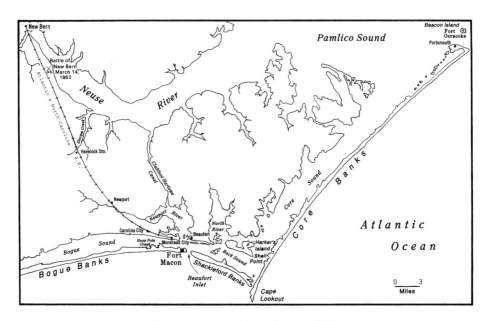

New Bern to Beaufort Harbor, 1862.

ing steamer hoisted the Confederate flag and passed through the inlet into
Beaufort Harbor. Soon she was safely tied up at the dock at Morehead City.
She proved to be the Confederate commerce raider *Nashville*, Captain Robert B. Pegram, bound from Southhampton, England, via Bermuda, to the
Confederacy. Pegram had tricked the *State of Georgia* by displaying friendly
signals and then suddenly dashing past the Union ship into the inlet at full
speed. Of further interest was the fact that while at Bermuda, Captain
Pegram had met the ever-present Captain Josiah S. Pender, who had run
the blockade from Beaufort to Bermuda in a schooner on Confederate
service. Pender offered Pegram his services and those of his pilot to take
the *Nashville* through the blockade into Beaufort Harbor, which Pegram
accepted. With the aid of local men and some clever tactics, the *Nashville*
was now safe at Beaufort Harbor for the time being.[9]

Aside from this event, everyone from Generals Gatlin and Branch down to the men in the ranks tensely waited for some sign as to Burnside's next movement. Although the most likely target was New Bern, the Confederate War Department was still preoccupied by the chance Burnside might threaten Southeastern Virginia. Incredibly, on 2 March it ordered the withdrawal of the Pamlico River defenses at Washington, North Carolina, and the transfer of the almost 2,000 troops defending them not to New Bern but to Southeastern Virginia. Meanwhile, off Fort Macon, the number of Union warships was increased and the garrison was in daily anticipation of an attack. On 12 March, the usual mail train did not come down from New Bern, arousing suspicions that something must be happening. Early on the morning of 13 March, the sound of heavy gunfire was clearly audible from the direction of the Neuse River. It began early in the morning and lasted for hours. There now was no doubt that the New Bern defenses were being attacked by Burnside. If the town fell, Fort Macon would be cut off and alone. Colonel White and his five companies garrisoning the fort would be left as the only major Confederate force remaining on the North Carolina coast north of Wilmington.[10]

FORT MACON SURROUNDED

As the Fort Macon garrison had suspected, on 12 March Union gunboats and transports had been sighted coming up the Neuse River. More than an month after the battle of Roanoke, General Burnside had at last begun operations against his second objective, New Bern. His troops had been loaded back into their transports and on the morning of 12 March moved up the Neuse River in company with the Navy gunboat flotilla. On the morning of the 13th, the troops were landed at Slocum's Creek, about eighteen miles below New Bern, and began marching along the river toward the town. The gunfire heard at Fort Macon during the day was from Union gunboats which as a precaution shelled the areas ahead of the troops as they landed and marched. The news of these activities finally prompted the Confederate War Department to order reinforcements for General

Branch, but it was too late. On the morning of 14 March, Branch's forces, numbering less than 4,000 men, fought Burnside's advancing troops from a prepared line of earthworks. Given the disparity of numbers with Branch's men outnumbered almost three to one, there was little doubt as to the outcome of the battle. Branch's men were overwhelmed and driven westward beyond New Bern toward Kinston. Union troops occupied the town. Burnside had taken his second objective.

The fall of New Bern sealed the fate of Fort Macon. There was no doubt that Burnside's next effort would be directed against it to secure the harbor. Unfortunately for Colonel White, the fort was now cut off with Burnside's army lying between it and any other Confederate forces in the direction of Kinston and Goldsboro. There was no way that any reinforcements could reach the fort. White and his men were on their own. They could expect Union troops to advance against the fort within only a few days once Burnside had consolidated his gains and disposed his forces to secure New Bern.

In the days that followed the fall of New Bern, there was intense activity and preparation in and around the fort. The picket force on Shackleford Banks was recalled back to the fort, sand bags were filled and placed to protect the guns, ammunition was prepared, outside buildings and quarters, including the hospital, were abandoned as everything was withdrawn into the fort itself, and dispositions were made inside the fort so that all five companies would be quartered within its casemates. Captain Pool's company, however, continued to maintain picket posts along Bogue Banks several miles outward from the fort. As for the railroad between Morehead City and New Bern, Colonel White was only too well aware of the problems it would cause him. Before New Bern fell it had been the fort's lifeline; now it would bring enemy troops and equipment to work against him. Accordingly, on 18 March he sent out a detachment from the fort which cut it by burning the 180-foot railroad bridge over the Newport River. On the way back the detachment also burned several buildings in Carolina City which might prove useful to the enemy, including the old winter barracks of the 26th North Carolina and the hotel which had been used during the winter as a hospital. Almost one mile of railroad track was pulled up at Morehead City and the iron rails carried back over to the fort.[11]

In the harbor, four ships found themselves blockaded from the ocean and now in danger of being taken when Union troops advanced from New Bern. Two of them, the British ships *Alliance* and *Gondar*, had been in the harbor since August but could at least argue against being taken by Burnside as prizes because of their British registry. A third was the prize bark *Glen* which was being fitted out as a privateer. Rather than allow her capture, the vessel was set on fire and destroyed during 23–24 March. The last ship was the steamer *Nashville*, which had entered the harbor only two weeks earlier. Only a skeleton crew under Lieutenant William C. Whittle remained aboard the vessel as the captain and most of the crew had been ordered to other duty shortly after the ship reached port. Rather than be caught at the docks when Burnside's troops advanced from New Bern, Whittle brought the *Nashville* down under the guns of Fort Macon on 16 March. His intention was to run the blockade even though three Union warships waited off the inlet to prevent his escape. Colonel White came aboard and suggested that Whittle destroy the *Nashville* and bring his men into the fort to aid in its defense. Whittle then informed White of his intention to take his chances to run the blockade. White bid him God-speed and left. After 7:00 P.M. on the night of 17 March, the *Nashville* got underway and started out of the inlet. Fortunately, only two blockaders, the *Gemsbok* and *Cambridge*, were on station that night off the inlet. Although the *Gemsbok* sighted the *Nashville* coming out and fired at her, the Confederate steamer easily evaded both Union ships and escaped to sea. In Fort Macon, the excited garrison had crowded the parapets to witness the attempt and cheered until the ship was out of sight.[12]

As all these activities were going on around Fort Macon, General Burnside was at New Bern deciding the fate of the fort. The capture of this, his third objective, would give him the use of Beaufort Harbor and thereby solve most of the logistical problems he was currently experiencing with his long, exposed supply line from Hatteras. He expected little trouble out of

Fort Macon's small garrison and decided to dispatch a portion of his Third Brigade under Brigadier General John G. Parke to accomplish the capture of the fort and harbor. Should the Confederates attempt to hold out, Parke would have the use of the expedition's siege train to take the fort by siege if necessary. Since most of the available large railroad rolling stock had been taken away or ruined by retreating Confederates when New Bern was taken, there was concern as to the fastest and easiest way to get the necessary troops, supplies, equipment, and siege guns to the area of Beaufort Harbor. On 18 March, the same day Colonel White's Confederates destroyed the railroad bridge at Newport, Burnside accompanied a reconnaissance force down to Slocum's Creek and determined a suitable landing site where the troops and guns could be put ashore only one and one-half miles from the railroad at Havelock Station. In this way, almost half the distance of thirty-five miles from New Bern to Morehead City could be covered by water.[13]

On the following day, 19 March, General Parke embarked two of his regiments, the 4th Rhode Island, Colonel Isaac P. Rodman, and the 8th Connecticut, Colonel Edward Harland, aboard transports for the voyage down the Neuse River to Slocum's Creek. At the same time, he directed the 5th Rhode Island Battalion, Major John Wright, to march directly to the same destination down the railroad. On the 20th, the transports carried the two regiments to Slocum's Creek, where they landed during the 20th and 21st. At Havelock Station on the railroad they joined the 5th Rhode Island Battalion, which had marched down from New Bern. Since it was not known if the siege train would be required, it was left aboard the vessels in the creek.[14]

Upon landing, General Parke learned of the destruction of the railroad bridge at Newport, about eight and one-half miles away. Since this and the regular county road bridge over the Newport River were vital to his operations, he gathered up about 700 men and pushed on with them as an advanced force to secure the bridge crossings over the Newport River, and the road and railroad as far as Carolina City. Parke reached Newport on the night of the 21st, finding the railroad bridge gone but the county road bridge intact. For the time being, he would have the use of the railroad for his supplies only as far as Newport. Beyond that, as he advanced on toward Carolina and Morehead Cities, everything would have to be transported by wagon on the county road. It was clear the railroad bridge had to be rebuilt as soon as possible, especially if it became necessary to bring up the siege guns to use against Fort Macon. He then moved on toward Carolina City, six miles distant, on 22 March with the advanced guard, leaving orders for the remainder of the 4th Rhode Island and 8th Connecticut to follow.[15]

Parke's troops reached Carolina City on the afternoon of the 22nd without incident. Being used to the large cities of New England, his men were much disappointed to find that something with such an important-sounding name as 'Carolina City' consisted only of a depot and siding along the railroad, with a few small houses, a wharf on Bogue Sound, and the ashes of the destroyed hotel. About one mile across Bogue Sound, however, lay Bogue Banks with Fort Macon, their objective, lying at its eastern end. Parke decided to make his headquarters at Carolina City and halted for the time being to allow the rest of his command to catch up. He also ordered the 5th Rhode Island Battalion to move down to Newport and rebuild the railroad bridge so that a regular system of supply would reach him from New Bern. On 23 March, he sent two companies on ahead three miles beyond Carolina City to occupy Morehead City and cut off any communication with the fort. Until the rest of his command and a sufficient supply of provisions arrived, however, he would not make an attempt to cross Newport River to occupy Beaufort.[16]

On this same morning of 23 March, Parke sent his adjutant, Captain Charles T. Gardner, and his ordnance officer, Lieutenant Daniel W. Flagler, to Fort Macon under a flag of truce with a note demanding its surrender "in order to save the unnecessary effusion of blood." The note stated Parke had an "intimate knowledge of the entire work" and that its fall was inevitable. The garrison was offered release as prisoners of war on parole provided the fort and its armament were not damaged. Colonel White, however, had no intention of giving up without a fight and sent a note back politely declining to surrender. There was nothing left for a disappointed General Parke to do but continue on with his operations and formally besiege the fort. Lieutenant Flagler, the ordnance officer, was sent back to Slocum's Creek to unload the siege train from the vessels in the creek. However, the guns could only be moved to Carolina City by rail and until the 5th Rhode Island Battalion finished rebuilding the railroad bridge at Newport, Parke would not be able to use them[17].

The remainder of the 4th Rhode Island and 8th Connecticut joined Parke at Carolina City on the 23rd, but even with both regiments at hand he refrained from venturing on to occupy Beaufort until he had enough provisions to support such a movement. On the following day, the 24th, the town officials of Beaufort were summoned, and ordered to cease any communication with the fort. The officials expressed fears that Colonel White would shell the town if they cooperated with Parke and left to hold a town meeting to discuss the situation. On the 25th they returned and stated they were powerless to cooperate with Parke. Colonel White had said he would never allow the Union troops to land in Beaufort and would shell the invaders and the town if necessary. Parke then dismissed them without telling them of his intentions. By this time he had received two loads of provisions back at Slocum's Creek and now felt he could seize the town. At midnight that night, Major John Allen of the 4th Rhode Island took two companies of his regiment across the harbor in some small boats and quietly took possession of Beaufort in the early morning hours of 26 March. There was no opposition or trouble. Later on the 26th, Allen was reinforced by one company of the 8th Connecticut because of the extensive waterfront area his force had to patrol. The soldiers found a surprisingly large number of the people who had not fled the town were loyal Unionist who eagerly welcomed the arrival of Burnside's forces. Among these was Ordnance Sergeant William Alexander, who had remained in Beaufort since having Fort Macon taken from him the previous April. As for Colonel White, no attempt was made to shell Beaufort itself but he had the fort's guns fire upon any boat which dared to cross the harbor between Morehead and Beaufort. Consequently, most communications between Parke's main body and Major Allen's force in Beaufort were made at night.[18]

The final steps to completely invest Fort Macon began during the last days of March, culminating in the occupation of Bogue Banks, on which the siege operations would be conducted. On 27 March, a couple of officers from Major Allen's command in Beaufort crossed over Shackleford Banks to the ocean where they succeeded in opening communications with the Navy blockading fleet offshore. On the following day, landing parties from the blockading fleet occupied the Cape Lookout Lighthouse and Shackleford Banks. On 29 March, under cover of a boat howitzer mounted on a launch, Parke sent a detachment from the 4th Rhode Island across the sound from Carolina City to Bogue Banks at a point about five miles west of Fort Macon to reconnoiter. No resistance was encountered. The detachment was joined on the banks the next day by the remainder of its company and later by two other companies. Parke now had a secure foothold on Bogue Banks and could proceed with formal siege operations against the fort. A request was made to the naval flotilla cooperating with Burnside that a shallow draft vessel be sent around through the sounds to aid in landing troops and equipment on the banks. A gunboat was also requested to secure access to Core Sound.[19]

On 29 March, Parke's one major concern, the rebuilding of the Newport River railroad bridge, was put to rest. Major John Wright and three companies of the 5th Rhode Island Battalion had moved down to Newport on 23 March under Parke's orders and had begun the reconstruction of the bridge the following day. The job might have easily lasted several weeks under normal conditions but the vital importance of the bridge to Parke's operation spurred the Rhode Islanders on to where in less than one week they had completed a railroad bridge able to bear the weight of fifty tons. The first loaded railroad car passed over it on the 29th. Now it was possible to have a regular system of supply by railroad directly from New Bern, as well as to bring up the guns of the siege train.[20]

As for the siege train, following the fort's refusal to surrender on 23 March, Ordnance Lieutenant Daniel W. Flagler had been sent back to Slocum's Creek to land it ashore. The train consisted of three 30-pounder Parrott Rifles in the care of Captain Lewis O. Morris, Company C, 1st U. S. Artillery, and four 10-inch siege mortars, all with implements and ammunition, but no cannoneers. Flagler did not believe the two batteries were sufficient for the job and obtained yet another battery of four 8-inch mortars from New Bern which he also had floated down to Slocum's Creek. To land the guns and transport them to the railroad at Havelock Station, Flagler obtained some wagons and a gang of Negro laborers from the division quartermaster. At the railroad, the guns were pushed aboard a couple of freight cars and pulled down the railroad by horses and mules. The railroad bridge at Newport having been completed by this time, the first battery of guns, the Parrott battery of Captain Morris, arrived at Carolina City on 31 March. The others soon followed and Parke had them sent to Bogue Banks over the days which followed. A spur line of the railroad branched off to the Carolina City wharf and enabled the guns to be loaded directly from the cars onto an old scow and carried in successive trips across to the banks. Bogue Sound was so shallow only one trip could be made during high tide through a shallow, narrow channel, so progress was very slow. At the banks, the landing place was at the head of a tidal creek through the marsh known as Hoop Pole Creek. Here the guns and their ammunition had to be offloaded and then manhandled through a wide marsh to reach dry land. It was difficult work which required days of backbreaking effort well into April.[21]

During the first days of April a number of events took place as the Union operations continued. On 3 April the Union gunboat *Ellis* came up through Core and Back Sounds northeast of the fort accompanying the light draft stern-wheel steamer *Old North State*, which would help land Parke's troops on Bogue Banks. That night the stern-wheeler made a daring dash across the harbor between Beaufort and the fort without being noticed and succeeded in reaching Parke at Carolina City. Her assistance proved to be limited, however, because she drew too much water to actually reach the banks. The *Ellis*, meanwhile, took up station at the mouth of North River near Harker's Island. In the meantime, the 9th New Jersey regiment was sent down from New Bern to assist Parke. It relieved the 5th Rhode Island Battalion at Newport and took position to guard the railroad bridge and the local roads approaching the line of the railroad against raids by Confederate cavalry. The 5th Rhode Island Battalion moved on to Carolina City on 4 April and then was moved across to the banks and the camp at Hoop Pole Creek two days later. The landings continued with several old scows and shallow draft vessels found in the area so that by 12 April Parke had on the banks seven companies each of the 4th Rhode Island and 8th Connecticut, the 5th Rhode Island Battalion, Captain Lewis O. Morris' Company C, 1st U. S. Artillery, and Captain John H. Ammon's Company I, 3rd New York Artillery. The latter two companies had just reported for duty to man the three batteries of siege guns. In addition, a detachment of the Signal Corps had arrived and set up signal stations in Beaufort, Morehead and Carolina Cities, on Bogue Banks, and even with the ships of the block-ading squadron offshore. In this way constant communications could be maintained with all parts of the far-flung Union forces. On 8 April, a blood-less skirmish took place as three companies of the 4th Rhode Island crowded Captain Pool's Confederate outpost forces back toward the fort and away from the area of Parke's expanding beachhead on the banks. It was the first actual shooting contact Confederates had had with Parke's forces other than occasional cannon shots at passing boats.[22]

Meanwhile, in Fort Macon, a great deal of activity was also taking place. Colonel White's refusal of Parke's 23 March demand to surrender met with great enthusiasm and approval throughout the little garrison. Their re-solve was that if Fort Macon was to be taken it would not be without a fight. But after taking stock of the situation, the picture that emerged was not completely encouraging. The amount of provisions in the fort was more than adequate since a seven-month supply had been built up before the siege. The supply of ammunition was in a fair quantity but the most serious deficiency was in gunpowder. A total of 35,000 pounds was on hand, which was enough for only three days of active sustained fighting. Much of the powder was old or of inferior quality. Of the five artillery companies and staff which comprised the garrison there was a total of about 440 men. The effective total was less than 300, however, because a great deal of sickness prevailed. A total of fifty-four guns comprised the fort's armament, which would be quite formidable in a standup engagement against ships or assault. However, no mortars had ever been provided for the fort in case of a siege. Regular cannons did not have the ability of mortars to reach into earthworks and entrenchments with a lobbing fire.[23]

Still, the preparations for battle continued. Artificial merlons of sand bags were created along the upper parapet's seaward and landward sides. Overall, the defenses on the landward side approaches were lacking. All the fort's digging tools had been requisitioned by General Branch long before the siege during the desperate effort to strengthen the New Bern defenses. Nothing remained to strengthen the fort's landward side or erect earthen traverses between the guns. On 24 March, Colonel White gave orders to his company commanders calling upon those stationed on the covertway to defend their batteries to the last. If forced to abandon them, these companies would fall back into the citadel. The ditch and doorways would be defended with small arms. The orders also called for those men not on duty to remain in their rooms but with a portion ready to relieve those on duty at any time. The men were cautioned to take careful, deliberate aim so that each shot would count. "Impress it upon the minds of the men," it concluded, "that they are now to show who they are and what they are made of."[24]

Over the next few days all structures which interrupted the fort's field of fire or might shield the enemy were destroyed. The Eliason House was burned to the ground on 26 March, leaving only its tall brick chimney to mark the spot. On the 27th some of the other buildings around the fort were torn down. The Bogue Banks Lighthouse northwest of the fort was toppled over. On the 28th a couple more buildings were burned and the beacon near the south corner of the fort pulled down. On the night of 29 March, Colonel White and Captain Pool were standing on the upper parapet when they noticed lights materializing all around the fort. They came from the ships of the blockading squadron offshore, and from Union camps at the towns, on Shackleford Banks, and now on Bogue Banks from the camp on Hoop Hole Creek as well. It was perhaps the first time the Confederates realized the magnitude of the forces arrayed against them and the seriousness of their position. Fort Macon was completely surrounded.[25]

The garrison could only watch as each passing day marked further progress of Union forces against them. The sight of the U.S. flag waving over Beaufort was of particular concern and anxiety because so many of the garrison were from there and the surrounding area. Being cut off in the fort, they were in sight of all that they held dear but were helpless to protect their homes and families against the invading enemy. Their loved ones were completely at the mercy of Union soldiers. In desperation they crafted toy boats, packed them with letters and messages to their families and launched them from the fort beach on the incoming tides in the hope they would be carried around to Beaufort. Union soldiers intercepted them frequently and turned them in to headquarters, but some of the letters perhaps reached the persons for whom they were intended. Seventeen local men in the garrison deserted at this time while on picket.[26]

It was during this time of growing frustration and desperation that an extraordinary event took place in the fort. It was found that one of the men had been a baker before the war and since the fort had a large supply of flour Colonel White ordered that the daily flour ration be baked into bread loaves for the men rather than issued to the companies for individual use. It was felt this would relieve the company cooks, provide a change of diet, and use less flour in order to preserve what was on hand longer during a siege. The men were receptive to the idea and the baker began turning out loaves of bread from the fort's large bake oven. Unfortunately, the loaves were blackened, hard, overdone, and generally inedible. At first there was much laughter and comment at the baker's expense, someone even suggesting the loaves be turned in to the Ordnance Department as ammunition. This quickly changed, however, as little improvement took place and the men requested the return of the flour ration for individual company use, which could be cooked in the kitchens or bakery at will. The five company commanders agreed and made their feelings known to Colonel White. The fort surgeon likewise warned that the bread was inedible and should be suspended. White prevailed, however, and continued with his order for baked bread. On 6 April, the company commanders tried again by presenting Colonel White with a formal request to suspend the baked bread. Again

White refused, and two more days passed in which the discontent of both officers and men grew without White seeming to realize the seriousness with which the garrison viewed the situation. On 8 April, the five company commanders had had enough. They sent White a note stating that they had tried everything consistent with honor and the good of the service, and that they were now prepared if necessary to take the normal flour ration fixed by regulation from the Commissary. An angry White summoned the company commanders at once. He threatened to arrest them and place a guard at the Commissary casemate. The officers expressed their readiness to undergo arrest if that was his decision but asked where he intended to obtain a guard for the Commissary from his angry soldiers. A heated discussion ensued but ended with no resolution of the problem. The company commanders departed and prepared to seize the amount of flour which the companies were entitled to requisition by 9 A.M. unless White reconsidered. Colonel White finally backed down at this point and signed the requisitions for the regular issue of flour only a few minutes before 9 A.M.[27]

The "Bread Incident" had ended, the entire matter undoubtedly blown out of proportion on both sides by the stress of the fort's situation. Discontent lasted some days afterward. Colonel White, for his part, was disturbed by the demoralization of the men over their present situation, the insubordination displayed during the Bread Incident and the failure of the officers to control and suppress the difficulties. For their part, the garrison was irritated by White's inflexibility and stubborn adherence to orders. That very night, 8 April, eight men from Cogdell's, Manney's, and Pool's companies who lived in Beaufort and who were fed up with the entire situation deserted from the fort under cover of a storm. The desertions had an even more demoralizing effect on the little garrison. Colonel White issued an address the next day calling on the men to stand firm in the face of their enemies.[28]

On the night of 9 April, more men left the fort, but this time with White's sanction. In a desperate bid to get important papers to Confederate lines and request forces to come to the relief of the fort and break the siege, Lieutenant Cicero Primrose of Cogdell's company and a crew of men were detailed to try to slip past Union blockading ships by open boat in the ocean. Late that night the boat left the fort wharf and got past Union gunboats unnoticed. Primrose and his companions safely reached Confederate lines and reported to Major General T. H. Holmes, now commanding the Department of North Carolina. Unfortunately, Holmes was unable to send any of his forces to the relief of the beleaguered fort. However, word of the problems of the Fort Macon garrison soon reached Richmond when Lieutenant Primrose was sent there to report to General Robert E. Lee, then serving as an army operations director for President Jefferson Davis. After hearing of the "discontent and insubordination which is reported to exist among the troops in Fort Macon," Lee was afraid the garrison would not offer a suitable resistance if the fort was attacked. On 15 April, he authorized General Holmes to abandon the fort and bring off as much of the public property as possible. Of course, the situation had gone past this, and Lee's fears were groundless. Despite the brief period of internal turmoil, the garrison of Fort Macon had no intention of giving up without a fight.[29]

THE SIEGE

Once General Parke succeeded in getting over to the banks the siege guns and troops which he would use against Fort Macon, his next step was to determine the sites for the batteries to reduce the fort. This would require a reconnaissance in force up close to the fort to choose their locations. Accordingly, on the morning of 11 April five companies from the 4th Rhode Island and 5th Rhode Island Battalion formed into line for an advance toward the fort. Accompanying the advance was Parke, Lieutenant Flagler, Captain Morris, and Captain Robert S. Williamson of the Topographical Engineers. In the ocean, the Union gunboat *Albatross* steamed in close and followed slowly along with the advance. About two miles from the fort was Captain Pool's line of the picket guard. As the Union troops came into view signals were made by the pickets to warn the fort. A sharp skirmish ensued as the Rhode Island troops gradually pushed Pool's men back toward the fort for about a mile by virtue of their superior numbers. The *Albatross* also opened fire, throwing a few shells at the Confederates and hastening their retreat. Soon the gunboat *State of Georgia* joined the *Albatross* and fired a few shots as well. Pool's men made a brief stand and then retired inside the fort. As the Union troops appeared within range the fort opened fire upon them and the two gunboats. Union troops took cover behind the sand hills about three-quarters of a mile away as Flagler, Morris, and Williamson selected sites for three batteries ranging from 1,280 to 1,680 yards from the fort. Once they were finished Parke ordered the force to withdraw back the way it had come. The action ended without loss to either side. That night Pool's picket guard ventured back out and reoccupied their old stations.[30]

Having seen the nature of the ground and gotten the information he needed, Parke now determined to repeat the advance on the following day but this time to permanently take position in front of the fort so that construction of the siege batteries could begin. On the morning of 12 April, five companies of the 8th Connecticut were deployed in line of battle. The advance began and as on the previous day a hot skirmish was soon in progress as the Union soldiers encountered Captain Pool's picket guard. The pickets were steadily pushed back and soon retired into the fort, bearing off one man who had been wounded in the engagement. The fort's guns opened fire and drove the Union soldiers under cover. The bluecoats established themselves about two-thirds of a mile from the fort behind the first line of sand dunes lying beyond the area which had been cleared and levelled during the previous summer. Here they would remain as a permanent line. During the afternoon, Captain Manney's company was sent out from the fort as skirmishers and suddenly encountered the Connecticut skirmish line concealed behind the first line of dunes about 1,200 yards from the fort. Another sharp skirmish ensued in which the commander of the Connecticut skirmishers, Captain Thomas Sheffield, and one private were wounded. Manney's men sustained no losses but retired back to the fort when they found themselves too heavily outnumbered to dislodge the enemy.[31]

While the land action was in progress, the gunboat *Albatross*, which

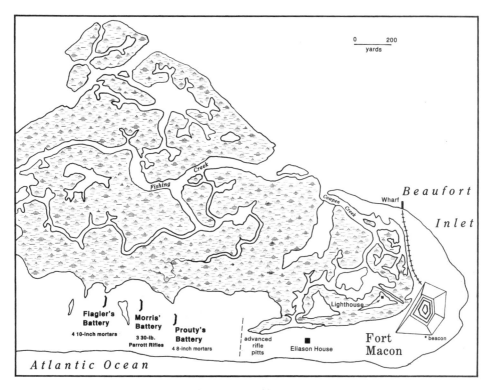

Map of the siege of Fort Macon.

had already engaged the fort at long range earlier in the morning, again steamed up close to shore and exchanged shots with the fort before retiring out of range. In all during the day the fort fired eighty shot and shell at the Union troops and the gunboat. There were no losses on either side beyond the one Confederate and two Union men wounded in the skirmishing. The siege of Fort Macon was formally underway.[32]

With a permanent line established west of the fort, work began in earnest in constructing emplacements for the three siege batteries, a system of trenches to connect and guard them, and a series of rifle pits in advance for the pickets. The men of the 4th Rhode Island, 8th Connecticut and 5th

Rhode Island Battalion shared the duties of guarding the batteries equally, serving one day out of every three on a rotating basis exposed to the heat of the sun, the damp wind, blowing sand, and a daily desultory fire from the fort's guns. A force of five companies was always required for this purpose. As they protected the work from attack, the task of constructing the batteries themselves was performed by Captain J. H. Ammon's Company I, 3rd New York Artillery, and work details from the infantry. The emplacements were made behind three large sand dunes, leaving the sides facing the fort intact but digging away the rear slopes to form a parapet about eight to ten feet high. The interior face was then revetted with sand bags for support. Behind the sand bagged interior face were laid the heavy timber platforms on which the guns would sit. The two mortar batteries were secure behind such emplacements but the Parrott battery required the addition of embrasures to be cut through the parapet to permit its guns to fire out. Because these would betray the battery's exact location they would be the last thing to be completed before commencing the bombardment. Magazines were also constructed for the batteries for ammunition and powder.[33]

The process of hauling the guns and ammunition a distance of about four miles from Parke's camp to the battery sites was very difficult. The wheels of the Parrott guns, and the wagons hauling the mortars, ammunition, and lumber, easily mired down in the loose sand. But with great exertion and many successive trips, the ordnance was transported successfully to the battery sites. Because the last half mile to the battery sites was badly exposed to the fort's guns, everything was brought up at night. Likewise the great majority of the work on the emplacements was performed at night. Some work was done during daylight hours but was less effective because of the disruptive fire from the fort. Men were posted as lookouts to watch for the telltale flash and puff of smoke from the fort's ramparts when a cannon was fired at the Union position. They would shout "Down!" to warn their comrades in the trenches or the batteries to get to cover before the shot reached them. Fortunately for the working parties and the men in the trenches this fire was not very effective as the fort had no mortars in its armament to lob shells down into their trenches and work areas.[34]

As work went on night and day the three batteries quickly took shape. At a distance of 1,680 yards from the fort and situated near the marsh of the sound side of Bogue Banks was the battery for the four 10-inch siege mortars, which would be commanded by Lieutenant Flagler. Some 200 yards in advance of this and slightly more toward the center of the island was the battery for the three 30-pounder Parrott Rifles, which was commanded by Captain Morris. Still 200 yards in advance of the Parrott battery, or 1,280 yards from the fort, and situated to the right near the ocean beach was the third battery for the four 8-inch siege mortars. This battery would be commanded by Lieutenant Merrick F. Prouty, an infantry officer who had been assigned to artillery duty with Flagler. All three batteries were connected with trenches to promote communication as well as shelter for the infantry companies guarding the batteries. Out in front of the trenches and batteries, a series of small rifle pits were made at various points to shelter the men assigned as the advance guard who were within about 900 yards of the fort. For flanking defense against assault, a rifled 12-pounder boat howitzer was placed into position to guard them and manned by a detachment of sailors from the steamer *Old North State*.[35]

On 18 April, General Burnside, newly-promoted to the rank of major general, came down from New Bern to see firsthand how Parke's operations were progressing. On the following day he crossed over to the Banks and inspected the batteries. The fort fired a number of shots at the ambulance in which he rode from one battery to another but no harm was done. Having seen the situation, Burnside left again for New Bern with the intention of returning through Core Sound by ship to be present at the final stage of the siege, and to bring down some armed canal barges to aid Parke's operations. Before leaving he ordered Parke to establish about 400 of his best marksmen ahead of the batteries about 500 to 600 yards from the fort to pick off the fort's gun crews on the ramparts.[36]

In obedience to this last request, on the evening of 21 April, Parke ordered a force from the 8th Connecticut under Major Hiram Appelman to advance beyond the lines to establish an entrenched position for sharpshooters. Appelman's force reached the ruins of the Eliason House, about

Union siege works during the siege of Fort Macon, April, 1862. The 10-inch mortar battery position is at left. The 30-pounder Parrott Battery is visible at left center. The 8-inch mortar battery is the long dark shape at right center. *From Frank Leslie's Illustrated Newspaper.*

600 yards from the fort, but the dark body of men moving up the beach was spotted by the Confederates. The fort opened fire, dispersing the group. Major Appelman and one private were wounded by canister and the force retired back to their lines. Parke made no further attempt to establish a line of advanced sharpshooters.[37]

In the fort, meanwhile, there had been a great sense of frustration in knowing the enemy was out in the sand dunes working on his siege positions but not knowing exactly where or what was being done. The fort's lookout was posted in the crosstrees of the fort's large flagpole and reported any movement or appearance of the enemy but it was simply impossible for him to see behind the sand dunes. On 13 April an unsuccessful effort was made to sneak men in a boat around on the marsh side behind the Union position to observe what the Union soldiers were doing. On 14 April, a group of the fort's pickets skirmished briefly with the advanced guard of the 8th Connecticut, slightly wounding three of the Connecticut soldiers. Again on the night of 20 April, a party from the fort went out and tried to dislodge the Union soldiers from their advanced positions. A lieutenant and a private of the 5th Rhode Island Battalion were wounded in the encounter but the Confederates were unable to accomplish their object. For the most part the fort's sick garrison simply did not have the numbers to drive the Union soldiers from their positions or seriously interrupt their work. The Confederate pickets remained in close observation, just out of range. Occasionally, some of them would venture close enough to the Union advanced guard to yell taunts in an effort to draw them out into the open but the Union soldiers would not accommodate them.[38]

The fort's guns fired upon the Union soldiers here and there as the occasion presented itself. Without mortars, however, the fire was less than effective because it could not reach behind the sand dunes where the enemy was concealed. The shells which were fired were set so that they might explode directly over the Union positions and rain their fragments down into the Union troops. But even this had its limits because of the old or inferior quality of the fort's gunpowder and fuses. In the sand dunes it was difficult to determine precisely where the Union troops were working or what effect the fort's fire was having on them. In desperation, Colonel White resorted to improvisation. He had the six 32-pounder carronades in the fort's counterfire galleries under the covertway removed and hauled up onto the terreplein of the northwest, or land, face of the covertway. Here they were remounted with the fronts of their gun carriages jacked up so that they had an elevation of about forty degrees to simulate a mortar. Captain Pool's company manned them and on 16 April began trying its luck at lobbing shells into the Union positions. Most of the shells seemed to burst too high to be effective and considerable experimentation was necessary if they were to achieve the desired effect. Still, Pool's men used them throughout the siege. In addition to these guns, the fort's two 10-inch columbiads on the seaward faces were turned around and likewise fired at high elevation with low powder charges to achieve a mortar effect.[39]

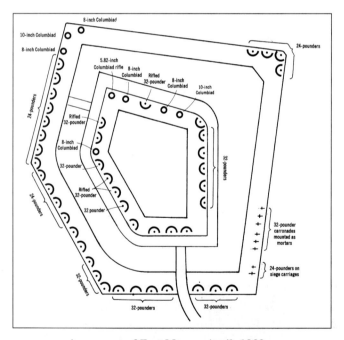

Armament of Fort Macon, April, 1862.

Aerial view of Beaufort Inlet looking eastward. Modern Fort Macon and Bogue Point in foreground, Shackleford Banks in background. Red-roofed buildings adjacent to Fort Macon are part of the U.S. Coast Guard Base.

C.J. Sauthier map of Beaufort, North Carolina, 1770, showing "Fort Dobbs in ruin." (North Carolina State Archives)

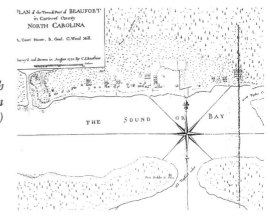

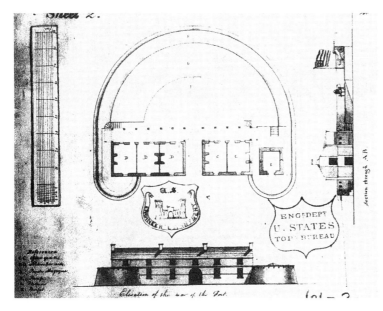

Plan and profiles of Fort Hampton by Major Alexander Macomb, 1808. (National Archives)

Nathaniel Macon, 1758 - 1837.
(North Carolina State Archives)

Aerial view of Fort Macon
from the southwest.

Bogue Point and Fort Macon looking northwest toward the harbor and Morehead City.

Bogue Point and Fort Macon looking northeast toward Beaufort.

Looking along the upper parapet of Fort Macon toward the inlet, Shackleford Banks, and the ocean. Replica rifled 32-pounder in position.

View looking eastward across the covertway toward Beaufort Inlet and Shakleford Banks. From this it is easy to understand how Fort Macon commanded the inlet with its guns.

Sally port entrance and bridge from the north angle.

Postern bridge looking toward the south angle of the covertway.

Looking along the southwest front toward southwest counterfire galleries. The mound of earth on the parapet at left is the remains of an earthen traverse which protected a battery of two 10-inch mortars in 1898.

Looking along the northwest front toward the north angle. Large patches of red brick along the upper edge of the citadel are repairs from battle damage from Union cannons. Rear postern entrance at right.

View looking into parade ground. Replica Hot Shot Furnace at right.

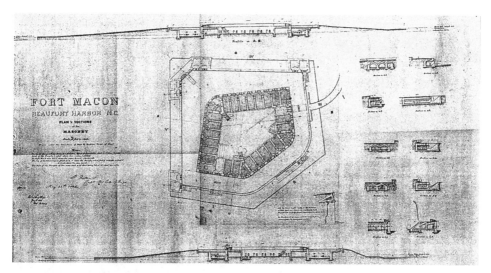

Engineer drawing of Fort Macon following completion of alterations and modifications of 1841 - 46. (National Archives)

Captain Josiah S. Pender. (North Carolina Collection, University of North Carolina Library)

Colonel Charles C. Tew.
(North Carolina State Archives)

Lieutenant Colonel John L. Bridgers.
(From NCT*)*

Colonel Moses J. White. (College
Archives, Earl Gregg Swem Library,
College of William and Mary)

Major General Ambrose E. Burnside.
(Library of Congress)

Brigadier General John G. Parke.
(U. S. Military History Institute, Carlisle Barracks)

Morehead City on March 24, 1862, as sketched from the balcony of the Macon House Hotel.
The bark Glen *is still visible burning at center. Fort Macon's flag can be seen at right center.*
(From Frank Leslie's Illustrated Newspaper*)*

Union siege works during the siege of Fort Macon, April, 1862. The 10-inch mortar battery position is at left. The 30-pounder Parrott Battery is visible at left center. The 8-inch mortar battery is the long dark shape at right center. (From Frank Leslie's Illustrated Newspaper*)*

The 10-inch mortar battery of Lieutenant Daniel W. Flagler in action during the bombardment of Fort Macon, April 25, 1862. (From Frank Leslie's Illustrated Newspaper*)*

The 30-pounder Parrott Rifle Battery of Captain Lewis O. Morris in action during the bombardment of Fort Macon, April 25, 1862. (*From* Frank Leslie's Illustrated Newspaper)

The Union Blockading Squadron in action against Fort Macon during the bombardment of April 25, 1862. (*From* Frank Leslie's Illustrated Newspaper)

The surrender of Fort Macon and lowering of the Confederate flag on the morning of April 26, 1862. (*From* Frank Leslie's Illustrated Newspaper)

The northwest wall of Fort Macon immediately after the battle showing the damage caused by Union rifled artillery. (From Battles and Leaders of the Civil War*)*

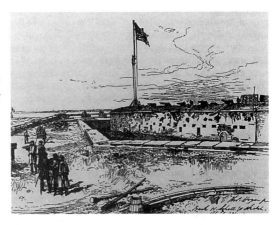

Photograph of Fort Macon's sally port entrance in 1867. Note the group of soldiers and ladies on the bridge. (North Carolina State Archives)

Photograph of Fort Macon's sally port entrance and bridge in 1867. (North Carolina State Archives)

Interior of Fort Macon looking toward the row of officers' casemates between the staircases, 1867. Muzzle of 8-inch Columbiad and sally port entrance at left. (North Carolina State Archives)

Interior of Fort Macon with Union troops drilling in the parade ground, 1867. Prisoners can be seen watching through the bars of the prison casemates at right. (North Carolina State Archives)

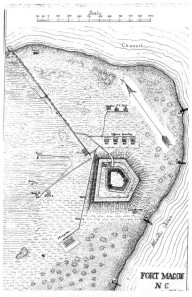

Map of the Fort Macon Military Reservation, 1877. (From RG 94, Medical Histories of Posts, National Archives)

Sketch of the 10-inch mortar battery near the south angle during the Spanish-American War, 1898. (By the author)

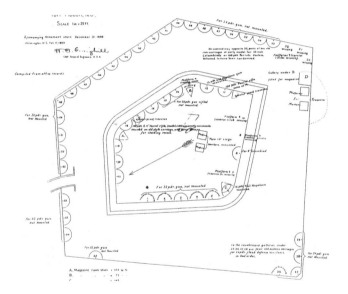

Armament of Fort Macon in the Spanish-American War. (National Archives)

Photograph of abandoned Fort Macon, early 1900s. Note doors and other interior work thrown outside by vandals. (North Carolina State Archives)

Lantern slide of abandoned Fort Macon about 1924. (Fort Macon State Park)

Parade ground of Fort Macon as viewed from the sally port following restoration by the Civilian Conservation Corps. (Fort Macon State Park)

Workers of the Civilian Conservation Corps re-laying one of the brick sidewalks, 1934. (Fort Macon State Park)

Photograph of the formal opening ceremony of Fort Macon State Park by Governor J. C. B. Ehringhaus, May 1, 1936. (North Carolina State Archives)

Photograph of 155mm gun on the beach at Fort Macon in early 1942 during World War II. (Courtesy of Joseph D. Sebes)

Photograph of Harbor Entrance Control Post tower on top of Fort Macon in 1943 during World War II. (Courtesy of Thomas McKeon)

Photograph of barracks complex outside Fort Macon looking from Harbor Entrance Control Post tower in 1943 during World War II. (Courtesy of Thomas McKeon)

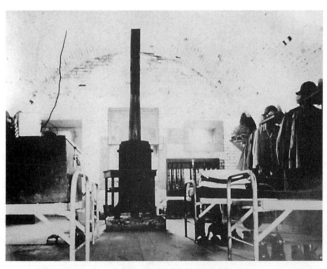

Photograph of the interior of Casemate 16 in 1943 during World War II. (Courtesy of Thomas McKeon)

As the days passed with the fort's guns shelling the Union positions from time to time, a new feeling of discontent arose among the five company commanders over the way in which Colonel White was conducting the defense. Probably in the interest of conserving ammunition, White insisted that the fort's batteries ask him for permission to fire each time an opportunity presented itself rather than allow the commanders to fire at will. Usually so much time was lost obtaining the order from White to fire that the opportunity was lost as well. The commanders felt this type of defense was too passive in the face of an enemy who was boldly making preparations for attack. They wanted to use the fort's armament aggressively to blast enemy troops whenever they appeared and to shell the enemy positions vigorously to cause as much disruption of their work as possible.

Colonel White listened to each of the commanders separately on the evening of 21 April as they expressed their views and agreed with them. From that time on the commanders would have authority to use their guns more aggressively and at their discretion. This new policy was put into effect almost immediately because this was the same night that Union troops attempted to establish the advanced sharpshooter position near the ruins of the Elaison House. The fort's guns repulsed the attempt handily. Captain Pool then treated the Union soldiers in the sand dunes to a sleepless, uneasy night as he fired his carronade mortars at intervals until daylight. During the next day and the two days which followed the fort's fire was much more aggressive, firing between thirty and fifty shots a day into the Union positions. One group of soldiers from the 5th Rhode Island Battalion was kept pinned down in an advanced rifle pit for forty-eight hours before they could be relieved.[40]

In the early afternoon of 23 April, a steamer appeared rounding Harker's Island to the northeast of the fort. It was the *Alice Price*, which had come down the Neuse River and Core Sound from New Bern carrying General Burnside and his staff to be present at the final stage of the siege. The ship had towed down with it the two armed canal barges *Shrapnel* and *Grenade* and a schooner loaded with ammunition. The two barges mounted a total of four 30-pounder Parrott Rifles and one 12-pounder Wiard Rifle, and were protected by bales of wet hay and cotton. Burnside intended to position them with the gunboat *Ellis* and her 80-pounder Dahlgren Rifle to the northeast of the fort near Beaufort to get the fort under fire from three sides with the blockading squadron and the batteries on the banks.[41]

Dropping her tow, the *Alice Price* steamed over to join the *Ellis* at the mouth of the North River, about three and one-half to four miles from the fort. The steamer's arrival had not gone unnoticed by the Confederates, and Captain Guion was ordered to fire upon the two ships with the fort's 5.82-inch rifled columbiad despite the great range. Two shots were fired, one landing between the two ships and the second within a few yards of the *Alice Price*. Guion's gunners were unable to load a third shot in time before the steamers retired back up the sound out of range.

Burnside now decided to give Colonel White one last chance to surrender the fort and at about 1600 that afternoon had the *Ellis* steam back toward the fort with a flag of truce flying at her masthead to convey the demand for surrender. Colonel White sent out a sailboat from the fort beach with Lieutenant Cogdell aboard to see what the enemy desired. Cogdell's boat met a cutter which put out from the *Ellis* containing Captain Herman Biggs, Burnside's Chief Quartermaster who was a friend of Colonel White since their days at West Point. Cogdell took Burnside's note from Biggs and carried it back to the fort as Biggs' cutter awaited the reply at Shackleford Banks. The note stated that General Parke was now ready to open fire but that Burnside had ordered him not to until the surrender demand could be made with a view to saving human life. Burnside offered terms that the garrison of the fort would be sent home on parole if the fort was surrendered in its present condition. If these terms were not accepted, Burnside warned, the consequences of attack and assault would rest upon White.[42]

Colonel White called his officers together to discuss the situation and all agreed to fight rather than accept the surrender demand. Lieutenant Cogdell took the reply back to Captain Biggs just before dark. At this point, Biggs made the offer that perhaps the two commanders themselves, Burnside and White, should meet on Shackleford at 6 A.M. the next morn-

further conference in person. The two boats went their separate ways. Cogdell reported the verbal offer of a conference to Colonel White, who accepted.

At 6 A.M. on 24 April, White and Captain Guion went out across the inlet in a sailboat under a flag of truce to Shackleford. The *Alice Price* approached and they were soon joined on shore by Burnside and Captain Biggs. The conference was conducted in a pleasant, gentlemanly manner, particularly with White and Biggs, who were glad for a chance to see each other again. Burnside reiterated his feelings that since his siege guns were ready to fire he felt compelled to make the surrender offer in order to save lives. White replied that he was prepared to take the consequences of attack and would surrender only when compelled to do so. Burnside also informed them the latest news of the war, including the surrender of Fort Pulaski at Savannah, Georgia, almost two weeks earlier. White and Guion were unaware of this and must have realized the ominous implications for their own fate if a larger, more powerful fort like Fort Pulaski could be made to surrender. Still, they were unshaken from their resolve to pursue the struggle to its end. There was little else to say on the subject and after about twenty minutes the officers parted company, White and Guion returning to the fort while Burnside and Biggs retired back up the sound in the *Alice Price*.[43]

Having satisfied himself that his course was clear, Burnside sent orders to be relayed by the signal stations for Parke to open fire with his batteries at once. Lieutenant Flagler had reported the batteries completed and ready for battle the previous night so he was determined to waste no further time. In actuality, Flagler's report proved to be slightly premature because a few more preparations were still necessary and the embrasures of the Parrott battery had not yet been cut through the front of the battery. Chafing at the delay, Burnside sent an order to open fire that afternoon if possible. Parke made an attempt to comply but by the time the two artillery companies arrived at the batteries from camp four miles to the rear it was already 3:30 P.M. By the time they would be able to open fire it would almost be dark. Because of this and the need for further work on Morris' Parrott battery, it was decided to delay until the morning of the 25th.[44]

Unaware of all these communications between Parke and Burnside, the fort's guns fired vigorously upon the Union positions at intervals during the day, wounding one soldier of the 5th Rhode Island Battalion. Several shots were also fired that evening at the Union gunboat *Daylight*, which had replaced the *Albatross* on station off Beaufort Inlet. It is not known what thoughts or preparations were made in the fort over 24–25 April, but after the meeting with General Burnside the garrison knew the Union forces would make their play within the next day or two. At some point iron railroad rails taken from the tracks leading down to the fort wharf and from the railroad in Morehead City were leaned upright in stacks against the walls over the doors and windows of the casemates of the three eastern fronts of the parade wall to protect them from the artillery fire which they knew would soon come. Indeed, on the Union side everything was ready to open fire soon after sunrise on 25 April, with the exception of the embrasures of Captain Morris' Parrott battery. Morris' company was at work on these throughout the night so that the Parrotts would also be ready to open fire with the mortars in the morning.[45]

THE BOMBARDMENT

In the early morning hours of 25 April, Captain Morris' company finished opening the embrasures of its battery position for the three 30-pounder Parrott Rifles. Most of Morris' company and nine men of Captain Ammon's company would man the Parrott battery. In their hurry to complete the embrasures before sunrise, it is doubtful any of these men reflected upon the fact they were about to make history. Because rifled artillery was still such a new innovation, once they opened fire on Fort Macon, it would be only the second time in history that rifled cannons were used in combat in a breaching battery against a fort. Two weeks earlier, rifled cannons had breached the walls of Fort Pulaski, Georgia, and forced its surrender. However, this fort was one of the "perpendicular fortifications" of the Third System based on the principals of Frenchman Marc-René Montalembert which had been embraced so enthusiastically by the Board of Fortifications in the three and a half decades before the war. Thus when actually put to the test in combat, such forts had no protection for their walls against direct fire. In contrast, Fort Macon's earthen glacis covering its walls might prove troublesome for Union gunners. Even with the great accuracy of fire associated with rifled artillery, how well could Morris' gunners expect to do with such a narrow, partially concealed target presented to them? The answer would soon be evident.[46]

In the two mortar batteries all was in readiness. Nine men of Captain Morris' company were detailed as gunners for the mortar batteries along with the remainder of Ammon's company. Captain Ammon would assist Lieutenant Flagler with the management of the 10-inch mortar battery. The trenches between the batteries were manned by companies of the 8th Connecticut, while the regiment's two flank companies would have the unenviable position of lying between two fires in the advanced rifle pits in front of the main Union position. Out in the ocean were four ships of the blockading squadron at their anchorage which would be available to participate in the bombardment, although they were unaware the bombardment would begin that morning. Union soldiers and sailors watched the sun come up at about 5:02 A.M. and waited until it was light enough to distinguish targets.[47]

The men in the fort sensed nothing unusual at first about this morning as sunlight slowly illuminated Bogue Banks. Roll call was held at 5:30 A.M. and showed that out of over 400 men in the garrison only 263 were present for duty. The rest were on the sick list.[48]

About 5:40 A.M., Captain Morris jerked the lanyard of one of the Parrott Rifles, shattering the morning stillness with an angry boom. The thirty-pound iron missile struck the fort's parapet a moment later. The other Parrotts quickly followed suit, followed by the mortars. The battle was on. As time passed, the initial excitement of the moment for the gunners changed to the steady rhythm and routine of loading and firing.[49]

In the fort, the first shots caused an immediate reaction. Men standing around leaped for cover. The fort's lookout posted up in the crosstrees of the flagpole found himself in a most vulnerable position as the first shells

**The 10-inch mortar battery of Lieutenant Daniel W. Flagler in action during
the bombarcment of Fort Macon, April 25, 1862.**
From Frank Leslie's Illustrated Newspaper.

whizzed by. Immediately he grabbed the halyards and slid rapidly to the
ground. Elsewhere, the garrison suffered its first casualty almost immediately. One of the first shots, a 10-inch mortar shell, mortally wounded a
sentinel at the brick roadway through the covertway.[50]

It was not until 6:00 A.M. or shortly thereafter that the fort returned
fire. The first shot was from one of two 24-pounder siege guns mounted on
platforms adjacent to the north angle of the covertway, commanded by
Captain Manney. Beside Manney along the northwest face Captain Pool
joined in with the carronade mortars, as did the four 24-pounders at the
southwest angle of the covertway called the Eliason House battery, manned
by a portion of Captain Guion's company. The columbiads of Pool's water
battery at the south angle of the covertway were also engaged. On the upper terreplein, Captain Blount opened fire with his battery of 32-pounders

on the northwest face while the remainder of Captain Guion's company worked the 10-inch columbiad on the southwest face at high elevation as a mortar. Captain Cogdell's company would normally have manned the guns bearing on the channel from the upper terreplein and therefore would not be engaged against the enemy land batteries. However, his company would be used to relieve the other companies as needed. Because of the reduced number of men available for duty, not all of the fort's available guns were actually in use. However, at least twenty-one guns were in action against the batteries.[51]

For the next couple of hours the battle raged. The fort's fire was very rapid during this period and was concentrated largely upon the Parrott battery since its embrasures betrayed its exact position and provided a good target at which to shoot. Gradually more of the fort's fire became directed at the mortar batteries. Flagler's 10-inch mortar battery was located more closely behind Morris' Parrott battery than was desirable and many of the fort's projectiles which overshot the Parrott battery hit Flagler's. The embankment of Flagler's battery began to suffer as shot and shell ploughed into it. The wooden stakes in the ground on top of the battery by which the mortars were aimed were displaced.[52]

The fire of the Union batteries was maintained during this period with somewhat mixed results. Lieutenant Prouty's 8-inch mortars, being nearest the fort, did the best in dropping shells in or over the fort. Also, early on a few Parrott projectiles skimmed over the upper parapet of the fort and disabled several guns on the opposite side bearing on the channel. However, the fort's rapid firing soon created so much smoke that the fort was obscured. The Union gunners quickly found themselves unable to distinguish what they were shooting at or tell where their shots were falling.[53]

Between 8:00 and 9:00 A.M. the struggle took on an additional element as the four ships of the Union blockading squadron entered the action. Commander Samuel Lockwood in his ship *Daylight* was in charge of the squadron and waited two hours before ordering it into action. At 7:45 A.M., he steamed toward the other three ships making signals for them to clear for action and form in line ahead behind the *Daylight*. By 8:30 A.M.

the four vessels were moving up toward the fort to take part in the engagement. In the lead was Lockwood in the *Daylight,* a screw steamer armed with four guns. Next in line was the *State of Georgia,* a side-wheel steamer armed with nine guns, commanded by Commander James F. Armstrong. Third in line was the screw steamer *Chippewa,* armed with four guns and commanded by Lieutenant Andrew Bryson. Last in line was the bark *Gemsbok,* armed with six guns and commanded by Acting Lieutenant Edward Cavendy.[54]

The sea was rough that morning. A southwest wind was blowing at between Force 4 and Force 5. The consequent rolling and pitching of the ships would be bad for gunnery. At 8:40 A.M. the gunboats opened fire on the fort. They moved past at a range of one and one-quarter miles at the edge of the shoals off the entrance to the inlet. The *Gemsbok,* being a sailing vessel, took position about a mile from the fort and anchored to deliver her fire. The steamers, however, turned around and passed back in front of the fort, shooting their starboard guns on the backtrack. In this manner, Commander Lockwood kept the three steamers moving back and forth in front of the fort in an elliptical course, firing the port guns on the first track and the starboard guns on the backtrack.[55]

In a confrontation with the gunboats, the fort was more than a match. Leaving Manney's and Blount's guns to keep up their fire against the land batteries, Captain Pool's men left the carronade mortars on the lower terreplein and ran around to man the guns of the water battery at the south angle and southeast front. Captain Guion's men at the Eliason House Battery in the southwest angle withdrew into the fort to man Guion's columbiads and rifled guns on the sea front of the upper terreplein. At 9:05 A.M. the fort opened fire on the fleet. The heavy projectiles from Pool's and Guion's columbiads and rifled guns splashed all around the vessels, passing well beyond them. Many shots went over the decks and through the rigging, in some cases only a few yards above the heads of the men on deck. At 9:25 A.M., an 8-inch shot from one of the columbiads hit the *Daylight* on the starboard quarter. The shot ranged through several bulkheads and a deck into the engine room, where it missed the machinery and main steam line by only six inches. The shot struck the opposite side of the engine room without passing through the hull again. Splinters of wood were showered upon the engine room personnel, one of whom had his right forearm broken. Aboard the *Gemsbok,* a shot from the fort cut some of her starboard rigging. The *State of Georgia* had a shot pass through her ensign. At one point the *Georgia* passed too close to the shoals and touched bottom, but did no damage to her hull.

After being in action over an hour, Commander Lockwood realized he was accomplishing little. The wind and sea were having a great effect on the gunnery of the ships. Believing the fort would hold out several days, he did not wish to use up the ships' ammunition all at one time, especially their long-range fuzed shells, of which the *Daylight* had already used half her supply and the *Gemsbok* her entire supply. In the hope that better weather would prevail in the afternoon to give the ships better battle conditions, Lockwood signalled at 9:54 A.M. for the squadron to retire. The four ships moved off out of range and returned to their anchorage. As it would turn out, however, an increase in the wind and sea that afternoon would prevent their further participation in the battle.[56]

Pool's and Guion's gunners watched the retirement of the fleet with jubilation. For months the blockaders had hovered off Beaufort Inlet without venturing close enough for anything more than an occasional shot or two. This had been the first time the enemy vessels had actually attempted to engage the fort and the fort had shown itself more than capable of handling them. But any celebrating was short lived. Pool's men returned to their carronade mortars while Guion's went back to the Eliason House Battery as before to resume the action against the enemy land batteries.

Scarcely had the blockading squadron retired than efforts were made to get into action the *Grenade* and *Shrapnel,* the two floating batteries which Burnside had brought down from New Bern three days earlier. These were towed out of the North River and moved up to fire upon the fort from the northeast. Because of the difficulties of the narrow channel and the increasing wind and seas, only the *Grenade,* Lieutenant Benjamin D. Baxter, was able to get into action. About thirty shots were fired from her two 30-

pounder Parrott Rifles, but with the unfavorable conditions and extreme range the vessel was soon withdrawn.[57]

Out at the Union batteries, Lieutenants Flagler and Prouty were having problems. The beach sand proved to be miserable stuff on which to situate firing platforms for mortars. Under the heavy concussions from the mortars the sand shifted out from under the sleepers supporting the planking of the platforms, leaving the sleepers without support. Consequently they began to split. In Flagler's battery, the sleepers of three of the 10-inch mortars broke and caused the planking to become damaged in taking the recoil without adequate support. Flagler stopped fire on them one at a time so that they could be repaired. Also, the wooden bolsters on the 10-inch mortar carriages which formed part of the support for the fronts of the mortar barrels all became split from the recoil and required repair. Similarly, at 11:00 A.M., one of Prouty's 8-inch mortars was rendered inoperable for a period of two hours from a broken bolster until it could finally be repaired.[58]

The most serious problem faced by Flagler during the morning was damage to the embankment of his battery parapet by the fort's fire. The parapet was well gouged and furrowed by numerous shot and shell, throwing up clouds of sand. The blasts from the 10-inch mortars themselves even helped shake down the crumbling parapet. By 11 A.M. so much damage had been done the mortar crews were uncovered and exposed. They were forced to lay down for their own safety so that for a time Flagler's battery was silenced. Fortunately for them, the turning point of the battle was at hand.[59]

For most of the morning the fort had given a good account of itself in battle and the smoke of its guns had provided great protection in hampering the aim of Union gunners. As a result a great deal of the Union fire was missing the fort. The 10-inch mortars tended to go past the fort and explode over the channel beyond. The Parrotts similarly overshot the fort while some of the 8-inch mortar fire fell short. The battle might have continued like this all day had it not been for an incredible bit of good fortune for the Union gunners. Over in Beaufort, Lieutenants William S. Andrews and Marvin Wait stood watching these events from the Union signal station on the upper piazza of the Atlantic Hotel on the Beaufort waterfront. This station was one of the chain of signal stations established by General Parke to relay messages between his scattered command. In this case, however, the Beaufort station was in a unique position to observe the fall of the shots from the Union batteries. Forward observation of artilleryfire, so common-place today, did not exist in 1862 and although they could clearly see the firing errors being made by the Union batteries, the two observers had no orders to help direct the fire. Still, Andrews and Wait were determined they must help somehow, and took it upon themselves to begin signalling the batteries to inform them of their firing errors. About 9 A.M. they got the attention of Flagler and signalled range corrections until his shells were dropping into or bursting over the fort. In turn the same thing was done with Prouty's and Morris' batteries until their fire was also on target. After 11 A.M. Flagler estimated more than five of every eight shells were on target.[60]

The correction of the Union fire disrupted the fort's return fire. Confederate gunners found the ramparts swept with exploding mortar shells. Some men were covered by sand and earth raining down out of explosion clouds; others were knocked down by flying clods of earth. Some men were wounded by shell fragments, broken bricks and splinters of wood. One man was blown twelve feet into the air and came down in shreds. One man beside a 32-pounder was blown to bits by an exploding shell while another man in front of him remained completely untouched. Under these circumstances the Confederate fire began to slacken. As it did so, the protective smoke cloud which had covered the fort likewise began to dissipate. The thinning smoke allowed the Union gunners to see their targets at last and increase the accuracy of their fire. By noon, every shot fired by the Union batteries seemed to fall into or over the fort.[61]

Once able to clearly see the target, the awesome power and accuracy of rifled artillery became abundantly evident as Morris' Parrott Rifles worked their destructive mischief on the fort. Morris' mission was to knock out the fort's guns and breach the walls. With the fort's guns mounted *en barbette* there was very little protection for them except for places where sand bag merlons had been constructed on the parapet. One of the Parrott rounds drilled though the gun carriage of one of Manney's 24-pounder siege guns near the north angle and killed its gunner. A rifled 32-pounder in Guion's sea face battery on the southwest front of the upper parapet was disabled by a Parrott round which went through the two uprights of the top carriage. Several guns bearing on the channel fronts of the fort were disabled by Parrott shots which glanced over from the landward side, one of them on the covertway being dumped completely over on its side. About 2 P.M. in Captain Pool's water battery at the south angle of the covertway, one of the Parrott projectiles bored diagonally through the wooden top carriage frame of an 8-inch columbiad on the right side of the angle then went through the wrought iron top carriage frame of a 10-inch columbiad on the left side of the angle. The shot then struck the breastheight wall and glanced off to damage the next gun. Finally, it tumbled off into the ditch. Three men were killed or mortally wounded by this one shot, and several others wounded, including Captain Pool's son. The surviving members of the gun crews for these pieces were knocked flat to the ground by the concussion. Such were some of the deadly effects of the Parrotts on the fort's exposed armament.[62]

Against the walls of the fort the effects of the Parrotts were equally as dramatic. Their fire shattered the wood and shingle interior slope covering of the crest of the parapets, gouged holes in the glacis and parapets, and sent chunks of brick and mortar flying with each hit. Some of the shots actually reached down inside the interior of the fort to strike the upper portion of the parade walls on the east side. One of these shots cut the ends off two railroad rails out of a stack leaning against the wall over one of the windows and went on to drill into the wall past its length. Another went through one of the solid stone steps of the northeast stairway. Yet another came through a casemate and cut off the leg of a man sitting on his bunk.[63]

As for the scarp wall on the two western fronts of the fort directly facing the Union batteries, the fort's glacis did much to provide cover against direct fire. Only about three feet of the scarp wall was actually exposed to view between the crest of the glacis and the upper parapet. Yet with an accuracy of fire never thought possible from artillery at the time General Simon Bernard designed the fort some forty years earlier, Morris' gunners were actually able to shoot into that tiny band of exposed wall from almost 1,500 yards away. Some of the Parrott rounds were deflected down to hit the scarp below the visual level of exposed masonry by being made to just graze the crest of the glacis in front of it. Soon, large patches of broken red brick began to appear in the yellow-washed facade of the scarp wall. In two places the upper part of the scarp was actually breached.[64]

There was one section of the fort's scarp wall which was of particular interest to Morris. Behind the southwest angle of this wall lay Fort Macon's largest gunpowder magazine. This bit of information had been provided to him by one of Burnside's other brigade commanders, Brigadier General John G. Foster, who for two years before the war had been an engineer

The 30-pounder Parrott Rifle Battery of Captain Lewis O. Morris in action during the bombardment of Fort Macon, April 25, 1862.
From Frank Leslie's Illustrated Newspaper.

officer charged with Fort Macon's maintenance and repair. Foster was completely familiar with the fort's layout and his information proved quite valuable to Morris. Thus, the fort's most vulnerable point lay within Morris' reach since this angle was the one nearest the Union batteries. If Morris could succeed in breaching the scarp wall at this point he would thus endanger the magazine. As the afternoon wore on, some of the fire of the Parrotts was concentrated at this angle of the wall trying to break through.[65]

The return fire from the fort had steadily dropped during the course of the afternoon. This was due partly from the heavy amount of fire sweeping the ramparts and keeping the Confederates from their guns, and partly from fatigue caused by the difficulty of supplying reliefs to the men at the guns from the rest of the sickly garrison. The fort's rate of fire dropped to intervals of from five to twenty minutes. The slackening of return fire enabled the men in Flagler's battery to hurriedly repair the ruined parapet of their battery and resume fire. Flagler himself soon felt it safe enough to stand out in the open on the battery to observe the fall of his shots. One of Ammon's men, Private William R. Dart, as detailed to come out and reset the aiming stakes for the mortars on the parapet of the battery. But there was considerable danger in taking the situation too lightly because the fort's guns were still in action. Each time a white puff of cannon smoke was observed to suddenly pop forth from the fort's ramparts, Dart would yell a warning to his comrades. One time, however, Dart failed to observe one of the fort's guns firing and continued setting an aiming stake. The danger now became all too real. Within moments the solid shot cannonball hit Dart squarely in the chest, mangling him and killing him instantly. Lieutenant Flagler was spattered with blood and flesh, as were the walls and platforms of the battery.[66]

In Morris' battery, although the front of the emplacement took many hits, damage was actually slight even with the exposed embrasures. Six 32-pounder shot and shell came whizzing through the embrasures during the engagement. One of these grazed the top of the barrel of one Parrott Rifle, dented the iron reinforce band around the breech and carried away the breech sight. A 32-pounder shattered the wheel of another of the Parrotts but the wheel was quickly replaced with a spare. Incredibly the only injuries to personnel suffered in the battery were a sergeant and a private who were injured by spent cannonballs. Prouty's battery escaped serious injury since most of the fort's fire seemed to be directed at Morris and Flagler. Two of the fort's shells burst directly over the battery but no loss to personnel occurred.[67]

Meanwhile, the Confederates were determined to keep up the fight even though as the afternoon progressed their situation grew more serious by the hour. Even Union observers in Beaufort and Morehead City who could plainly see them with binoculars and telescopes were forced to remark over their determination and tenacity as they steadfastly worked their guns. At times they were hidden by explosions and clouds of smoke and dust only to reappear as if by magic as the wind swept it all away. Amidst flying shell fragments, bricks, wood and debris they kept to their work. At times they were force to take cover as the shelling became too intense, yet not many minutes would pass before one by one they began firing their guns again.[68]

Until early afternoon Colonel White himself was in the thickest of the fighting. Unmindful of the danger, he coolly passed from gun to gun, battery to battery, even to those most exposed, shouting encouragement to his men and reminding them of their duty to state and country. By 1 P.M., however, these great exertions had taken a toll on his frail health and he was exhausted. At this point he requested Captain Guion to take command while he retired to his quarters to regain his strength.[69]

At about 2:30 P.M., Captain Manney and Pool came up to Captain Guion to report the condition of their batteries. Manney had only one gun left in action and had been temporarily forced to withdraw his men from it due to its exposed condition. Captain Pool reported that two of his three columbiads had just been knocked out with the loss of three men, and felt it was time the company commanders held a council to discuss the situation. Guion agreed and the five company commanders met in one of the casemates. The chance of holding out much longer looked dim. Many guns were knocked out, the gun crews were exhausted, and there were not enough men to afford reliefs. Even if resistance continued, the garrison faced the far greater threat of complete annihilation because two of the magazines were now endangered. With one of the stone steps of the northeast stairs perforated there remained a good chance another Parrott round might find the same hole and pass easily through into the parade wall behind it where the northeast magazine was located. Far more serious, however, were the Parrott rounds being concentrated on the scarp wall of the southwest angle, behind which lay ordnance storage rooms containing ammunition, and the fort's largest magazine containing five tons of gunpowder. The scarp wall at the angle and the ceiling arches of these two small ordnance storage casemates between it and the magazine were cracking from repeated hits outside and would not last much longer. If the wall and arches collapsed, the magazine wall would be uncovered and exposed. Any attempt by the garrison to move the ammunition and gunpowder from this endangered area in the midst of battle was neither possible nor feasible, and it went without saying that a detonation of the magazine would mean the sudden and catastrophic end of the entire garrison and fort.

The officers were in agreement that surrender seemed their only option inasmuch as they had no control over the threat to the magazines. They then went to Colonel White's quarters to lay the matter before him for his decision. White told them he had been deliberating upon these issues himself and had come to the same conclusion. Surrender was inevitable and further resistance would only mean a useless waste of life. Accordingly, Captains Guion and Pool were delegated to meet with the enemy to offer terms upon which the fort would surrender.[70]

THE SURRENDER

At about 4:30 P.M. a white flag was displayed over the fort. All three Union batteries ceased firing while an acknowledgement was made. The white flag disappeared briefly and then reappeared coming out of the sally port with a group of men. Captains Pool and Guion and twelve soldiers bore the flag from the fort to the chimney and remains of the Eliason House, where they were met by a group from the batteries consisting of Lieutenant Prouty, Captain Duncan Pell of Burnside's staff, and Lieutenant Moses A. Hill of Parke's staff. Guion stated his purpose of holding a suspension of hostilities to discuss the terms on which the fort's surrender would be accepted. A considerable delay took place until General Parke could be brought over from his headquarters at Carolina City. Once he arrived, Guion and Pool stated Colonel White's offer to surrender the fort in its present state to him on condition that the garrison be paroled and allowed to go home. These were the terms originally offered by Burnside on 23 and 24 April, and by Parke himself on 23 March.[71]

Parke now stated he had no authority to grant these terms and said that surrender must be unconditional. Guion and Pool said they would not accept this, whereupon Parke replied that hostilities would recommence at once. However, he then agreed to extend the suspension of hostilities until the matter could be referred to General Burnside for his final decision. With that the two groups departed with the understanding everything was to be left in its present condition. Curiously, despite this last agreement, during the night all three of the Union batteries were repaired and stocks of fresh ammunition brought up in case hostilities resumed the following morning. In the fort, the garrison complied with the agreement against making repairs. An unpleasant night was spent making crude coffins for the seven men killed during the battle and wondering what might become of the rest of them should the enemy insist on unconditional surrender.[72]

During the night of 25–26 April, considerable delay was caused by strong winds and seas in getting word to General Burnside on the steamer *Alice Price* concerning the request for terms of surrender. Finally, an impatient General Parke started for the *Alice Price* to meet with General Burnside in person, arriving on board at 4 A.M., 26 April. Burnside's decision was to grant the terms the Confederates requested. There was no reason why these could not still be offered, especially as the practice of release on parole was something Burnside had consistently used for Confederate prisoners during the campaign up to now. The *Alice Price* got underway after sunrise and came down to Shackleford Point under a flag of truce. A boat was put out with two staff officers who went over to the fort beach and entered the fort. Colonel White was read the terms of surrender, which were simply that the fort would be surrendered and the garrison released on parole with their private effects and baggage. This was what had been requested and a greatly relieved Colonel White knew they were the most favorable terms he could hope for. He and Captain Guion accompanied the Union officers back to the boat and were taken over to the *Alice Price* to formally sign the terms with Generals Burnside and Parke.[73]

Aboard the *Alice Price*, the meeting was quite cordial and the terms were quickly drawn up for signatures. They were as follows:

TERMS OF CAPITULATION

The following are the terms of capitulation agreed upon for the surrender to the forces of the United States of Fort Macon, Bogue Banks, NC:

ARTICLE 1: The fort, armament, and garrison to be surrendered to the forces of the United States.

ARTICLE 2: The officers and men of the garrison to be released on their parole of honor not to take up arms against the United States of America until properly exchanged and to return to their homes, taking with them all their private effects, such as clothing, bedding, books, &c.

M. J. White
Colonel, C. S. Army, Commanding Fort Macon
Saml. Lockwood
Commanding U. S. Navy, and Senior Officer
Jno. G. Parke
Brig. Gen. Vols., Commanding Third Division, Dept. NC

Fort Macon, NC April 26, 1862.[74]

With this done, the two Confederate officers accepted the offer of breakfast with Burnside and Parke. After breakfast, White, Guion, Burnside, Parke, and some staff officers climbed into the boat to go over to the fort. As the boat left, White sat for a time with his face in his hands. It was obvious to all the mortification he felt at having to surrender the fort. The boat reached the fort beach and while the Union officers walked briskly up the beach to bring up their troops, White and Guion returned to the fort to convey the news to the garrison. The men were overjoyed and relieved that they would be paroled rather than taken off to a prisoner of war camp. They were ordered to fall in with arms and at 9:00 A.M. the garrison was marched out of the fort by companies onto the glacis. Here they stacked their muskets and artillery short swords, and waited in line for the arrival of the Union troops to take possession of the fort.[75]

Meanwhile, Burnside, Parke, and staff officers made their way along the island back to their lines. In the trenches and rifle pits they found the 5th Rhode Island Battalion, which had just relieved the 8th Connecticut a short time before. Even though the Connecticut soldiers had endured the entire bombardment in the trenches and rifle pits the previous day with shells passing over them, bursting nearby and covering them with sand, it was the luck of the draw in the rotation of duty that they were relieved and the Rhode Islanders would be the ones to receive the fort's surrender. The battalion was ordered into line and with new flags just received from Rhode Island unfurled started up the beach for the fort with Burnside and Parke at their head. The battalion approached the fort and marched around the glacis, halting near the sally port entrance. At this point the Confederates filed past back into the fort one last time to pack and retrieve their personal effects and baggage before being taken away. Once they were inside, the 5th Rhode Island Battalion marched around the perimeter of the covertway ramparts, each company taking position until the entire perimeter was encircled.[76]

At 10:10 A.M. the large Confederate garrison flag was lowered from the flagstaff. There followed some awkward moments for Major John Wright, commander of the 5th Rhode Island Battalion, as he sought to find a suitable U.S. flag to raise in its place. It turned out Fort Macon's original twenty by thirty-six-foot U.S. garrison flag of prewar days had been made into the Confederate Stars and Bars by the resourceful garrison. The red and white

**The surrender of Fort Macon and lowering of the Confederate flag
on the morning of April 26, 1862.**
From Frank Leslie's Illustrated Newspaper.

stripes of the original flag had been removed and resewn together to form
the large red-white-red bars of the Confederate flag. Wright's dilemma was
soon solved when someone located a U.S. flag. It was the flag taken from
the wrecked steamer *Star of the Union* the previous November. At 10:22 A.M.
this flag was hoisted up the flagstaff while a Rhode Island bugler played the
"Star Spangled Banner." Fort Macon was now formally retaken by the Union.
The men of the 5th Rhode Island Battalion could barely restrain themselves from cheering at this important moment, but General Burnside felt
such sympathy for Colonel White he had given strict orders to the Rhode
Islanders against cheering or any similar outburst. However, distant cheering could be heard echoing across the harbor from Union troops in Beaufort, while in the ocean the steamer *State of Georgia* fired the National Salute of twenty-one guns.[77]

The Confederate garrison flag of Fort Macon was retained by Major

Wright of the 5th Rhode Island Battalion after it was taken down. Afterward, Wright secured Burnside's permission for the battalion to keep the flag for the purpose of presenting it to Governor William Sprague and the General Assembly of Rhode Island. This was subsequently done. At least one other large Confederate flag from the fort, perhaps used as a storm flag, was retained by General Parke and his staff.[78]

It now remained for the Confederates to sign their parole lists and be given transportation back to their lines. They marched out of the fort for the last time, bearing their personal possessions and baggage. The dead were carried out in wooden boxes as the Union soldiers entered the fort. Two badly wounded Confederates, including the man whose leg was taken off by a Parrott shot while sitting on his bunk, had to be left in the fort for the time being with a third man to attend them as a nurse. The first of the garrison to leave were Pool's and Manney's companies and part of Cogdell's, all from the local area, which were transported over to Beaufort for release late in the afternoon aboard the steamer *Old North State*. About one hundred others from the New Bern area, mostly Guion's company, were taken aboard the *Alice Price* to be released when Burnside returned to New Bern. The *Alice Price* left Beaufort late on 27 April and arrived at New Bern the following afternoon. The remaining 156 members of the garrison, including Colonel White, were taken aboard the gunboat *Chippewa* on the afternoon of 27 April and carried to the mouth of the Cape Fear River. Under a flag of truce the prisoners were transported to a Confederate steamer from Fort Caswell and returned to Confederate lines.[79]

After taking possession of Fort Macon, Union officers had time to assimilate all the facts and figures associated with the battle. The three siege batteries fired a total of 1,150 shots at the fort, of which 450 were from Morris' battery and the rest from the mortars. Of these, officers counted 560 actual hits made on the fort. There were forty-one hits by Parrott shots in the tiny band of visible scarp wall of the western face. Some of the Parrott rounds penetrated to a depth of two feet into the masonry. Forty-eight mortar shells exploded in the ditch, many on the ramparts and at least a score in the parade ground, of which one broke through into one of the fort's cisterns. The parade walls were scarred, pocked, and covered with dirt and burned powder. Thousands of shell fragments littered the fort. Fifteen of the fort's guns had been knocked out by Morris' Parrotts while at least five others were damaged by exploding mortar shells which splintered their gun carriages or blew up their traverse circles. In the words of Colonel White: "Two more days of such firing would have reduced the whole to a mere mass of ruins."[80]

The fire of the four warships of the blockading squadron during the bombardment probably amounted to about 125 shots, most of which apparently fell short along the seaward portion of the glacis. Union observers in Beaufort felt at least a few of the squadron's shells burst over or within the ramparts but no damage of consequence was done to the fort by this fire. Of the thirty shots fired by the floating battery *Grenade*, most were ineffective due to unfavorable water conditions and extreme range.[81]

The spoils of victory to the Union forces included the fort's armament of fifty-four guns, 20,000 pounds of gunpowder, a considerable quantity of ordnance, commissary and quartermaster stores, forty horses, and 500 rifles and muskets with accouterments. Despite the intensity of the bombardment, losses were light on both sides. The Union loss was one man killed, three men (two Army and one Navy) wounded. The Confederate loss was seven killed, eighteen wounded.[82]

REVIEW AND CONCLUSIONS

In reviewing Fort Macon's first and only battle, it might be a fair question to ask whether it fulfilled what was expected of it from a defensive standpoint as a Third System fort. It certainly fulfilled the mission of any fortification in that it provided a stronghold which enabled an inferior force to hold out for a period of time against a force of considerable superiority in numbers and equipment. In so doing it caused the superior force to exert a substantial investment in time and effort to effect its eventual capture. Originally, Third System forts were expected to hold out from thirty to fifty days against an attacking force, which would allow time for relief forces to arrive. From 23 March, the first Union demand for surrender, until the fort did finally surrender on 26 April, thirty-five days elapsed. Unfortunately, the situation was such that no relief forces were available to march to its aid. It was never intended that Third System forts should stand alone against an enemy but that support from friendly ground and naval forces should be a part of its overall defense. Fort Macon had none of this after the battle of New Bern. It would seem, then, that the fort did fulfill what the Bernard Board of Fortifications would have expected of it as a Third System fort, and did so in a situation of isolation which was not part of the Board's original vision.

Whether the garrison could have done more in its own defense is more difficult to assess. Their inexperience in this early stage of the war was probably an important factor, and one could easily say that the defense might have been conducted somewhat differently had the battle occurred in 1865 rather than early 1862. Excluding such factors as lack of mortars, poor ammunition, sickness and lack of numbers, any mistakes made in resisting the siege were probably the result of inexperience. Of course, in any situation such as this, more could have been done when one looks back in hindsight. There are three major areas which could have affected the outcome of the siege: resistance to Union landings on Bogue Banks, disruption of Union siege operations in front of the fort, and artificial alteration of the fort to minimize damage to the walls and armament. Whether the garrison had the resources to seriously alter the course of events in any of these three areas is difficult to determine. Overall, whether it could have done enough to change the eventual outcome of the siege is a moot point.

Of the many factors which contributed to the fort's downfall, one of the most important was the fort's lack of mortars. Even the best efforts of the six improvised "carronade mortars" were nowhere near as effective as an actual mortar would have been. A couple of siege mortars with a suitable supply of good ammunition would have enabled the fort to disrupt Union operations during the siege and send an effective counter-battery fire against the Union siege batteries during the bombardment. Why such weapons were never provided for the fort is difficult to say, but the major focus of Confederate authorities always seems to have been directed toward acquiring the heavy long-ranged guns needed to defend against the Union Navy, especially after the battle at Hatteras Inlet. The Union Navy, unquestionably, was judged to be the major threat to the fort. There seems to have been no worst-case scenario developed as to how the fort would defend itself in a situation where it was surrounded and under siege from the land. Once Burnside's mode of amphibious attack was demonstrated at Roanoke Island it was too late to try to requisition mortars from the hard-pressed Confederate Ordnance Department for the landward side. The subsequent withdrawal of Confederate infantry from the area of Fort Macon just prior to the battle of New Bern took away the fort's main hope of resisting a Union approach by land.

The single most important factor working against Fort Macon, however, was the use of rifled artillery. Rifled cannons were one of the many innovations of modern warfare which made its first appearance in the Civil War and it was so new that its use against Fort Macon was only the second time in history it had been used in breaching batteries against a fort. While almost every Union participant seems to have believed the fort would hold out longer than it did, the astounding power of rifled guns accomplished in hours what would have taken days of bombardment by smoothbore guns at close range, or weeks of siege by regular approaches. The accuracy and power of these guns which enabled Union gunners to disable so many of the fort's guns and endanger its magazines was the key factor in the fort's downfall. In the larger sense, rifled artillery was now firmly established as a force to be reckoned with and thus ensured the decline of a major era in military history. The art of masonry fortification, manifested in the use of thousands of castles, fortified cities, and forts during the course of centuries of warfare throughout the world, was now passing into obsolescence as a means of primary defense. In this sense, the bombardment of Fort Macon was part of a happening which would change the history of warfare.

7

UNION OCCUPATION

The capture of Fort Macon meant the opening of Beaufort Harbor for exploitation by both the Union Army and Navy. Neither wasted much time in doing so. In anticipation of future operations into the interior, General Burnside requested reinforcements, railroad locomotives and cars, and wagons from the War Department, pointing out on 3 May 1862: "All the troops destined for this department can be transported to Beaufort Harbor in large vessels and landed at the wharf at Morehead City, where there is some 17 or 18 feet of water." Two days later, Burnside again wrote to the Secretary of War that the "possession of Beaufort Harbor renders the transportation of troops to this department very easy, and if a movement in force into the interior, with a view to occupying Goldsboro and Raleigh . . . be desirable, the necessary force can easily be brought to this point . . . . " However, before any such movement could take place, General McClellan's army was defeated in Virginia in June, 1862, causing the transfer of Burnside and a portion of his command to Virginia as a reinforcement. The further operations of the Burnside Expedition in North Carolina thus came to an end.[1]

As for the Union Navy, Commander Samuel Lockwood wrote to Flag Officer L. M. Goldsborough, commander of the North Atlantic Blockading Squadron, four days after the surrender of Fort Macon that Beaufort

Harbor "would be a good place of deposit for coal, provisions, small stores, and lubricating oil, which is in constant demand by the engineer's department for the vessels stationed here and blockading off [Cape] Fear River, North Carolina." On 2 May, Flag Officer Goldsborough ordered 1,000 tons of coal, and a full supply of provisions, stores, and clothing to be sent to Beaufort Harbor for the use of the vessels of the North Atlantic Blockading Squadron. Thereafter, Union supply vessels were always maintained in the harbor for resupplying Union warships and, later in the war, a naval storehouse building was erected near Fort Macon's wharf. Orders were given that Navy vessels stationed off Beaufort or Wilmington were to go to Beaufort for their supplies rather than Hampton Roads, which considerably reduced the amount of time ships would have to be off station for resupply. At the request of the Army, arrangements were made so that at least one Union warship was always on hand in the harbor obtaining coal or supplies which could assist Fort Macon's Union garrison with the defense of the harbor, if necessary.[2]

GARRISON DUTY

Immediately after taking possession of Fort Macon in April, 1862, General Parke shifted his forces to occupy the area and give his men a well deserved rest. Morris' and Ammon's companies were moved into the fort itself. The camp at Hoop Pole Creek was broken up and moved to the fort. The 5th Rhode Island Battalion went into camp outside the fort for a time while the other regiments were distributed to the towns or sent back to New Bern. As rapidly as possible, the damages done to the fort during the bombardment were repaired. Once the walls were patched with masonry, the grounds restored and the fort thoroughly cleaned and policed, life settled down to routine garrison duty once again.[3]

For the remainder of the war the fort was continuously occupied. Morris' and Ammon's companies served as the fort's garrison for the remainder of 1862. From 1863 until the end of the war the garrison was usually increased to between three and five companies of infantry or artillery

at any given time. Once repairs were completed, the fort changed little
from when the Confederates had occupied it. Most of the armament which
had been used by the Confederates in the battle was retained by Union
troops, with the exception of a few of the 24-pounders which were shipped
elsewhere. By July, 1862, three 10-inch siege mortars were obtained by the
garrison and placed on the fort's landward side, thus curing the problem
of no mortars which had so plagued the Confederates during the siege.
Union troops distrusted the rifled cannons inherited from the Confederates. None of them were banded with a breech reinforce and therefore
might burst if full service charges were used. In the spring of 1863, three
100-pounder Parrott Rifles on iron carriages were installed in the fort to
give the garrison reliable rifled guns. Curiously, Union garrisons made no
effort to solve the major problem the fort had faced during the battle–the
vulnerability of both the armament and the gunpowder magazines to the
fire of rifled artillery in battle.[4]

For the remainder of the war, the occupation of Fort Macon was largely
one of comfort and ease for Union soldiers. In the day to day routine of
garrison duty, soldiers were drilled both as infantry and artillery, and frequently practiced with the fort's big guns. On one occasion while practic-
ing with the guns, a shell with a defective fuse exploded soon after leaving
the cannon's muzzle. Its fragments shredded a row of uniforms and clothing drying on a clothesline and killed two mules and five pigs grazing outside. When off duty, soldiers sometimes visited Beaufort and Morehead
City for what little diversions could be found there. An old Negro boatman
came across the harbor to the fort each morning to take over any soldiers
who wanted to go into town. The arrival twice a week of the mail steamer
from the North was an event eagerly awaited by all with the hope of receiving letters and packages from home. With a war going on, a certain degree
of vigilance was constantly maintained. A picket station was established about
two miles from the fort and soldiers frequently patrolled as far as five or six
miles from the fort along the island. However, the most serious encounters
experienced by soldiers on picket duty were not with Confederate soldiers
but with snakes. One man on picket duty, for instance, noticed a rustling

under a pile of cedar leaves on which he was lying and found three copper-heads keeping warm under him.[5]

In addition to the usual duties of soldiers, the garrison of the fort had another duty required of them during the course of the war—that of guarding prisoners. It was only logical that Fort Macon should be considered an ideal place at which to confine prisoners by virtue of its remote location and strong, cell-like casemates. The fort's garrison not only served as guards, but also kept the prisoners at hard labor performing various operational and maintenance tasks around the fort. In July of 1862, the first group of prisoners arrived at the fort for confinement, a practice which lasted for the next fourteen years. The prisoners consisted of one officer and twenty enlisted men, all Union soldiers undergoing sentence imposed by court martial for various military offenses. Most of the prisoners confined at the fort during the war would be the Union Army's own court martial cases rather than Confederate prisoners of war. As the months passed, the number of prisoners present at any one time fluctuated as new prisoners arrived and old ones were released at the expiration of their sentences.[6]

Living conditions for the prisoners were not pleasant. They were turned out of their quarters at reveille, after which they would answer to roll call, empty all slop tubs in the fort, and put their quarters in order. After breakfast they were kept at hard labor at least ten hours a day with one hour for lunch. They were kept under guard and shackled with ball and chain. They were forbidden to speak nor were any of the garrison allowed to speak to them other than the guards, except on authority. They were made to answer roll call after supper and then were immediately locked up for the night. No lights were allowed in their cell during the night. Slop tubs were provided for them when locked up. The prisoners were confined in Casemate 26 in the north angle of the fort which was set up as a prison cell. One report in March, 1863, mentioned the poor conditions offered by the casemate and noted "sunshine never enters to such an extent as to make printed matter discernible in all parts of the room, consequently the place is constantly damp." The report also found after examining the medical returns for the post over a one month period the proportion of sickness among prisoners was five times greater than among soldiers of the garrison. The fort commandant was ordered to attend to the health of the prisoners.[7]

Not all the prisoners confined in Fort Macon during the war were Union Army court martial cases, however. On 9 June 1864, the Confederate block-ade runner *Pevensey* was chased ashore on Bogue Banks about nine miles west of Fort Macon by the Union gunboat *New Bern*. Thirty-six crewmen were captured and confined briefly in Fort Macon before being sent north to prison of war camps. Similarly, in August, 1864, fifty-one crewmen of the blockade runner *Lilian* were brought into Beaufort and confined in Fort Macon for several weeks. One of the crew recorded the conditions as follows: "There was not sufficient space in our quarters for us all to lie down at once, and consequently I slept nightly for several weeks with my head upon my neigh-bor on one side and my legs over another. Our food was served twice daily and was of the coarsest description, but we were permitted to buy butter, crackers, sardines and the like at high prices from the sutler. We were al-lowed to march out upon the parapet for an hour daily, under guard, from which we gazed with longing eyes upon the opposite shore of Dixie's Land."[8]

THE SPECTER OF WAR

For almost two years following the capture of the fort, Union garrisons enjoyed a relatively easy existence at Fort Macon with little chance of direct involvement in the war. The garrison watched as Union Navy vessels con-stantly entered the harbor for supplies and left to resume blockade duty elsewhere on the coast. Army supply vessels landed their cargoes at the railroad depot in Morehead City to keep Union forces occupying the North Carolina coast supplied. At times Union troops passed through Beaufort Harbor in transports, frequently in large numbers, bound for some other front. In January, 1863, a large expedition was fitted out to operate against Charleston which filled Beaufort Harbor with gunboats, monitors, and dozens of transports. Many of the Union troops serving in the Department of North Carolina took part in the expedition, embarking at Morehead City and sailing with it when it left on 29 January 1863.[9]

In these instances, troops and vessels were in motion to go fight at other locations. Even many of the operations within the Department, including two large-scale raids in force into Confederate territory during November and December, 1862, seemed far removed from Fort Macon. But the presence of war was still very much a reality. In March and April of 1863, Confederate Major General D. H. Hill made unsuccessful attempts to recapture New Bern and Washington. For a time afterward, it was feared his forces would renew their attempts while Confederate forces from Wilmington would threaten the Morehead City area and the railroad to New Bern. Union troops spent the summer fortifying vulnerable points, which included erecting entrenchments to defend Morehead City. No further attack came. However, later in the year disquieting reports were received about Confederates building two powerful ironclad rams for the eventual purpose of eliminating Union gunboats in the sounds and aiding in the recapture of Union-held enclaves in the coastal area. These were the CSS *Albemarle* on the Roanoke River and the CSS *Neuse* on the Neuse River. Even though construction of these vessels dragged on for months, by the beginning of the year 1864 the two ironclads were nearing completion and would be operational in the early part of that year. Union troops in all the enclaves of North Carolina could expect trouble at some point as a result, including Fort Macon.[10]

As Union commanders feared, the first five months of 1864 proved to be ones of intense pressure and anxiety as Confederate forces took what was to be their last chance to try to recapture some of the territory of coastal North Carolina lost in 1862. Although Fort Macon would not come under direct attack during these operations the fate of its garrison hung in the balance along with that of other Union enclaves in the face of Confederate attacks. Fortunately for the Union, the two Confederate ironclads were not ready at the end of January, 1864, when the forces of Confederate Major General George E. Pickett made an attack to recapture New Bern. While several Confederate columns of Pickett's troops converged on the city to invest it, yet another column commanded by Brigadier General James G. Martin was to advance from Wilmington as a diversionary force to threaten the Morehead City area and the railroad to New Bern. As Pickett's main forces engaged the New Bern defenses during 1 and 2 February, 1864, General Martin's column overran Union outposts below Newport on 2 February. After a brief engagement Union troops were then driven from the post of Newport Barracks. On 3 February, Martin pushed portions of his force out to within six miles of Morehead City, but refrained from continuing his general advance against it until he could learn of what progress had been made by Pickett's main effort against New Bern.[11]

At Morehead City, Union Colonel James Jourdan, commanding the Sub-District of Beaufort, prepared as best he could with what meager forces he had to resist against Martin's advance. A detachment of one hundred men were taken from Fort Macon's garrison and divided to reinforce the troops in Beaufort and Morehead City. Jourdan later concentrated his forces during the night of 2 February into the entrenchments built the previous year to guard Morehead City. A Navy gunboat in Bogue Sound secured his left flank. Should he be compelled to abandon this line and evacuate Morehead City, his only recourse would then be to withdraw to Fort Macon itself. In the meantime, women and children of Union soldiers' families were sent to Fort Macon or placed aboard ships in the harbor for safety. Most of the naval stores on hand at Morehead City, Beaufort, and the naval store house at Fort Macon were transferred to the ships. A large quantity of stores were also destroyed.[12]

Fortunately for Colonel Jourdan no attack against Morehead City came to pass. On 3 February, General Martin had started some of his forces toward Morehead City when he received word that Pickett's main operation against New Bern had failed and that Pickett was withdrawing his forces. As a result, Martin likewise withdrew back to Wilmington. Union soldiers reestablished their positions in the Sub-District of Beaufort, doubtless with a new respect for the havoc even a small force of Confederates such as General Martin's could cause to the security of Morehead City, Beaufort, and Fort Macon.[13]

With large forces of Confederate soldiers continuing to remain in eastern North Carolina during February and March, continuous rumors of impending Confederate attacks on the Union enclaves kept Union forces on constant edge and alert. The enclaves of New Bern, Washington, and Plymouth felt themselves in danger of renewed Confederate attack at any time. Even at Beaufort Harbor fears were entertained that Confederate naval forces in launches might possibly slip into the harbor to attack Union shipping. These fears were reinforced when, on the night of 3 April, a Confederate commando team succeeded in slipping through Union lines and badly damaging the lighthouses at Cape Lookout with gunpowder charges, all within sight of Fort Macon. However, the main fear of Union authorities was that posed by the Confederate ironclads. It was known that following the failure of the New Bern operation, Confederate forces were now concentrating on finishing the ironclads *Albemarle* and *Neuse* to aid their operations to recapture Union coastal enclaves. Large numbers of soldiers were being detailed to help rush these vessels to completion. Union commanders received reports on their progress with growing apprehension and anxiety. In belief that the *Neuse* would soon be able to come down the Neuse River to attack New Bern, during March of 1864, one of the three 100-pounder Parrott Rifles at Fort Macon was transferred to strengthen New Bern's river defenses. Major General John J. Peck, commanding the District of North Carolina, noted that in the entire Union-held section of the North Carolina coast there were only seven large caliber rifled cannons capable of causing any significant damage to an ironclad (two at Plymouth, one at Hatteras, two at New Bern, and the two 100-pounders remaining at Fort Macon). Soon the worst fears of Union commanders concerning the formidability of the Confederate ironclads was to be confirmed.[14]

During 17–20 April 1864, Confederate forces of Brigadier General Robert F. Hoke attacked and captured the Union enclave of Plymouth. Assisting was the ironclad *Albemarle*, which sank one Union gunboat defending the town, damaged another, and aided Hoke's ground forces by shelling Union fortifications defending the town. The success of this operation seriously threatened the security of New Bern and Fort Macon with the possibility that, with the assistance of the ironclads, Confederates might actually manage to recover the coastal sections lost by them in 1862. Again hurried preparations were made for defense by Union forces. Some of the troops of the Sub-District of Beaufort were withdrawn to reinforce New Bern, which stripped local defenses around Beaufort Harbor. To do the guard and picket duty around Morehead City, fifty artillerymen were taken from Fort Macon's garrison. These were replaced for a time by a party of sixty sailors from the Union warships *Grand Gulf* and *Cambridge*, in the harbor to help man the fort's guns. As anticipated, General Hoke's Confederates now planned to renew their effort against New Bern and to unite the ironclads by bringing the *Neuse* down from Kinston and the *Albemarle* down through the sounds into the Neuse River. Word reached Union commanders that Confederates were also preparing pontoons for a contemplated movement down the Outer Banks against Fort Macon as well.[15]

Just when everything seemed darkest for Union troops, however, General Hoke's plans came apart. The *Neuse* grounded hopelessly on a sand bar on 22 April and could not support an advance against New Bern. Hoke then intended to wait for the *Albemarle* to transit the sounds and come up the Neuse. On 5 May, however, the ironclad was attacked by a number of large Union gunboats as she came out into Albemarle Sound and was forced to return to Plymouth for repairs after a severe engagement. Hoke's forces in the meantime advanced against New Bern on 4–5 May, but were then recalled to Virginia and forced to break off operations because of the opening of the Union Army of the Potomac's spring offensive in Virginia. Thus ended the last Confederate chance to recapture New Bern and Fort Macon.[16]

There was one interesting sidelight resulting from Confederate operations against New Bern and Plymouth which did have a direct effect on the garrison of Fort Macon. Among the Union soldiers taken prisoner by General Pickett's Confederate forces during the February attack on New Bern were soldiers of the 2nd North Carolina Union Volunteers. This regiment, along with the 1st North Carolina Union Volunteers, were composed of North Carolinians who were loyal to the United States and who had taken up arms against their fellow North Carolinians in Confederate service. The soldiers of these two regiments were contemptuously termed 'Buffaloes', and were always regarded with a particular disdain by Confederates. However, twenty-two of the Buffalo prisoners taken by Pickett were found to be former *Confederate* soldiers who had deserted and joined the enemy. General Pickett had all twenty-two tried as deserters and hanged in Kinston despite protests by Union authorities. The controversy touched off by this incident had a demoralizing effect on the soldiers of the two regiments who were still in Union service. Following General Hoke's capture of Plymouth and subsequent efforts to take New Bern, they were in a state of near panic as to the treatment they would receive if they too were captured. Union commanders expressed no faith in them as front line troops in a battle but felt if these two regiments could be stationed in some quiet sector where they could feel secure against capture they would settle down and return to effectiveness. The Sub-District of Beaufort was felt to be as safe a sector as could be had in the District of North Carolina, especially with its remoteness from front lines and the security offered by Navy ships, Fort Macon, and the entrenchments protecting the different towns and posts. As a result, in April and May of 1864, both regiments, along with their wives and children, were stationed in Beaufort, Morehead City, Newport, and Fort Macon to get them away from front line duty. Here they served out most of the remainder of the war in relative safety. From May, 1864, until March, 1865, four or five companies of the 1st North Carolina Union Volunteers comprised Fort Macon's garrison.[17]

FINAL MONTHS OF CONFLICT

The last year of the Civil War at Fort Macon was one of comparative quiet as large-scale operations in Virginia, Georgia, Tennessee, and finally South Carolina took precedence. However, Beaufort Harbor was used as a rendezvous point by the Union Navy in its final operations against Fort Fisher, North Carolina, in December, 1864, and January, 1865. In the last weeks of the war, as Major General William T. Sherman's Union Army pushed General Joseph E. Johnston's Confederate Army through North Carolina in March and April of 1865, Beaufort Harbor and the railroad from Morehead City became the main supply line for Sherman's armies. The wharf facilities at Morehead City were increased to handle the staggering amount of supplies necessary to sustain Sherman's force of 70,000 men and 40,000 animals. Fort Macon became the place of incarceration for dozens of Sherman's soldiers undergoing court martial sentences. The number of military prisoners held in the fort jumped as high as 119 convicts in April, 1865. With the surrender of Johnston's Confederate Army at Bennett House near Durham that month, the war was essentially over. Perhaps the last military function of Fort Macon in the Civil War came on 8 May 1865, when the fort received orders to prepare to defend against possible attack by the Confederate commerce raider *Stonewall*, which was still at sea and unaware of the war's end. No attack materialized and with this the most tragic period of American history finally came to an end. The last volunteer unit to comprise the fort's garrison in the war, Company G, 2nd Massachusetts Heavy Artillery, left the fort in June, 1865, to muster out of service.[18]

8

POSTWAR YEARS

With the end of the Civil War, the U.S. Army was to remain in occupation of the South for the next twelve years during the period of Reconstruction. As the units of the U.S. Volunteers mustered out of service, their places at the various military posts which remained occupied were taken over by U.S. Regulars. Fort Macon was one of the posts which was to remain occupied as a garrison station after the war's end and in June, 1865, elements of the 14th U.S. Colored Heavy Artillery took over garrison duty. This unit's occupation of Fort Macon was notable for two reasons. First, it marked the first time black troops occupied the fort (albeit, with white officers), and second, it marked a record for the most troops ever to actually live in Fort Macon at one time. Post returns for November, 1865, show the entire regiment with 864 officers and men present for duty occupying the fort, along with forty-five prisoners, to make a total of 909 men living in the fort. Each company occupied a single casemate.[1] Fortunately, the regiment mustered out of service the following month and was replaced by two companies of the 37th U.S. Colored Troops. These companies comprised the fort's garrison until the beginning of 1867, when this regiment also mustered out of service. In March, 1867, elements of another black regiment, the 40th U.S. Infantry, then garrisoned the fort until August 1868, after which time white infantry or artillery units garrisoned the fort during the remaining years of the Reconstruction Era.[2]

ARMY LIFE DURING RECONSTRUCTION YEARS

The life of soldiers garrisoning Fort Macon during the Reconstruction years was little changed from that of previous years as the fort resumed the role it had before the war as a typical Army military post. Day to day military duties were carried out, training and drill continued, prisoners were guarded and kept at labor. In spare time the usual diversions such as hunting, fishing, and visits to local towns were open to the soldiers. A post library containing over 200 books was established in one of the casemates. Following the end of the war, married officers and soldiers once more brought their wives and families to live on the post. Married enlisted men and their families, and the post laundresses, occupied six rundown frame cottages scattered around the reservation, with more than one family sometimes being forced to share the same cottage. Officer's families usually occupied casemates. In 1869, four frame buildings used as soldier quarters at Goldsboro were dismantled and shipped to Fort Macon to serve as officer's quarters. Once these were finally erected some of the overcrowding in the fort was alleviated when officers and their families moved into them.[3]

In what appears to be the only recorded impressions of life at Fort Macon from a woman of this period, Mrs. Jane Augusta (McKenny) Coues, wife of Assistant Surgeon Elliott Coues, found two aspects of life in so small a place as Fort Macon somewhat annoying. At any hour of the day or night the sergeant of the guard could be heard constantly shouting in his "stentorian voice" to challenge anyone entering the fort, or to turn out the guard when the officer of the day passed. "All day and all night long," she wrote her sister, "the sentinel with his horrid voice is either saying: 'Commanding Officer, turn out the guard,' or else: 'Who goes there, Halt!'" Far more nerve-wracking for her, however, was the fact that the cannon used to fire the morning and evening salutes was situated over her casemate. Every day she dreaded with nervous anticipation its bone-jarring boom directly overhead. She wrote that "every day when the time comes I get so nervous expecting it that I feel as though I should fly." However, in other letters she wrote of more pleasant aspects such as riding horses on the beach with her husband, taking excursions with him in a sailboat, and going fishing. Sewing and reading occupied other portions of her time, and almost every day she made the rowboat trip over to Beaufort to go to market.[4]

The 1870 Census lists sixteen children living at Fort Macon who were under the age of twelve years. What an exciting place an Army fort with an ocean beach just outside must have been for them! One small toddler, the daughter of Assistant Surgeon Elliott Coues, established a routine for herself to go around each morning after she dressed to the different casemates of the other officers for candy, which the officers kept in expectation of her visits. Still, all was not just fun and games for children living at Fort Macon. In the library casemate (Number 6) a post school was established. Here the children were gathered and tutored in their studies by one of the soldiers.[5]

Fort Macon in these years was a small military city where men, women and children lived, worked, and played. In addition to its tiny school and modest library, it had a hospital, a cemetery, storehouses, stables, and a wharf with a railroad line leading to it. A regular mail was established through the Beaufort post office. A local boatman was contracted to carry mail and freight between the fort and Beaufort. As for supplies, fresh beef and fuel were obtained locally by contract while all other supplies were usually shipped from the North by steamer to New Bern and then by rail to Morehead City, if not directly by steamer. To supplement their provisions, soldiers at times cultivated vegetable gardens outside the fort. During the fall fishing season, the soldiers sometimes were able to seine large amounts of fish. Most of the catch was sold and the rest salted and kept for the men to eat during the winter. With married soldiers at the post it was only natural that babies were born here occasionally. Sometimes there were also deaths at the post, usually by disease or accident. There was no chapel at the post, however, and any funerals or religious services were usually conducted by the post commander. In the case of a death at the post an effort was usually made to send the body back home. If this was not possible, the body was interred in the post cemetery about half a mile west of the fort.[6]

Throughout much of the Reconstruction period, however, there was a general sense of neglect and frustration. The post had seen constant hard use during the entire decade of the 1860s with little done for its upkeep and maintenance. During the war, attention had been concentrated on repairing the fort's battle damage while the day to day routine maintenance and upkeep for the quarters, buildings, and grounds was largely ignored. With the end of the war, the trend of downsizing and economic cutback in the military led to a spirit within the War Department to make do with what it had and a reluctance to incur expense except when absolutely necessary. At Fort Macon the result of these years of hard use and neglect was that, in general, virtually everything at the post was completely worn out. In the fort itself the bridges over the ditch were decayed. Many casemate doors had no locks. Many of the windows had shutters, blinds and panes of glass missing. The wooden floors of the casemates were rotten while the plaster and lathing of the walls and ceilings in many places had fallen in hunks and patches. There were many leaks in the casemates while the officer's casemates were said to be "infested with rats, mice, centipedes, and bugs of all kinds." Shot beds on the ramparts to hold cannonballs were falling to pieces with decay, leaving loose cannonballs lying around.[7]

The wharf was mentioned a number of times in reports as needing attention due to the attack of worms and erosion but nothing was done. It collapsed by 1870, and the garrison's supplies and provisions had to be landed ashore in lighters. Of the buildings outside the fort, the post hospital was said to be a "disgrace to the service." It was an old building floated over to the fort from Morehead City in sections near the end of the war and re-erected 250 yards southwest of the fort. Its foundations had settled unevenly in the sand, causing the walls to bulge outward, the roof to sag inward, and the floor to have a rolling surface. Gaps in the floor, walls, and roof planking allowed wind, rain, and sand to come down freely upon those inside. Unless a man was very sick, it was best to keep him in the casemates rather than send him to the hospital. As for the small shacks used as quarters for married enlisted men and the post laundresses, they were in the same dilapidated condition as the hospital. They gave an odd appearance where they had been repeatedly patched up by the occupants with odd boards and pieces of canvas to keep out wind and rain. Even the four sets of officers' quarters dismantled from Goldsboro and shipped to the fort in 1869 had problems. They arrived as a mass of lumber with little plan or organization and were erected by the inexperienced garrison. It took almost a year to complete all four. It was stated that "these cottages are badly built and the rooms are too small for the climate, being . . . less than two-thirds the size of regulation rooms." Another report stated the "boards of the kitchen floors are an inch apart and the kitchens are so cold, and full of drafts in winter as to be untenable." Like the other buildings, they were leaky and worn out.[8]

Successive post commanders complained of these distressing conditions while officers making routine inspections of the post likewise pointed out the conditions in official reports. Few changes were made, however. Much of the lack of response to change the conditions was due to the postwar trend of Congressional cutbacks and military economizing. To the minds of politicians and bureau chiefs in the War Department, this all made complete sense, but to a sick soldier at Fort Macon huddling on a bunk in the hospital with sand and rain blowing in on him through gaps in the weatherboarding, it did not. The sentiments and frustrations of every post commander at Fort Macon during the Reconstruction years were doubtless expressed in a hot letter written by Lieut. Colonel Walter S. Poor, 14th U.S. Colored Heavy Artillery, who had been unable to obtain lumber from the Quartermaster Department to make repairs at the post. Poor wrote: "The nominal excuse for not furnishing this lumber is the recent order from the [Quartermaster General] directing expenses be reduced to the minimum. It is a penny wise but pound foolish policy that permits a permanent fort that has cost the Government hundreds of thousands of dollars to become dilapidated and unserviceable merely that an officer may have the credit of a saving of a few pounds of nails and a few feet of lumber during the short time he is in charge of a depot or post. The fort in its present condition reflects little credit upon the government and it cannot be repaired unless the Quartermaster's Department furnish the means."[9]

The fault was not entirely that of the Quartermaster Department. While this department was responsible for the furnishing and upkeep of military buildings, barracks, and troop quarters, it was the Engineer Department which was responsible for the maintenance of fortifications. In the case of Fort Macon, the situation was complicated by the fact the troop quarters were located inside a fortification and thus mingled the responsibilities of these two departments. Understandably, there was a reluctance for one department to pay for repairs which might properly fall within the domain of the other. Ultimately, however, it was the Engineer Department which was responsible for repairs to the casemate quarters. In these postwar years, the Engineer Department was in the process of giving consideration to modifying the seacoast forts for improved weaponry. An 1866 report, presently to be described, addressed the modifications necessary for Fort Macon, which included the recommendation to repair and revamp the casemate quarters. Until a decision was reached as to what repairs and modifications were necessary to upgrade Fort Macon for modern armament, the Engineer Department held off from committing itself to a full scale overhaul of the fort's casemate quarters. Since these would have to be repaired anyway, it seemed best to do all the repairs and modifications at one time. Unfortunately, years dragged on before a decision was reached regarding repairs and modifications of the fort. As a result there was little relief for soldiers living in the fort's damp, decaying casemates.[10]

The lack of a decision by the Engineers regarding the modification of Fort Macon also meant no upgrading of the fort's armament during the Reconstruction years. The same guns used during the war, including ten of the old 24-pounder smoothbores which had been at the fort since 1835, were still present, with their wooden carriages rotting slowly away. In September, 1866 Brig. Generals James A. Hardie, Inspector General, and Albion P. Howe, Inspector of Artillery, made an inspection of the fort's ordnance and ordered the ten 24-pounder and eithteen 32-pounder smoothbore guns at the fort condemned, along with their old ammunition. It was not until October of the following year that these guns, ammunition, and some other scrap metal, amounting to about 200 tons in weight, were finally shipped from the post to be turned in to the New York Arsenal on Governor's Island, New York.[11]

Of the guns left at the fort, two 100-pounder Parrott Rifles, two 10-inch siege mortars, and six 24-pounder flanking howitzers in the counterfire galleries were serviceable. By 1871, two 12-pounder Napoleon field guns had been added to the armament and were also serviceable. With these few guns, practice firing and drills were at least possible for the garrison. However, by 1872 the condition of the carriages of the columbiads and rifled 32-pounders which remained was such that it was felt too threatening to life to work around them. The post commander requested permission to dismount them and place them on skids so that they could be properly cared for and thus eliminate the risk of falling over on someone.[12]

After 1870, in the face of much correspondence over the condition of the post, the Quartermaster and Engineer Departments began to remedy the deplorable condition of some of the buildings on the reservation. In 1871, the Engineers built a new wharf. This lasted only a year and then was badly damaged by shore erosion. The wharf was repaired and over the next several years considerable work was necessary for the Engineers to construct a breakwater and crib jetty to control the erosion around it. In 1872, the Quartermaster Department built a new two-story storehouse, bakehouse, stables, and a hospital at the post. During 1873-74, two new small houses, one for the post ordnance sergeant and the other for the commissary sergeant, were built. Also in 1873, a fence was erected across the reservation for the purpose of keeping out wayward livestock which local farmers were in the habit of turning loose on Bogue Banks to pasture. Prior to putting up the fence, the garrison experienced considerable trouble with sheep raiding the post vegetable gardens and cattle herding at night on the fort glacis around the officers' quarters and under the officers' porches.[13]

In the matter of quarters for the officers and soldiers, however, there was to be little change. As time went on with no decision by the Engineer Department as to when or if Fort Macon was to be modified and repaired for the reception of modern armament, recommendations were made in 1873 for the Quartermaster Department to build new barracks for two companies outside the fort, along with a new set of officers' quarters. Plans were submitted for these proposed quarters but they were never acted upon. As it appeared outside quarters would never be built, on 1 September 1875, recommendations were sent requesting funds at least to place new floors in the casemates to improve the living conditions. The Quartermaster Department finally acquiesced in assuming the responsibility for the new floors in the casemates, which was done during 1875–76.[14]

During the final years of Reconstruction the fort was garrisoned by two companies of the 2nd U.S. Artillery. As these companies continued to remain at the fort year after year without the usual rotation to other posts, Captain John I. Rodgers, post commander, felt a growing sense of frustration over the situation with his command for a number of reasons. He felt the food being supplied was substandard, the living quarters for the officers and men were inadequate, and perhaps of greatest concern was that no effort was being made by regimental headquarters to keep the strength of his two companies up to normal quotas. Through expiration of enlistments and normal attrition his companies were allowed to dwindle in size so that by September, 1875, they contained only thirty-two and twenty-six enlisted men, respectively. With normal guard and provost duties and the presence of military prisoners to guard, the men were on duty almost constantly with little chance for rest. In his annual report for 1875, Rodgers summed up his frustrations: "My company and myself have been at the Post continuously since November, 1872. We are worn out with the discomfort of the place. It is impossible for me to convey a just idea of the discomfort of this Station, to which the enlisted men are subjected during the warm weather: in their damp confined quarters, there is no air, outside on the glacis, or elsewhere, there is no shade to rest in, and no shelter from the direct or reflected heat, with saturated clothing, and the poorest beef for food, and tepid water. There is no escape or recreation in the vicinity. The men are losing their power of resistance to disease, and require a change . . . As for myself, I will say I have never before been subjected to so many deprivations of the necessities of life. Money has not been able to buy good food and water at this station."[15]

Shortly afterward one of the garrison companies was replaced by a fresh one and another year passed. By 1876, however, Reconstruction was nearing an end and the decision was made to close Fort Macon as a regular garrison post, pending a decision from the Engineer Department as to the prospect of modifying the fort for modern armament. In September, 1876, the regular garrison was withdrawn and replaced by a small detachment. The detachment remained at the post until 27 April 1877, when it was also withdrawn. From this point the fort was left in caretaker status again as it had been before the war, with only Ordnance Sergeant Adolphus Smith on duty.[16]

MODIFICATION FOR MODERN ARMAMENT

The innovations of tactics and weaponry brought about by the Civil War demonstrated the need for a radical modification of the country's existing fortifications if they were to continue to offer national defense in the changing face of warfare. As a result, the War Department began to look at its seacoast fortifications to reassess their defensive potential and determine what changes were necessary to upgrade them to meet future contingencies for national security. In December, 1865, Engineer Captain Peter C. Hains made an inspection of Fort Macon with a view to determine what requirements were necessary to make it suitable for modern defense. In a seventy-one page report submitted in January, 1866, Hains concluded that the "ease with which [Fort Macon] was captured is a practical demonstration of its weakness." He went on to examine changes to the fort's physical structure and armament which would make it a much stronger fortification capable of meeting the challenges of improved military technology. The report is particularly interesting as an illumination of just how much the defensive needs of forts like Fort Macon had changed in only just over forty years since the days of General Simon Bernard.

To protect Fort Macon's landward side, its weakest point, Hains recommended the construction of a glacis of normal slope on Front IV rather than the steep "glacis coupe" which presently existed. Also, the long stretches of the covertway along Fronts IV and V needed to be broken up into a number of small, indented salient angles to provide more direct fire on the landward approaches. The parapets of the citadel on these fronts should be raised eighteen inches to reduce the effect of reverse fire on the channel guns on the opposite side of the fort. Fourteen 20- and 30-pounder Parrott Rifles were proposed to defend the two landward fronts. In addition several howitzers, eight or ten siege mortars and at least ten Coehorn mortars were needed to defend the two landward fronts against siege. To protect the fort's scarp wall from being breached on the landward sides by rifled siege guns and endangering the magazines, as had happened to the Confederates during the 1862 battle, the exposed portion of the upper scarp wall on Fronts IV and V should be protected by a belt of three-and-one-half-inch thick armor plating extending five to six feet down below the cordon. Hains estimated a total of 127 tons of wrought iron were required for this. To withstand the penetration power of rifled cannons at short range, the parapets of the fort had to be increased to a thickness of eighteen feet. On the seaward fronts, Hains recommended an armament of heavy rifled guns capable of dealing with armored warships. He called for a 6-gun water battery built at the foot of the glacis, thirteen guns on the covertway and six more on the citadel. To further deny entrance to the harbor of an enemy fleet, mines should be planted to destroy enemy vessels as they passed through the inlet.

One of the most serious problems faced by anyone defending Fort Macon was the exposure of its armament all mounted *en barbette*, as demonstrated by the large number of guns knocked out or damaged during the 1862 bombardment. To prevent enfilade fire from sweeping the terrepleins and knocking out multiple guns in a row, Hains felt the guns should be provided with earthen traverses between them to localize the effect of any hit. Additionally, he felt the fort's heaviest and most important guns facing the sea should be mounted in armored turrets similar to those of Navy ships, or at least semi-turrets (semi-circular iron shields which protected the guns). The remaining guns should be protected by merlons. Those on the landward side should be further protected by iron shutters to close the embrasures when the guns were being loaded. Hains examined the fort's present armament and decided it largely needed to be replaced by heavier updated guns since most of the fort's 24- and 32-pounder smoothbores on their weatherworn gun carriages were not effective against armored warships. The fort's columbiads were unserviceable due to rotten platforms and the fort's unbanded rifled cannons were "feared by the garrison."[17]

Captain Hains' illuminating report was an accurate, if costly, assessment of Fort Macon's weaknesses and the solutions to overcome them to keep it defensible in a newly dawning age of military technology. It was duly filed with the Office of the Chief of Engineers for consideration, along with similar reports of the country's other seacoast fortifications. Of course, in the postwar era, the war-weary nation's thoughts were mostly of downsizing the military rather than continuing to pour money into massive, expensive modifications of forts. Although some modifications of some of the larger, more important forts were carried out during this period, it is not surprising that the subject of modifying Fort Macon was not a pressing concern of the War Department. In many of the annual reports submitted by the Chief of Engineers during the Reconstruction years, the statements concerning Fort Macon appear: "Projects for the modification of this work, in order to the introduction of an armament of the heaviest caliber of guns, are now under consideration, and appropriations will be asked as soon as the detailed estimates are received," or "The subject of the modification of this work is still under consideration." Unfortunately for the garrison of Fort Macon, anxiously awaiting the decision in the hope it might result in repairs and renovation of their casemate quarters, the Engineer Department never resolved the matter during all the years of the Reconstruction. A complete renovation of the casemate quarters never occurred. When the garrison of Fort Macon was withdrawn at the end of Reconstruction in 1877, the matter of the modification of Fort Macon for modern warfare was still being considered by the Engineers.[18]

THE PRISON PERIOD AT FORT MACON

The end of the Civil War did not mean the use of Fort Macon as a prison came to an end. On the contrary, prisoners were to remain in confinement at the fort throughout the Reconstruction years. Until 1867, the fort was used as it had been for most of the war for the confinement of military convicts–U.S. Army personnel undergoing sentences of general court martial. With the passage of the Reconstruction Acts of 1867, however, the South was carved up into military districts and placed under martial law. The Army now assumed the function of maintaining law and order, and tried civilians charged with civil or federal crimes by military commission. North and South Carolina were designated the Second Military District under this arrangement. Because neither state had a state penitentiary at which to confine civil prisoners convicted of offenses by the military commissions, Fort Macon became designated by the Army as a federal penitentiary for the confinement of both the civil and military prisoners of the district. The entire northwest wing of the fort was to be devoted to making quarters for an estimated 200 or more prisoners. In June, 1867, a large order of iron was requisitioned to fabricate grated prison doors and bars for the windows of the casemates on this wing. Soon civil prisoners began joining the military convicts imprisoned at Fort Macon.[19]

During this period, the military prisoners at Fort Macon were in confinement for various charges. Many were deserters, some had violated the Articles of War, and others were charged with such things as "conduct prejudicial to good order and discipline," or "Behaving in a contemptuous manner toward his superior officer," or "Sleeping on Post," etc. Some of the soldiers were charged with major civil offenses such as murder, manslaughter, rape, and robbery. An examination of the civilian prisoners in confinement shows charges such as murder, assault with intent to kill, highway robbery, larceny, burglary, and receiving stolen property. Most of the sentences seem to have ranged from six months or one year at hard labor for the lesser crimes, and up to ten years at hard labor for the more serious crimes. As Fort Macon was intended solely to be a place of confinement at hard labor, no executions of prisoners charged under serious capital crimes were carried out.[20]

As during the war, prisoners were made to wear the ball and chain around their ankles and were kept under armed guard. "Hard labor" continued to be such daily chores as emptying the slop tubs in the fort, drawing water and distributing it to the casemate quarters and kitchens, chopping and distributing firewood, general police and cleanup, and any work or maintenance which was needed around the post. In the hot days of summer the prisoners were usually recalled from work during the hottest part of the day from 11:00 a.m. until 2:00 or 3:00 p.m.[21]

In the summer of 1867, as the number of prisoners began to increase following the Reconstruction Acts, the post commander, Captain Charles B. Gaskill, 40th U.S. Infantry, felt that the potential of the growing number of prisoners was being wasted. On 24 July 1867, Gaskill proposed the visionary idea of what is known today as "prison industries", to have prisoners work to produce something useful which might defray the expense of feeding and confining them. In this case, Gaskill proposed that prisoners manufacture shoes and underclothing for the Army. With a minimum initial outlay for tools, materials, and superintending foremen, he felt the manufacture of shoes and clothing by the convicts would not only cover the expense of their confinement, but would in time also turn into a profitable operation which would realize a savings to the Army. Gaskill stated: "Further—if advisable, this fort could be used more extensively than it now is for the confinement of prisoners by increasing the garrison and preparing (which can be done cheaply) additional quarters for the troops. The location is excellent in all respects—including considerations of health, and in time it might be made the receptacle for all military prisoners from the Atlantic Coast, with a manufactory sufficiently extensive for the supplying of the Army with a large amount of necessary clothing, &c. Why not make this labor of practical use in addition to the matter of punishment?"

Unfortunately for Gaskill, the Army did not see fit to carry this interesting proposal into effect.[22]

The largest number of prisoners confined at Fort Macon was during the years of 1867 and 1868. During the months of July, August, and part of September, 1868, the number of prisoners in confinement at one time peaked at 120. Large numbers of prisoners at the fort presented considerable problems because the small, understrength companies garrisoning the fort frequently did not have sufficient numbers of men to perform normal garrison duties and guard the prisoners at the same time. As a result, a dangerous situation developed where large squads of prisoners had to be put to work with only two or three guards to watch over them. In May, 1867, Captain Charles B. Gaskill, commanding the post, was so concerned for the safety of his guards he requisitioned fifty revolvers for the purpose of having "a weapon sufficiently formidable to equalize the disparity in numbers between the guard and those guarded." The most serious problem remained the insufficiency of soldiers to guard the large prison population. On 1 and 2 September 1868, when two different escapes took place, there were 120 prisoners at the fort and only thirty-three privates available for duty to guard them. There is little wonder that the prisoners had ample opportunity to take advantage of the situation.[23]

In the life of any prison, some of the most interesting stories are those of attempted escapes by the inmates. Fort Macon is no exception. The prisoners made many attempts to escape and frequently were successful. For escapees, getting away from the fort was only part of the problem. Being on an island they also had to get across Bogue Sound back to the mainland in order to complete their escape. Scattered along the opposite end of Bogue Banks were a number of homes of local fishermen, who frequently conveyed escapees across the sound in their boats. It is not clear from the records if the fishermen were actually aware the men were escaped prisoners from the fort or if the fishermen did this to defy the U.S. Army. Whatever the case, a number of prisoners successfully got to the mainland with the help of the fishermen and sometimes were not immediately recaptured. Some of the escapes from the fort were quite interesting and are recounted here.

During the summer of 1866, five prisoners succeeded in breaking out the iron grating in the rear embrasure of their casemate cell but were quickly recaptured. The commander of the post requested iron to repair and properly secure the windows but was ignored by the Quartermaster Department. On 19 October, two other prisoners succeeded in breaking out the grating of another window and made a successful escape without being recaptured. In order to properly repair the window the post commander was forced to borrow some iron from the Navy and requested the services of a blacksmith and mason to repair the other cell window grates.[24]

In the dark, stormy early morning hours of 3 February 1867, six prisoners cut out the panels from the door leading to an adjoining unoccupied casemate. They then passed through into a storage casemate and exited by an unsecured door into the parade ground. From here they hurried up the steps to the parapet and then climbed down the scarp wall into the ditch outside by means of lightning rods which were bolted down the wall to protect the magazines. Their absence was not discovered until reveille. It turned out part of their success was due to the negligence of the Sergeant of the Guard who had not passed through the prison cells periodically to count the prisoners and check their fastenings as he was required to do. Had he done so, the escape would have been detected earlier. The post commander mentioned that another factor involved was the lack of light at the fort because of the failure of the Commissary Department to properly furnish candles to the post.[25]

In the early morning hours of 1 September 1868, two prisoners detailed to help at the post kitchen slipped away from the cooks and escaped through loose bars in the embrasure window of the neighboring casemate. Investigation disclosed that the bars in the embrasure could be pushed out or replaced at will due to loose bricks forming the bottom of the embrasure. The window had been in this condition for some time and had been used by soldiers of the 40th U.S. Infantry previously stationed at the fort to sneak out. Some of the prisoners became aware of the window's condition and had been merely biding their time until a chance was presented to escape through it. The window was secured by the garrison.

The very next morning, however, four other prisoners on kitchen detail slipped away from the cooks and escaped by unlocking the postern gate. The gate had been secured by a padlock but one of the escapees had acquired a duplicate key. A subsequent search of the remaining prisoners turned up several other duplicates of this key. After these two back-to-back incidents involving the kitchen detail, a guard was placed to watch over prisoners on kitchen duty. Of the six prisoners who escaped on these two days, only two were recaptured.

Scarcely two weeks later, on the afternoon of 17 September 1868, a guard escorted four prisoners (including one who had been recaptured in the earlier escapes that month) to the sink (privy). Three of the prisoners did their business quickly and came out. When the guard looked in on the last prisoner, whom he felt was taking too long, he was jumped and pushed into the sink. Here the four prisoners handcuffed the guard to a post, stuffed a plug of tobacco into his mouth and gagged him with a handkerchief. Taking the guard's gun the four prisoners dashed away, two of them easily slipping off the ball and chain they were wearing. Only two of the escapees were recaptured. A subsequent examination of the remaining prisoners wearing balls and chains disclosed all but three could easily slip them off their legs. A blacksmith was then hired to secure all the balls and chains.[26]

On the evening of 9 February 1869, four prisoners at work in the kitchen washing supper dishes escaped by climbing down the scarp wall by the magazine lightning rods. Afterward guards were placed on the covertway opposite the angles where the lightning rods came down the wall to secure this mode of escape. Several weeks later, on 2 March 1869, the prisoners in one of the casemates tried a different method of escape. They were discovered busily cutting away the bricks in one of the loophole windows to make a hole large enough for a man to pass through. The window was secured and afterward lamps were ordered to be kept burning in the prison cells at night so that the guards could see what was happening in each cell.[27]

Several weeks after that attempt, on the night of 28 March 1869, the sentry stationed on the covertway opposite the lightning rods on the southeast angle of the citadel suddenly heard several alarm shots being fired from other sentry posts around the fort. In a matter of moments the dark figures of two men mounted the parapet of the citadel at the angle opposite him and crouched low as if trying to get to the lightning rods without being noticed. The sentry called out the challenge but the two men gave no response. Prisoners escaping! The sentry fired his rifle and hit one of the men. He then challenged the other man and once again received no response. With unerring aim the sentry shot down the second man. Within minutes what appeared as a failed prison escape turned into tragedy. The two men on the wall were not prisoners but instead were Lieutenant W. S. Alexander, the officer of the day, and Private William Downey, one of the guards. It turned out the alarm guns had not been fired because of a prison escape, but rather for a casemate chimney on the parapet of the southeast angle which had caught fire. Alexander and Downey had jumped onto the parapet to extinguish the blaze and in the howling wind did not hear the challenges of the sentry on the outer wall opposite them. Private Downey was killed instantly while Lieutenant Alexander lay mortally wounded with a shot through the lungs. Mrs. Jane Coues, wife of Assistant Surgeon Elliott Coues, stayed by the side of the dying Alexander until the end. In a letter to her sister she wrote: "Such a night I never passed. I was the only lady at the fort and he wanted me with him. I never witnessed such excruciating agony in my life. He lingered twenty-four hours. He was a young boy—only twenty years old—and life looked very bright. But when I told him he was dying he met it very bravely, and after I had talked with him a while he seemed perfectly resigned. I had never thought to be permitted to point a dying soul to Christ . . . Such an occurrence would be shocking enough in a community, but when it happens among a few people shut up in a fort and isolated from the rest of the world, it seems doubly awful." In the inquest which followed the sentry was ruled to have carried out his duties properly and was cleared of any blame.[28]

The largest escape to be made from the fort, and the last, took place on the night of 8 February 1874. It is also the most remarkable escape because of how it was carried out. Despite sentries posted both in front and rear of the prison cell, eleven prisoners escaped from the cell by passing up one by one through the tiny 12-inch rear ventilator opening in the crest of the ceiling arch. The prisoners then made their way up the island and were assisted by local citizens across to the mainland. Only three of the eleven were recaptured.[29]

Throughout these incidents there apparently was no official censure of the post commanders or garrison for so many escapes. In the main, the steps taken to guard and manage the prisoners were adequate. But working against them were such factors as the insufficient number of soldiers available from the small garrison to guard the prisoners; the physical limitations of old or worn bars, locks or restraining devices, and the sheer desperation and ingenuity of the prisoners themselves. Beginning in 1869, however, the situation began to improve. Following the escape of the four prisoners in February, 1869, the post commander pleaded his case for more soldiers to be stationed at the fort. At the time only one company (four officers and thirty-eight men) comprised the garrison to perform all normal daily garrison duties and look after fifty-six prisoners. His efforts were successful and a second company was stationed at the fort the following month. From then until the end of the prison period two companies comprised the garrison of the post. Another factor which eased the prison situation was a lessening of the Army's role in civil affairs. North Carolina was readmitted to the Union in 1868 and efforts were made to reestablish permanent state and local governments. The Army in turn began to divest itself of responsibility for civil prisoners, who could now be turned over to the control of civil authorities. A state penitentiary was authorized for confinement of North Carolina's civil prisoners in 1869 by the General Assembly. As a result, the number of prisoners held at Fort Macon dropped as the civil prisoners in confinement were turned over to civil authorities and the focus thereafter shifted back to using the fort as a place of confinement for military convicts only.[30]

For a time even the number of military convicts at Fort Macon steadily decreased after 1868, until by October, 1871, only one prisoner remained. During the following year, the number of prisoners rose again until September, 1872, when there were as many as sixty-three in confinement. There-after, the numbers steadily decreased until by the summer of 1876 only eleven remained. During July, 1876, as the post was about to be deacti-vated, seven of these prisoners were transferred to Fort Levenworth, Kan-sas, for confinement. The remaining four were retained because their sen-tences were about to expire. The last of the four was discharged at the end of his sentence in December, 1876. With the closing of Fort Macon at the end of Reconstruction, the prison period likewise came to an end.[31]

CARETAKER STATUS AGAIN

In the period of 1877 to 1898, Fort Macon was ungarrisoned and left in caretaker status in charge of an ordnance sergeant as it had frequently been before the war. The only personnel on the reservation were the ord-nance sergeant and his family, and the families of Signal Corps telegra-phists operating an Army telegraph station on the post until 1885. In these years the fort was made a satellite of the post of Fort Johnston, and later of Fort Caswell, on the Cape Fear River. During these years there were a few incidents of note.

Hardly had the garrison left the post in 1877 before some local citi-zens began to petition the War Department for permission to lease the fort to turn it into a summer resort for the area. Other petitions were made to obtain the abandoned buildings on the post. The War Department refused to grant any of these petitions.[32]

On 18 August 1879, a violent hurricane battered the area doing much damage to the buildings at the reservation and forcing the personnel there to take shelter in the fort. Chimneys and fences were blown down, the foun-dations of many of the buildings were undermined and damaged by storm surge, and the plank sidewalks around the reservation washed away. Ord-nance Sergeant Adolphus Smith was greatly concerned about the amount of work needed to clean up and clear away debris. He was also concerned that the damage sustained by the 4000-foot long fence across the reserva-tion would allow the cattle placed on the island by local citizens to en-

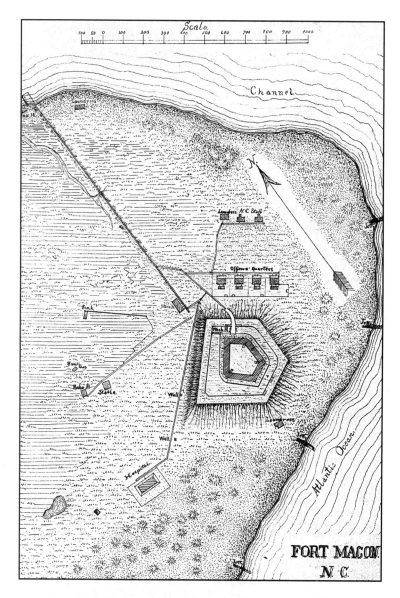

Map of the Fort Macon Military Reservation, 1877.
From RG94, Medical Histories of Posts, National Archives.

croach upon the reservation as they had done in the past. Smith was ordered to prepare estimates of what was needed for repairs, cleanup and to secure any buildings which might be in danger. Ultimately, however, the decision of the War Department was that since it was unlikely the fort would be occupied again except in emergency, there was no necessity of incurring expense to repair the buildings. It is interesting to note that this is how the future usefulness of Fort Macon had come to be regarded at the War Department.[33]

Despite the War Department's viewpoint, armament continued to be retained at Fort Macon. The two 100-pounder Parrott Rifles, two 10-inch siege mortars, and two 12-pounder Napoleons were still present for the fort's defense should some future emergency arise. The Parrotts and mortars were still mounted, the Napoleons were now dismounted and without carriages. The other guns which had been present during the Reconstruction years (the columbiads, rifled 32-pounders, and 24-pounder flank howitzers) were also still present but were unmounted and considered worthless. They were catalogued by ordnance officers for disposal and sold.[34]

In the meantime, the Engineer Department was quite busy at Fort Macon during most of the decade of the 1880s. The Engineers were working on improvements to Beaufort Harbor and had projects in motion to stabelize shore erosion at both Shackleford Point and Bogue Point. At Bogue Point a number of stone jetties, spur jetties and rip-rap of the shore of the inlet beach were built, as was a concrete breakwater. The purpose of these measures was to slow shore erosion encroaching on the inlet beach east of the fort and around past the area of the wharf. On the beach, brush and sand fences were used to halt wind erosion. Other repairs were made to the fort itself, a few repairs were also made.[35]

It was also during the 1880s that the subject of modifying old seacoast forts for modern armament was finally resolved. In 1885, President Grover Cleveland named a special board of civilians and officers of the Army and Navy, headed by his Secretary of War William C. Endicott, to examine and report on this matter. The purpose of the Endicott Board was essentially the same as General Bernard's Board of Fortifications had been almost seventy years earlier, to examine and plan the country's seacoast defenses. It was intended to modify and upgrade those fortifications of the most importance with modern armament, utilizing the revolutionary advances in breech-loading smokeless powder weaponry and seacoast defenses. These advances included large-caliber breech-loading seacoast guns, quick-firing breech-loading guns and mortars of medium and small calibers, massive gun emplacements of reinforced concrete, mines, searchlights, and torpedo boats. In the same way that the Bernard Board had operated, the various posts and harbors of the United States were assessed by the Endicott Board as to their defensive importance and a list formulated as to which harbors would receive modern defenses. When the list was released by the Board, twenty-six sites were listed for defense on the coast and three on the Great Lakes. Of these, Fort Caswell on the Cape Fear River, was one of the stations slated to be modified for modern defenses in order to protect North Carolina's largest seaport, Wilmington. Fort Macon and Beaufort Harbor were not judged to be of enough national importance by the Endicott Board to warrant modification for modern armament. Thus Fort Macon's days as a garrison station were unquestionably over. Temporary armament and defenses could always be put into place for its defense should some war emergency arise.[36]

In the final decade of the nineteenth century, there was little change. Several ordnance sergeants came and went. Buildings continued to molder away. Engineers sometimes appeared to work around the fort and continued their efforts to stabilize the beach. Occasionally, an officer appeared to inspect the fort. Otherwise, Fort Macon was largely forgotten by the Army.

THE SPANISH-AMERICAN WAR

In the late 1890s, the country's attention turned to the island of Cuba, where an outpouring of sympathy was given by the United States for Cuban rebels engaged in a lengthy struggle to achieve independence from Spain. Concerns for the success of the Cuban rebels led to growing political trouble between the United States and Spain. Increasing tensions soon led to the prospect of United States intervention in the interest of Cuban independence. On 15 February 1898, the U.S. warship *Maine* was destroyed in Havana Harbor by an explosion attributed to Spanish sabotage. This led to a rapid deterioration of relations between the United States and Spain, and the prospect of war. As this unfortunate specter loomed on the horizon, the danger was realized that for the first time since the War of 1812, the Atlantic Seaboard of the United States might become subject to attack by a foreign naval power. Spain possessed a battle fleet in the Atlantic which was very formidable at the time. It was entirely conceivable that this fleet might make its way to the U.S. coastal to attack at any point. Thus the need for seacoast defense was very real, but the U.S. coast defenses were again found lacking. Only a small portion of the new defenses authorized by the Endicott Board had been started and many smaller ports which had been ignored by the Endicott Board, such as Beaufort Harbor, had little defense. In anticipation of trouble, on 9 March 1898, Congress passed the National Defense Act, which appropriated a sum of fifty million dollars to push Endicott fortifications ahead and boost all areas of national defense.

On 15 February 1898, the day the *Maine* was destroyed, the editors of the *Beaufort Herald Dispatch*, Charles L. Abernathy and E. W. Hill, sent a letter to North Carolina Senator Marion Butler concerning the lack of defense at Beaufort Harbor. The editors pointed out that Fort Macon was "in a dilapidated condition with a lone sentry in charge of it . . ." and that "our bar has from 18 to 20 [feet] of water and this port, in the event of a naval engagement, would be of easy access." The editors also pointed out that Beaufort harbor had been passed by for modern defenses and that Fort Macon ought to be garrisoned. Despite this plea for political influence to draw attention to Beaufort Harbor, most of the Congressional attention toward defenses on the North Carolina coast went to the completion of Endicott defenses at Fort Caswell. The Army felt Beaufort Harbor's defensive needs could be answered by the establishment of a temporary defense with smaller classes of weapons. Accordingly, the share of the National Defense Bill of March 9 which was to be allotted to the defenses of Beaufort Inlet was a total of just $3,000.[37]

On 6 April 1898, Engineer Captain William E. Craighill and an assistant arrived at Beaufort from Wilmington to determine what could be done to defend Beaufort Harbor. The possibility of using a flotilla of torpedo boats had been raised, but when Craighill inspected Fort Macon the next day he determined the best defense would be to remount and restore the fort's existing old armament. At this time only the two 100-pounder Parrott Rifles, two 10-inch siege mortars, and two 12-pounder Napoleons remained at the fort. Craighill ordered the Parrott Rifles and siege mortars to be remounted. He also sent off a requisition for ammunition and ordnance stores needed for these guns, and for a battery of six muzzle-loaded rifled field guns. The Ordnance Department was unable to furnish the latter, however.[38]

For the remainder of April, Captain Craighill had forty workers at Fort Macon preparing it for the possibility of war. The reservation was closed to the public, much to the curiosity of the local people. The two 100-pounder Parrotts at the fort were cleaned and put into serviceable order. One of them previously facing the land side was moved so that both would face the inlet and bar. Earthen traverses were thrown up on the right side of each piece to prevent their being enfiladed from the sea. On the covertway, the two 10-inch siege mortars were mounted on platforms on the southwest front near the south angle and were similarly protected by an L-shaped traverse which covered them in front and from possible enfilade fire from the channel side. The windows of the South Counterfire Gallery under them was bricked up, and the gallery turned into a shell magazine for them. Two alternate platforms for these mortars were constructed in the parade ground. The entire ditch of the fort was filled in about one foot all around to help control drainage. The fort's casemates were cleaned out and given some minor repairs to make them ready to receive troops. The cost of these war preparations amounted to $2,783.35 of the $3,000 allocated for the fort's defense.[39]

The local people of Beaufort and Morehead City were at first pleased that something was being done for their defense. That quickly changed,

**Sketch of the 10-inch mortar battery near the south angle
during the Spanish-American War, 1898.**

By the author.

however, when they learned nothing more had been done than to remount the old Civil War guns and shovel some sand into the ditch. The work of the "Tin Bucket Brigade", as they derisively dubbed the engineer workers, was a "farce" as far as they were concerned. No modern guns, torpedo boats, or anything else had been provided for the fort. As the *Raleigh Morning Post* complained: "If Beaufort Harbor is of sufficient importance to have three millions recommended for harbor improvement, it does seem it is worth better protection than this."[40]

On 25 April 1898, the United States finally declared war on Spain. On the same day, Captain Craighill reported to the Chief of Engineers that the

Parrotts and mortars at Fort Macon had been placed in serviceable condition and that except for awaiting ammunition, the fort was ready to receive troops. He felt a sufficient garrison was one battery of artillery and two companies of infantry. He also mentioned the need for small caliber guns at the fort. On 30 April the Chief of Engineers requested from the Secretary of War a detail of troops to man and care for the armament. On 7 May, Company C, 6th U.S. Artillery, was ordered from Washington Barracks to North Carolina in response for both Forts Macon and Caswell. A detail of twenty-one men from this company commanded by Lieutenant Harry G. Bishop was sent to occupy Fort Macon while the remainder of the company reinforced the garrison of Fort Caswell. Bishop's detachment arrived at Fort Macon 16 May 1898. As for small guns for Fort Macon, none were supplied by the Ordnance Department. The problem was finally solved by reusing the two dismounted 12-pounder Napoleons at the fort. To mount them on the upper parapet, two of the old, empty 24-pounder flanking howitzer carriages taken from the counterfire galleries were used.[41]

As the days went by, it was obvious the small detachment of artillerymen was insufficient to adequately garrison Fort Macon. At this point, a bit of political intrigue directly affected Fort Macon.

When President William McKinley issued a call to the states to furnish troops for federal service to prosecute the war in April, 1898, North Carolina responded with two regiments of white infantry (State Guards) and a battalion of black infantry (volunteers). The black battalion was unique because it was the first volunteer unit offered for federal service in the war with all-black officers. The prevailing notion in the U.S. Army from the Civil War until now had been that black soldiers must fight only under white officers. This notion ran contrary to the desires of the black community at this time which, although anxious to prove its patriotism and valor on the battlefield, wanted the simple privilege of having black officers in command of black troops. "No Officers, No Fight" was a motto taken up by the black community in protest of the prevailing Army policy. In the case of North Carolina, however, the all-black battalion (officers and men) was authorized by Republican Governor Daniel L. Russell as a political favor for the large black vote which had helped win his election to governor in 1896. Despite its political motivation, the creation of the all-black unit was progressive at a time when prejudice was still high nationwide. "Russell's Black Battalion" was to be organized with three black companies selected from a large number which offered their services to the state. Its commander was Major James H. Young, a prominent black Republican legislator.[42]

At the end of April, meanwhile, Colonel B. S. Royster of the State Adjutant General's Office, left on a tour of the coastal section to determine a suitable location for a rendezvous point and camp for the battalion. Political opponents of Governor Russell had stirred up considerable suspicion and prejudice against the battalion so that it was felt advisable to mobilize the battalion in the more remote coastal section of the state. Royster visited several key places but after consultation with Army officers and engineers at Fort Caswell decided to rendezvous the battalion at Fort Macon, which had no garrison other than the detachment of artillerymen.[43]

Prior to ordering the companies to rendezvous, a camp of fifty tents was established outside the fort for their reception during May by Army Lieutenant Francis C. Marshall and all preparations were made for their arrival. On 30 May, the three companies of the battalion (one each from Raleigh, Charlotte, and Wilmington) left by rail for the rendezvous point at Fort Macon. On the following day they occupied their camp. Curiously, the black soldiers were not allowed to go into the fort itself, which was occupied by Lieutenant Bishop's detachment of Regular artillerymen. For a time, they were also not allowed to go into Morehead City or Beaufort.[44]

In the meantime, President McKinley issued a second call to the states in May, 1898, for more troops. To satisfy part of North Carolina's quota for troops Governor Russell decided to expand the Black Battalion into a full regiment by enlisting seven additional black companies. These companies were raised during June and on 30 June were ordered to rendezvous at Fort Macon. The full regiment was designated the Third North Carolina Volunteers and Major Young was promoted to be its colonel. As the battalion had been, all regimental officers and staff were black. At first it was thought that half of this regiment of over 1,000 men would have to be camped at Morehead City because of a lack of space at Fort Macon, but Young gave assurance that the entire regiment of ten companies could be encamped at the fort. More tents and equipment were sent to the post in preparation for the arrival of the new companies. After the new companies arrived at the post, Lieutenant Bishop and his artillery detachment left to rejoin their company at Fort Caswell on 19 July. In his place came a smaller detachment of Battery I, 2nd U.S. Artillery from Fort Caswell.[45]

For the remainder of the summer after the new companies were mustered in, the Third North Carolina Volunteers remained at Fort Macon, drilling and training in anticipation of orders which they hoped would come directing them to join the fighting in Cuba. Unfortunately, the relationship between the black troops and the local people was not good due to the racial atmosphere of the times. Of course, black troops at Fort Macon were nothing new. For several years after the Civil War black troops had been stationed here with no problems with the locals. For one reason, the presence of white officers in those units reduced any local feeling of suspicion and fear. Another reason was that in these postwar years the local people under martial law had no say over what the Army did. In 1898, the situation was different, and the local people were sometimes at odds with the black troops. Each time an incident took place, the Democratic press took the opportunity to belittle and vilify the regiment to spite Governor Russell. Insignificant incidents were blown into major ones to incite passions against the regiment.

For instance, on 13 August two soldiers got drunk in Morehead City and were arrested. Both managed to escape from the authorities back to the fort, but were later tried and fined. When one could not pay his fine an altercation took place at the post when civil authorities attempted to carry the offender back to jail. Colonel Young intervened. He preferred, instead, that military authorities take care of the man's punishment and did not release the man to the civil authorities. The local newspaper, *Morehead City Pilot*, loudly cited this and other "outrages", proclaiming that the "negro soldiers at the Fort Macon camp within the past week have given unmistakable evidence of a disposition to involve the white people of this city in a riot. . . " The article was quickly republished by other newspapers all across the state. A few days later, the *Pilot* then complained again when Colonel Young apparently ordered his soldiers to stay away from the town and its merchants after the drubbing the newspaper had given them.[46]

Fortunately for both parties, this situation did not continue much longer. Following American victories in Cuba and the Philippines, Spain and the United States signed a peace protocol on 12 August 1898, ending the brief Spanish-American War. The Third North Carolina was bitterly disappointed they would not get a chance to prove their patriotism and courage. For them the prospect of service now appeared to be reduced to camp and garrison duty. With the war emergency over, there was little point in maintaining a garrison at Fort Macon and the Army wasted little time in deactivating the post. In September the Third North Carolina was given orders transferring it to Camp Poland at Knoxville, Tennessee. On 14 September, the regiment broke camp at Fort Macon, crossed over to Morehead City, and boarded special trains sent down to transport them. With throngs of black well-wishers on hand to see them off, Fort Macon's most controversial garrison departed. By October, the detachment of white artillerymen from Fort Caswell were also gone so that once again the personnel on hand at the fort was reduced to the ordnance sergeant and his family.[47]

FINAL YEARS

Following the Spanish-American War, life at Fort Macon returned to the slow, lonely pace which had characterized the years prior to the war's outbreak. After the turn of the century, there was less for the ordnance sergeant in charge to have to take care of, as the last of the guns comprising Fort Macon's armament were disposed of. Under a Congressional Act of 22 May 1896, authorizing the donation of obsolete iron ordnance to towns and veteran organizations, Fort Macon's Parrott Rifles and siege mortars were placed on a list of condemned ordnance available for donation following the Spanish-American War. On 22 February 1900, the city of Spartanburg, S. C., sent an application to the Ordnance Department for the fort's two 100-pounder Parrott Rifles, which was approved by the Chief of Ordnance the following day. City officials arranged to have the guns removed from the fort and transported from Morehead City to Spartanburg on 26 April 1900. The following year the fort's two 12-pounder Napoleons were ordered turned in to the Augusta Arsenal, Georgia, and on 9 December 1901, were transported over to the railroad at Morehead City by a hired contractor. Only the two 10-inch siege mortars now remained in the fort, and even these were not to remain long. In May, 1902, Mayor A. M. Powell of the city of Raleigh, North Carolina, applied for the two mortars from the list of condemned guns with the help of North Carolina Senator Furnifold M. Simmons to serve as monuments for the city's Soldier Home. This was approved and the mortars were transported by rail to Raleigh in August, 1902. All the fort's guns were now gone.[48]

Meanwhile, an inspection of Fort Macon in January, 1902, resulted for the first time in the the War Department's consideration of completely abandoning the post. Major J. A. Lundeen, commanding Fort Caswell, reported on 30 January 1902, an inspection of Fort Macon which disclosed the dilapidated condition of Ordnance Sergeant Philip Coffenberg's quarters at the post. Lundeen recommended new quarters be built for Coffenberg or that quarters be rented for him in Beaufort since the old, obsolete ordnance stores at the fort posed no necessity for him to be quartered on the post. As the report passed up the chain of command, consideration was given to the necessity of continuing to retain an ordnance sergeant at the post at all. It was recommended the old ordnance stores remaining at the post should be condemned and sold off, which would then allow the transfer of the ordnance sergeant to another post. At this point, the Adjutant General's Office referred the matter to the Chief of Engineers on 14 March 1902, as to the necessity of even retaining Fort Macon at all for national defense.

The Chief of Engineers replied on 19 March that Fort Macon defended Bogue Sound, which was a link in the important inland navigable route stretching between Norfolk and Florida, and also controlled the admittance of small draft vessels into Pamlico Sound. For these reason the reservation should be retained for national defense even though no plans for construction of defenses were recommended. These considerations proved sufficient to warrant the Army to continue retaining the post. The question now returned to whether to withdraw the ordnance sergeant rather than build him new quarters.

At this point yet another problem arose. The commanding general of the Department of the East pointed out that under the terms of the original 1826 legislative act under which the State of North Carolina ceded the Fort Macon reservation to the United States, the reservation had to be "continuously occupied" or the land would revert back to the state. Thus, with the ordnance sergeant being the only military personnel on the post, it appeared he could not be withdrawn without the reservation being given up by the Army. As a result, it was decided the ordnance sergeant was to remain at the post for the time being. As for his quarters, the Quartermaster Department had one of the four old officers' quarters buildings completely renovated and repaired for him.[49]

Once more the months passed, and on the night of 26 July 1903, an incident took place which could have had serious consequences at Fort Macon. About 8:45 p.m. that evening, a fire of undetermined origin sprang up in the grass on the ramparts of the citadel of the fort and began to burn out of control. It also spread to part of the covertway. Ordnance Sergeant Philip Coffenberg and his son attempted to battle the blaze by drawing water from one of the parade ground cisterns and pulling it up to the terreplein by a bucket and rope to douse the flames. They were almost exhausted when help suddenly arrived. A boatload of five men from the U.S. Fish Commission Laboratory across the harbor near Beaufort came over to help extinguish the fire. Also, the Keeper of the Core Banks Lifesaving Station, who happened to be in Beaufort that night, hired a boat and came over with eight men to help. These fourteen men, along with Coffenberg and his son, succeeded in extinguishing the fire. Ominously, they noted the flames had burned to within only ten feet of one of the fort magazines.[50]

This incident sealed the fate of Fort Macon as an occupied military post. The question was raised at the War Department once again as to the necessity of retaining ordnance stores at the post and an ordnance sergeant to look after them. This time the Chief of Ordnance decided on 22 August 1903, to dispose of the old stores which remained and withdraw Ordnance Sergeant Coffenberg for duty at another post. This would mean the post would no longer have military personnel stationed there. However, the concern of the previous year that abandonment of the post would cause the reservation to revert back to the State of North Carolina was no longer an issue. In a completely separate action, the Secretary of War granted a request on 15 August 1903, by the Treasury Department to establish a government lifesaving station and boathouse on the reservation. The presence of a U.S. Lifesaving Station at Fort Macon would also serve to satisfy the clause concerning continuous occupation of the reservation by the U.S. Government even without personnel present at the old fort.[51]

Thus Fort Macon was to be abandoned. Ordnance Sergeant Coffenberg submitted an inventory of ordnance stores still on hand at the fort and was instructed on 28 September 1903, to arrange shipment of it to the arsenal at Watertown, Massachusetts. A local contractor was hired to transport the old stores and ammunition to the railroad at Morehead City and on 4 December 1903, the stores were shipped off. On 14 December the Army Chief of Staff directed that the fort be turned over to the jurisdiction of the Wilmington District, Corps of Engineers, whereupon Ordnance Sergeant Coffenberg would be free to proceed to his new duty station at Fort Assiniboine, Montana. Turning the reservation over to the Engineer Department was simply an administrative function which held the site in real property inventory control and recognized it as being in inactive status. On Christmas Day, 1903, Coffenberg signed over property transfer receipts and invoices to Captain R. P. Johnston, Wilmington District Engineers, for the fort, buildings and such property as remained. With this action, Fort Macon was formally closed and abandoned by the Army as a military post.[52]

9

THE TWENTIETH CENTURY

The beginning of the twentieth century found the United States standing for the first time as a world power with foreign territories and possessions, and with an Army and Navy capable of offering support and defense to them. The changing face of warfare had now shifted from internal struggles with Indians and the passive defense of huddling behind a chain of fixed seacoast fortifications of the previous century to more global concerns. As a result, Fort Macon and many other forts and old frontier posts lay abandoned and almost forgotten in the changing role of the U.S. military.

FORT MACON AS AN ABANDONED POST

Under the jurisdiction of the Engineer Department, Fort Macon sat abandoned with grass, vines and shrubs slowly overtaking it. It was not totally forgotten, however. On 9 March 1904, the Engineers auctioned off the old buildings which still remained standing on the reservation: the hospital, commissary storehouse, ordnance sergeant's and commissary sergeant's quarters, and three of the four officers' quarters. The net proceeds of the sale were $334.19. The fourth officer's cottage which had been repaired as quarters for the ordnance sergeant to live in during 1902 was retained as

213

quarters for the use of the foreman of the Engineers' ongoing harbor improvement project at Beaufort Harbor for the next two years. The foreman served the added purpose of looking after the property as a "fort keeper". While working on the harbor improvements for Beaufort Harbor, the engineers also erected and maintained extensive sand fences at the reservation to control sand erosion. Meanwhile, late in 1904, the U.S. Lifesaving Service completed the lifesaving station and boathouse which had been requested by the Treasury Department in the summer of 1903. The station was located northwest of the fort near the mouth of Cowpen Creek.[1]

On 20 March 1906, Major E. St. John Greble made an inspection of Fort Macon which once again brought the old fort to the attention of the War Department. Greble reported that two of the fort's magazines still contained several thousand pounds of old gunpowder which had never been removed. The old powder barrels had now rotted down so that the powder lay mostly spilled out on the floor of two magazines mixed up with powder bags, and barrel staves and hoops. When closing down the fort in 1903, the railroad had refused to ship this powder with the other ordnance stores and somehow in the process of turning the fort over to the Engineer Department it had never been disposed of. The powder lay forgotten until the summer of 1905, when some men from a Naval Reserve encampment held at the fort went exploring and ventured into the magazines with lighted matches.

The danger in allowing the old powder to remain was too serious to be ignored. The Chief of Ordnance recommended the nearest military post should send an ordnance sergeant to Fort Macon to destroy the powder by throwing it into the sea. Accordingly, Ordnance Sergeant Ludwig Leiner was sent from Fort Caswell on 17 May 1906, for this purpose. Leiner was unable to secure any assistance and performed the work alone by shoveling the powder into a wheelbarrow and pushing it about 500 yards to dump it into the sea. In this manner he made twenty-six wheelbarrow loads for an estimated 3,000 pounds of mortar powder and 1,000 pounds of cannon powder. After sweeping out the magazines he returned to Fort Caswell on 22 May.[2]

In December of 1906, severe shore erosion on the inlet beach came within two feet of undermining the new Fort Macon Lifesaving Station and dumping it into the water. In 1907, the station buildings were moved further up Cowpen Creek to a new site west of the fort which was granted by the War Department. To stabilize the inlet beach, the Engineer Department constructed a series of four new jetties along the inlet beach during 1907 and 1908 which checked further erosion.[3]

In 1908, the subject of upgrading Fort Macon and the defenses of Beaufort Harbor with modern armament was brought up again. Back in 1906, the seacoast defenses of the United States, as well as its foreign territories, had been reevaluated by the National Coast Defense Board, headed by Secretary of War William Howard Taft. As with the Endicott Board in the mid-1880s, Beaufort Harbor had been left off the list of harbors for which fortifications would be provided.[4] By 1908, however, North Carolina Congressional leaders felt the case of Beaufort Harbor deserved a reevaluation because of its increasing importance. Under Rivers and Harbors projects, the Engineer Department had just deepened the channel through the inlet to the harbor during the previous two years to increase its use as a deepwater port. The harbor and channel improvements were also intended to provide a deepwater outlet for the proposed leg of what was to become the Intercoastal Waterway between Norfolk and Beaufort to facilitate inland commerce. These improvements were felt certain to increase the value and trade potential of the harbor to the point that some defense should be provided for it.

On 20 February 1908, North Carolina Congressman Charles R. Thomas sent to the Secretary of War a copy of a bill for the House Appropriations Committee he had drafted to fortify Fort Macon again, and requested a report as to the cost of such an action. The Wilmington District, Corps of Engineers, gave its report eight days later, recommending as a suitable defense two 6-inch breech-loading guns on disappearing carriages, four 3-inch rapid-fire guns, four 6-pounders, and mines. The cost of constructing the emplacements was estimated at $160,000. The Ordnance Department later estimated the cost of the recommended armament at $139,400, and another $56,000 for ammunition. Added to this would have to be costs from the Quartermaster Department for barracks and quarters, storage facilities, hospital, roads, sewage system, and so forth. As Wilmington District Engineer Captain Earl I. Brown pointed out, "in this instance the cost of fortification would nearly equal the value of all property and real estate in the two neighboring towns [Beaufort and Morehead City]."[5]

The War Department, however, simply did not feel the fortification of Fort Macon and Beaufort Harbor was warranted or justified from a military standpoint. Too many other posts and installations of much greater importance needed fortifications or to have existing fortifications completed before small ports such as Beaufort could even be considered. The Chief of Engineers, for instance, in whose province the matter of fortifications rested, wrote on 14 March 1908, that "in its present condition . . . Beaufort Harbor is of practically no military or naval importance." He further stated that:

> "Even assuming that all the proposed improvements are completed, the entrance to Beaufort Inlet would, on account of insufficient depth, be prohibited to all except moderate sized cruisers and gunboats. Once inside of the harbor, further naval operations could only be carried on by torpedo boats or launches, and the first stage of a journey through the inland waterway would be through a narrow canal several miles in length, which could easily be blocked.
>
> There is nothing at the present time, in the immediate vicinity of Beaufort to encourage an enemy to enter. There are no dockyards, shipyards, or any similar structures of value to an enemy. The towns are small, and the portable property insufficient in value to become a military objective . . .
>
> For the above reasons, the construction of defensive works at the entrance to Beaufort Inlet is not considered desirable at the present time, or until the improvements now in progress or authorized have proceeded further, and until the commercial importance of the place shall have shown a large increase."

Despite simultaneous introduction of identical bills to secure a $1,000,000 appropriation to fortify Fort Macon in the House of Representatives by Congressman Thomas, and in the Senate by Senator Furnifold M. Simmons, the measures did not pass. Undaunted, in March, 1909, Congressman Thomas reintroduced the same legislation, but once more it failed to pass. As with the Endicott Board of the mid-1880s, Fort Macon was not to be included in the modern permanent defenses of the United States.[6]

The early 1900s passed with Fort Macon continuing to decay. Still the old fort attracted attention of local people over the years. There were occasional visitors to the silent ramparts: mostly hunters and fishermen, but occasionally boatloads of inquisitive excursionists. Even women and children eagerly made the trek through the snaky bushes and weeds to see this curiosity hidden in the brush. Vandalism became a problem. People broke windows, tore down doors and rotting woodwork, left graffiti, and carried off anything which might remotely be of value. At some point, people sawed and pried off many of the bronze hinges, gratings and metalwork which had survived. The Engineer Department took up the issue of theft of these articles with the U.S. District Attorney, but the thieves were never caught. In 1913, requests were made by local businessmen to buy the last old officer's quarters cottage which was the only military structure remaining on the reservation other than the fort itself. Late in the year, the War Department finally agreed and sold it for fifty dollars. In 1917 the Southern Life and Trust Company applied for and received permission to lease part of the reservation for five years as a seasonal retreat for its employees in return for maintaining a watchman on the property. In 1919, another man was granted a similar lease to erect a small cottage on the reservation.[7]

The Army itself had one occasion to show a passing interest in the reservation during these years, but not from a military standpoint. In 1915, the Chief of Engineers sent out a circular to the engineer districts inviting recommendations for any of the old 19th Century fortifications which might be worthy of historic preservation. Fort Macon was recommended from the Wilmington District and an estimate of $2,000 was submitted to effect repairs, clean and fence in the fort, and build a house for keepers. Unfortunately, global concerns soon took precedence and nothing toward this project ever materialized.[8]

On 16 April 1917, the United States entered the First World War. This time no troops were sent to Fort Macon and no frantic efforts were made to prepare it for war. The German Navy was not judged to be a threat to the coast of the United States so even temporary defenses were not considered by the Army for Beaufort Harbor. At the urging of local citizens, however, North Carolina Congressmen did petition the War Department for the establishment of defenses for the harbor but were unsuccessful. They were told that an attack was unlikely because the draft of the modern warships exceeded the controlling depth of the harbor, and that the area had little strategic value to encourage an enemy landing. The War Department said that should the defense of the harbor become a consideration it could readily be accomplished with heavy railroad artillery rather than fixed fortifications.[9] Despite the initial lack of a threat to the U.S. seaboard, in the summer of 1918 German U-boat submarines did cross the ocean to operate against shipping off the U.S. coast, including the coast of North Carolina. This new form of warfare carried with it the potential for coastal raids and shore bombardment, but the threat was not taken seriously enough for the Army to think about occupying Fort Macon, and other small harbor defenses.

Following the end of the war the United States military went through another period of cutback and downsizing. There was a general belief at this time that this "war to end all wars" had secured peace and harmony in the world, and that there was no further need to continue hanging on to such large inventories of military weaponry and property. In this spirit the U.S. Army took a long look at its vast holdings of aging forts, camps, frontier posts, and other military property in the early 1920s to decide what was still needed for national defense. The decision was made that much of it was not. Lists were prepared by the War Department to dispose of those properties no longer considered necessary for national defense. The Fort Macon Military Reservation was one of the sites so listed.

By Act of Congress of 4 March 1923, the Secretary of War was formally authorized to sell off and dispose of the surplus military properties listed. The Act provided that the individual properties would be appraised to determine their value. Once this was done the governors of the respective states where the properties were located would be notified and given an option of six months in which to effect a purchase by state, county or municipality should the property be desired for public purposes. If not, the properties would be offered at public sale.[10]

During August or September, 1923, government appraisers valued the Fort Macon Military Reservation at $7,500. On 4 October, North Carolina Governor Cameron Morrison was given notification of this fact and that the state had six months in which to purchase the site before it went up for public sale.[11]

A STATE PARK

Scarcely had the announcement been made in March, 1923, of the Army's intention to sell off Fort Macon than interest in acquiring the fort began to build across North Carolina. Inquiries about the status of the fort were made at the War Department by North Carolina Senator Lee S. Overman and even the Beaufort, North Carolina, Chamber of Commerce in April, 1923. The North Carolina Geologic and Economic Survey Board, charged with the management of the state's natural resources, at once began to urge that the old fort be acquired by the state for its historic value and its great potential to the state for recreation and tourism as a park. The Board foresaw this as a unique opportunity to form the beginnings of a statewide park system, which it advocated. No state park system yet existed in North Carolina at that time although in 1915 the first area to be designated a "state park", Mount Mitchell, had already been purchased. The acquisition of Fort Macon on the coast would give North Carolina two state parks at its opposite extremes. These would serve as the nucleus for what the Board hoped would eventually culminate in a whole system of state parks by the future addition of other sites of natural and cultural importance to the state.[12]

Once the Army notified Governor Morrison of the appraised value of Fort Macon, Morrison had to admit, however, that the state had no funds available to secure the property. Morrison and Doctor Joseph H. Pratt, Director of the Geologic and Economic Survey Board, decided the best way to raise the money was by public subscription. In January, 1924, Pratt announced that voluntary contributions in any amount would be gratefully accepted from the public. At the same time requests were sent to a number of prominent, wealthy citizens to contribute heavily to meet the appraised price as well as to provide a source of funds for maintenance and upkeep of the site until the General Assembly had the opportunity to assume the responsibility. It turned out, however, that the public subscription was unnecessary.[13]

Aware of the historical importance of Fort Macon to the state and the interest which had been shown in it, North Carolina Congressman Charles L. Abernathy and North Carolina Senator Furnifold M. Simmons introduced legislation in Congress in February, 1924, for the War Department to cede the reservation back to North Carolina without cost. These bills were successfully amended to the general legislation authorizing the sale of property no longer needed for military purposes. The legislation passed in the House on 21 May 1924, and in the Senate on 23 May 1924.[14]

On 4 June 1924, President Calvin Coolidge signed into law Public Number 193, 68th Congress, "Sale of Real Property Not Needed For Military Purposes", with its provision that the Fort Macon Military Reservation be ceded to North Carolina for public purposes. The terms of this provision stipulated the reservation must be used for public purposes, and that the United States always retained the right to erect such structures as may be necessary for the Treasury, War, Navy, and Commerce Departments. It was further stipulated that of the approximately 412.3 acres of land comprising the reservation, a tract of 22.6 acres was specifically exempted and reserved for the use of the Coast Guard Lifesaving Station. The only cost to North Carolina in all of this was for the legal consideration of one dollar, which Congressman Abernathy paid. The quitclaim deed from the United States formally conveying the reservation to North Carolina was delivered 18 September 1924.[15]

Thus by fortunate circumstances, clever political footwork and the vision of state leaders, Fort Macon passed into state hands and became the second state park, after Mount Mitchell. On 17 July 1925, a formal presentation ceremony was held at Fort Macon before about 300 people with North Carolina Governor Angus McLean, Congressman Abernathy, Senator Simmons and other dignitaries in attendance. Congressman Abernathy made a formal presentation of the deed to Governor McLean, who accepted on behalf of the people of North Carolina.[16]

From 1925, Fort Macon's formal administration was placed under the State Forestry Division of the Department of Conservation and Development, along with Mount Mitchell State Park and a number of other properties which the state now began to acquire as state parks. In the years which followed the fort changed very little. A little cleanup and other work was done in the fort and a couple of picnic tables were put out inside for the use of any visitors. Visitors and excursionists continued to come by boat until 1928, when a new form of transportation to the park took precedence. In that year, a toll bridge was completed from the mainland to a beach resort several miles west of the fort which eventually became the town of Atlantic Beach. From this point excursionists came to the fort by automobile by making the short drive down the beach. Rather than leave the fort completely unattended with this increased visitation, in the summer of 1928 the Forestry Division began to maintain a part-time warden as funds permitted to go over to the fort each week. The Forestry Division also took advantage of the reservation to plant thousands of pine seedlings and experiment to determine the adaptability of different types of pine trees to the coastal environment. Unfortunately, these plantations were all subsequently destroyed by a fire carelessly started by some park visitors on 3 August 1932.[17]

By the early 1930s, the United States was in the midst of the Great Depression. This was a trying time for almost everyone in the country, but strangely it proved to be a blessing for the handful of state parks which

North Carolina had acquired. Without the Depression there is no way of knowing when North Carolina might have been in a position to do something with its parks to establish public facilities, staffing, and proper administration. However, the public works programs which were created by the Federal Government from the early 1930s to the beginning of World War II made all these things possible and left North Carolina with a functional system of state parks.

In an effort to put the country back on its feet and provide employment during the Depression, the Federal Government began a series of relief programs utilizing unemployed workers to build public facilities and perform work toward development and conservation of resources. The most important of these was the Civilian Conservation Corps, which worked through the United States Forest Service and National Park Service to establish "camps" of workers to perform resource conservation projects. Relief programs such as this provided an excellent and badly needed vehicle by which not only to put people back to work, but also create valuable public facilities.

Taking advantage of this relief assistance, a resolution of the North Carolina General Assembly passed on 30 March 1933, authorized the state to apply for federal assistance through the government relief programs to develop Fort Macon State Park. Following this, initial efforts by Forestry Division officials to secure a camp of the Civilian Conservation Corps from the National Park Service to effect the development of the park were at first unsuccessful, but in November of 1933, state officials were able to have construction of a road begun from the settlement of Atlantic Beach to the park under another federal agency known as the Civil Works Administration. This was the first step toward the park's development. In January, 1934, a separate project was approved under this agency to allocate $30,000 for the restoration of Fort Macon itself.[18]

Unfortunately, the Civil Works Administration was disbanded by the Government in March, 1934, leaving the road to the park unfinished and nothing else done toward the fort itself. However, state officials in the meantime had secured authorization through the National Park Service for a

Civilian Conservation Corps camp to work at Fort Macon. On 19 April 1934, a forty-eight-man detachment of Company 432 of the Civilian Conservation Corps arrived at Fort Macon to set up a camp for the remainder of the company which would soon arrive to begin work. When completed, the camp would consist of military barracks buildings provided by the Army, a mess hall, equipment storage buildings and administrative offices. The work which the C.C.C. company was to perform was divided up into a number of projects. The clay automobile road from the Atlantic Beach settlement to the fort begun under the Civil Works Administration was to be completed. The fort and its grounds were to be cleared and the fort restored in part to its nineteenth century appearance. The roadside and fort grounds would be landscaped. On the beach, erosion control work would be done to stabilize the shore and sand dunes. Finally, public recreation facilities were to be built, along with a house for a caretaker to operate the park. The rest of Company 432 arrived on 11 June 1934, and the work began.[19]

From April, 1934, to October, 1935, the C.C.C. workers toiled at Fort Macon. The men lived in tents during that first summer until their camp, located about 1,000 yards southwest of the fort, was completed in September. Until the unfinished road from Atlantic Beach was completed their supplies and building materials were brought over by boat. The road was finally completed in March, 1935, extending three and three-quarter miles from Atlantic Beach to end at a parking lot between the northeast side of the fort and the inlet. In the fort, the tangle of vegetation which had grown up over the last three decades was removed with the exception of several of the large trees. The old collapsed plasterwork and rotten woodwork were removed from the casemates by the wheelbarrow load. All the parade fronts of those casemates on the three eastern fronts had doors, jambs, and windows restored. In some cases completely new woodwork was used for this, and in other cases the original woodwork was repaired and reinstalled where possible. One casemate was completed restored inside with lathing and plastering, while two others were partially restored inside.[20]

Other things accomplished by the C.C.C. workers included much work to stabilize the shoreline by erecting brush fences and planting beach grass to build sand dunes. A well was dug and a water system installed. A picnic area was established in the sand dunes southwest of the fort with a shelter building, parking lot and a road leading to it. Public toilets were built both at the picnic area and near the fort. A boat dock was built beside the Coast Guard boat basin to serve visitors arriving by boat. Finally, a house was built west of the fort for a caretaker to run the park. With these facilities completed the work of Company 432 was done. The company as given another project and left Fort Macon in October, 1935.[21]

The departure of the Civilian Conservation Corps left Fort Macon as North Carolina's first functioning state park with public facilities. The North Carolina Department of Conservation and Development resumed its administration of the park and hired Mr. Lott W. Humphrey to serve as its full-time caretaker. It seemed only fitting that the state's first functioning state park should have a formal opening and dedication ceremony to herald this important event in North Carolina's modern history. Accordingly, state officials planned a dedication ceremony with much publicity. On 1 May 1936, the ceremony was held with North Carolina Governor J. C. B. Ehringhaus giving the keynote address for a crowd of about 1,000 dignitaries and visitors. Thus Fort Macon State Park was formally opened to the public.[22]

The next five years were eventful as the new park felt its growing pains. An effort during the first summer of operation to charge an admission fee of ten cents a person met with such discontent the fee was discontinued until 1938. Bad weather caused so many problems with the new clay road from Atlantic Beach that it was paved in 1937. An ongoing problem of serious proportions was the sudden onset of severe shore erosion on both the ocean and inlet beaches of the park in 1936. By 1938, the ocean shoreline receded so much the site of the old C.C.C. camp was completely under water. The picnic area in the dunes southwest of the fort was also lost and the picnic shelter building had to be dismantled and removed. Early in 1939, the public toilet buildings serving the picnic area were moved to keep them from the reach of the sea. Thus the ocean had succeeded in

destroying the public recreation facilities built by the C.C.C. four years earlier. It was also in 1939 that the park caretaker, Lott W. Humphrey, died.
His wife, Virginia B. Humphrey, was retained by the Department of Conservation and Development to take over his position, becoming one of the
first women in the country to hold a park superintendent position.[23]

The loss of the park's recreational area was only a temporary problem.
Numerous requests had been made to establish a free bathing beach at the
park and state officials took steps to fulfill them with federal assistance. In
February, 1940, the Federal Government authorized a public bathing beach
development project for the park through the Works Progress Administration. The "Beach Development" project called for the construction of a
public bathhouse, concession stand, picnic area, boardwalk, water and sewage systems, parking areas, and access road. So that this area would be less
threatened by shore erosion problems associated with the inlet, it was located near the western boundary of the park almost a mile from the fort.
Construction began and considerable progress was made during 1940.
However, with the war going on in Europe and the increasing likelihood of
the United States' involvement, increasing numbers of local workmen in
W.P.A. projects were being diverted to build a number of Army and Navy
installations at Morehead City, Jacksonville, Cherry Point, and Holly Ridge.
Construction of the Beach Development dragged on until the summer of
1941 and then came to a standstill when all W.P.A. workers were ordered
diverted solely to military installation projects. At that time, the bathhouse,
concession stand, boardwalk, access road, and one parking lot were mostly
completed. Unless the United States went to war, the Beach Development
would open to the public for the summer of 1942.[24]

The Japanese attack on Pearl Harbor on 7 December 1941, brought
the United States into World War II. Ten days after the attack, the North
Carolina Adjutant General's Office received word from Brigadier General
Rollin L. Tilton, commanding the Third Coast Artillery District, that it would
be necessary for the Army to occupy Fort Macon once again for the duration of the war emergency. The State Port Terminal established at Morehead
City and a new Navy Section Base under construction just west of Morehead

City required defense from possible coastal raids and offshore bombardment. As a result the Army intended to establish a temporary harbor defense at Fort Macon State Park with a shore battery and troops.[25]

For state officials the prospect of Fort Macon being taken back over for war was something for which they were not prepared. The 1924 deed which gave the fort to North Carolina carried the provision that the departments of the Federal Government could return at any time to carry out activities on the park in the national interest, which is exactly what the Army was about to do. Beyond this, however, lay unanswered concerns such as how to prevent damage to the park or alteration to the fort's historic integrity by Army occupation. Also, what was to become of park buildings, property and employees? Finally, would the state be able to reclaim the park once the war emergency ended? While officials in Raleigh pondered these concerns, on 19 December 1941, a party of Army officers from General Tilton's command arrived to make a preliminary reconnaissance of the park. They called on Mrs. Humphrey, the Caretaker, studied the fort and terrain of the park and then left.[26]

There was no further development until about dawn on 21 December 1941, when a long convoy of Army vehicles full of soldiers came rumbling into the park. First Battalion, 244th Coast Artillery, had arrived after an all-night drive from Camp Pendleton, Virginia, to occupy Fort Macon for war.

WORLD WAR II

In keeping with the basic policy it had followed in the last part of the nineteenth century, the Army's intention in occupying Fort Macon again was to provide a temporary defense for Beaufort Harbor only for the duration of the war emergency. A detailed reconnaissance of the area had been made by the Army in November, 1941, when construction of a Navy Section Base began west of Morehead City. The plan resulting from this called for one mobile battery of Coast Artillery to be established at Fort Macon State Park to guard the inlet, and another to be stationed west of Atlantic Beach covering the Section Base located back on the mainland side of Bogue

Sound. Once notification of the intended occupation of Fort Macon was given to North Carolina state officials on 17 December 1941, movement orders were issued three days later to First Battalion, 244th Coast Artillery (155mm guns, tractor drawn) to proceed from Camp Pendleton, Virginia, to Fort Macon. The orders specified very briefly what was to be its mission:

"INFORMATION—

a, Naval and air raids are probable in the vicinity of BEAUFORT INLET (N.C.).

b, The principal objective in this area is MOREHEAD CITY with its port facilities, and the Naval and Marine installations in the vicinity (now under construction).

DECISION OR MISSION—

a, The TEMPORARY HARBOR DEFENSE OF BEAUFORT INLET is activated to deny entrance to BEAUFORT HARBOR to hostile ships, protect shipping and harbor facilities from Naval attack, and insure freedom of movement in and out of MOREHEAD CITY harbor to our Naval forces and shipping."[27]

The First Battalion, 244th Coast Artillery, moved as ordered by road on 20 December, leaving its eight 155mm guns to be brought down by rail. Upon crossing over to Bogue Banks early on the morning of 21 December, Battery A established itself in the sand dunes two and one-half miles west of Atlantic Beach off Salter Path Road while the remainder of the battalion, Battery B and Headquarters Battery, occupied Fort Macon State Park. At Fort Macon, the old casemates became alive with soldiers once again as Battery B and Headquarters Battery occupied the old fort. Troops threw field cots on the cold brick floors and lived under field conditions with the December winds whistling through the empty doorways and windows. As soon as possible in the weeks which followed, contractors were brought in with the cooperation of state parks officials to install wooden flooring and temporary doors and windows to make the casemates habitable for the troops.[28]

Almost immediately after the arrival of the troops an accident took place which raised concerns with both the Army and State Parks for both the soldiers and the fort. Soldiers removed some of the fort's old Civil War cannonballs which had been on display for park visitors in one of the casemates and carelessly placed them in the fireplace of their casemate quarters to serve as andirons for firewood. One of the projectiles happened to be an unexploded shell. Once the fire got hot enough it promptly exploded in the fireplace. By some miracle no one was killed in the crowded casemate. There were minor injuries and only one soldier had burns serious enough to require hospitalization. Although no one felt it was humorous at the time, the cannonball-in-the-fireplace incident achieved considerable notoriety afterward as one of those interesting ironies of war. The 244th Coast Artillery was formerly the 9th New York National Guard and thus provided the ironic twist where Northern soldiers could return to a former Confederate fort and be injured by an old Civil War cannonball seventy-six years after the Civil War ended. The incident is still jokingly referred to as the "last shot of the Civil War."[29]

Soon the battalion's eight 155mm guns arrived by rail at Morehead City. They were unloaded and pulled by their tractors over to Bogue Banks. On 24 December, Battery A's four guns took position in the sand dunes west of Atlantic Beach while Battery B's four guns similarly took position in the sand dunes southwest of the fort between the ocean and the Caretaker's House. The gun pits had timber platforms and walls concealed behind sand dune embankments and sand bags. Live ammunition for the guns was hauled up from the Ordnance Depot at Charleston, South Carolina. They were proof fired on 27 December and were ready for battle. Other defensive measures included the placement of sixty-inch searchlights and steel towers known as Base End Stations both in the park and on Shackleford Banks. A guardhouse and gate were established near the park entrance and the park was closed to the general public. For the time being the park staff, Mrs. Humphrey, the Caretaker, and Ranger Jesse Long, were allowed to stay. With the park closed down, however, their continued presence was pointless and they were eventually withdrawn.[30]

In the meantime, the takeover of the park by the Army from the State of North Carolina was formally accomplished in the form of a lease agreement drafted by the Real Estate Branch of the Engineer Department. The lease incorporated a complete inventory of all state property being taken over and a description of it. The lease stipulated the park and its property would be returned to North Carolina at the end of the war emergency and made provision for the restoration of the property to its prewar condition by the Army if deemed necessary. It stated that any alteration or damage to the park and buildings was to be kept to a minimum consistent with national defense. The annual "rent" to be paid by the U.S. Government for this lease was one dollar. The lease was prepared and after a number of additions by the state was formally executed 27 April 1942.[31]

Despite the clause about minimal damage and alteration, it was inevitable the fort would suffer damages by troop occupation. Holes were bored through walls by the soldiers to pass through pipes and wires. Wires and electrical conduit were nailed to walls and ceiling arches. Old original zinc downspouts in the gutter chases of the parade walls were ripped out, replaced with terra cotta pipe and bricked up. In places where water trickled out of the walls, patches of cement stucco were smeared to try to seal it off. A doorway leading to Casemate 2 from the sally port was partially bricked up. A small fireplace and oven which constituted the old officers' kitchen was demolished for space. Tragically, despite protests from the state, the big bake oven in Casemate 12 where the near-mutiny of the "Bread Incident" had originated during the 1862 siege, was also demolished for storage space. Throughout all of this, state officials corresponded regularly with the troop commander regarding the impact the occupation was having on the fort and made a number of inspections to check on state property. However, they were really powerless to do much more than look on in sadness as the Army went about the business of war.[32]

As the troops settled in during the first months of 1942, efforts were made to relieve the congested conditions. A formal troop housing area was established for Battery B personnel in the dunes west of the Caretaker's House adjacent to their gun position. A mess hall, latrine, and officers' barracks were erected below the northwest glacis of the fort, with a trestle footbridge built across the fort's ditch at the southwest angle to provide easy access to them. In the fort itself, the Headquarters of the Harbor Defenses of Beaufort Inlet were established. The casemates of the three eastern wings were used as administrative offices, supply offices, plotting rooms, dispensary, and so forth. Headquarters personnel were quartered in the two western wings and in tents outside. By now the casemates were all enclosed, floored, and heated with coal space heaters.[33]

During this time, the war was actively in progress just offshore and at times within sight of the fort. German U-boat submarines first began to destroy Allied shipping off the U.S. East Coast in January of 1942, extending as far south as Cape Hatteras, North Carolina. By March, 1942, the U-boats began sinking ships between Cape Lookout and Cape Fear. Although these attacks took place beyond the reach of guns at Fort Macon, everyone was keenly aware of what was happening. On the night of 14–15 March, a U-boat attacked two tankers just below Cape Lookout, the flashes and noise of gunfire plainly evident. On 18 March, two more tankers were sunk southwest of Cape Lookout, the fire from one of them being visible for miles. Some days later, Navy tugs towed the stern portion of yet another tanker blown in half off Cape Fear into Beaufort Harbor for salvage. The burned hulk of another tanker shelled off Cape Lookout on 2 April was towed into Beaufort Harbor for salvage while still another tanker torpedoed on 10 April off Cape Lookout was towed into the bight between Cape Lookout and Beaufort Inlet where it burned for weeks. Other reminders of the carnage were the oil and debris which washed up along the beaches, as well as the occasional body of an unfortunate seaman.

There was little the forces at Fort Macon could do to help in the U-boat fighting other than maintain the constant beach patrols in conjunction with Coast Guard and infantry units in the area. This type of warfare against submarines was mainly the responsibility of aircraft and the small fleet of Coast Guard cutters, Navy subchasers, and British armed trawlers which operated from Morehead City's port and Navy Section Base. Still, while not directly engaged, the forces at Fort Macon could take pride in the fact their presence insured a deterrence to any U-boat shelling of the Navy Section Base or the ships in port with deck guns. On 10 April 1942, the responsibility of the Harbor Defenses of Beaufort Inlet were expanded when the Navy established a net-protected merchant ship anchorage in the bight between Cape Lookout and Beaufort Inlet. Here merchant ships would be gathered up to anchor overnight in shallow water in a safe anchorage rather than travel in the sea lanes at night when they were most vulnerable to attack. The guns of Battery B at Fort Macon, and two 155mm guns of Battery A transferred in May to a position on the west side of Cape Lookout, commanded this anchorage and covered the ships within the limits of their ten and one-half mile range.[34]

First Battalion, 244th Coast Artillery, remained in the defenses of Fort Macon and Cape Lookout throughout part of the summer of 1942. In July, however, the battalion received notification of its impending transfer to Iceland, with its guns and searchlights to be left in place. To replace the personnel of the battalion stationed at the gun position on Cape Lookout, Battery H, 2nd Coast Artillery, was sent down from the Chesapeake Bay area. To replace the rest of the battalion at Fort Macon, a battalion of the 54th Coast Artillery from nearby Camp Davis was chosen. This caused a controversy. The 54th Coast Artillery was a black regiment with white officers, and here began the same kind of trouble which had prevailed with the 3rd North Carolina Volunteers in the Spanish-American War. There quickly arose local protests over the stationing of black troops at Fort Macon. Congressman Graham A. Barden and Governor J. Melville Broughton both contacted the sector headquarters and the War Department in reaction to ask that another battalion of white troops be substituted in their place. The War Department replied no other troops were currently available. On 2 August, Battery G, 54th Coast Artillery, arrived at Morehead City and relieved the men of the 244th Coast Artillery, who departed for Boston on 15 August. The troops of Battery G remained at Fort Macon during August but in the meantime the War Department finally agreed to replace them with white troops. Accordingly, Battery K, 2nd Coast Artillery, was activated and replaced Battery G, 54th Coast Artillery, early in September. For the next year and a half, Batteries H and K, 2nd Coast Artillery, along with a Harbor Defense Headquarters and searchlight detachment, constituted the permanent garrison of the Harbor Defenses of Beaufort Inlet. These acted in cooperation with field artillery and infantry units also stationed in the area as Sector Mobile Forces.[35]

During 1942 and 1943, there were other changes as efforts were made to upgrade weaponry and living conditions. The old 155mm guns defending the inlet and anchorage were really not suited for naval defense where a wide traverse of fire against moving targets was necessary. As a result, the Army acquired from the Navy Department a battery of two 5-inch Navy guns on pedestal mounts for Cape Lookout and two 6-inch Navy guns on pedestal mounts for Fort Macon. The new Cape Lookout 5-inch battery was completed 17 September. The two 6-inch guns for Fort Macon were situated in the sand dunes west of the 155mm gun position and completed on 26 November 1942. Once these two batteries were completed the 155mm guns were withdrawn.[36]

In addition to new guns, a Harbor Entrance Control Post (HECP) tower was built on top of Fort Macon to identify and control all shipping moving through the inlet. Also, a radio direction finder team was headquartered in a cottage outside the fort with outposts established in the area to track radio transmissions of U-boats offshore. In 1943, a large marshy area north of the fort was filled in, creating ten to twelve acres of new land. The Army then erected a large complex of barracks, machine shops, warehouses, recreation hall, mess hall, and other support buildings and roads on this new area. The fort was once again the centerpiece of a thriving military city on Bogue Point. The troops on Cape Lookout also got a barracks complex, which enabled them to move out of tents. A coastal radar station was also established on Cape Lookout.[37]

After July of 1942, the U-boat menace off the East Coast dropped to nothing more than an occasional nuisance raid. The danger had grown so minimal that by early 1944, a reorganization and downsizing of the coastal defenses of the Eastern Seaboard took place. As a result, the elements of the 2nd Coast Artillery in the Harbor Defenses of Beaufort Inlet were withdrawn in March, 1944, to undergo a regimental reorganization and were replaced by Batteries A and B, 246th Coast Artillery. By fall of 1944, the Army was so confident of no further coastal threats that it began to close some of its defensive posts. One of these was Beaufort Inlet. Accordingly, in November, 1944, the troops of the Harbor Defenses of Beaufort Inlet were withdrawn and the post closed. On 1 April 1945, the station was deactivated and custody turned over to the Engineer Department for disposition. For Fort Macon, the war was over. However, much remained to be done before the Army relinquished the property.[38]

With the deactivation of Fort Macon and the war in Europe ending, State Parks officials hoped to soon terminate the Army's lease of the park, remove Army property, restore the park to prewar condition, and reopen to the public. Unfortunately, this would not prove to be an easy matter. Considerable Army property still remained in the form of barracks, support buildings, towers, gun emplacements, barbed wire, etc., all of which had to be removed. The sand dunes, grounds, and vegetation had suffered considerably from soldiers and vehicles. The fort had tremendous repairs to be made, including the removal of the Army's temporary flooring, doors, and windows in the casemates as well as repainting and general cleanup. According to the lease agreement the Army was responsible for repairs and restoration of the park to prewar condition but the extent of damage costs had to be assessed and negotiated. Numerous meetings and conferences were held between state officials and agents of the Real Estate Branch of the Engineer Department on the matter which dragged out for a year and a half. In early 1946, the Army finished selling off and having removed all its property in the park with the exception of a number of items of equipment which the State wished to retain. These included various pumps, a heating system installed in the Caretaker's House, and an extensive water system in the park far superior to the old 1935 water system which existed before. In the final settlement, the State was given ownership of the equipment items and a lump sum restoration payment of $11,450. The Army's lease on the park was formally terminated at midnight on 1 October 1946.[39]

Once again Fort Macon belonged to the State of North Carolina. The Army's temporary flooring, doors, and windows were gone and the state now assumed responsibility for the remaining repairs and finish work to return the fort back to its prewar appearance. However, it was inevitable that some of the damages could never be repaired. The big bake oven, for instance, which had been such an interesting feature of the fort could never be rebuilt as before. Fort Macon had gone through yet another phase in its history with a whole new set of scars and marks. These were now part of the historic fabric of the fort and in time would become historic in themselves.

A MODERN PARK

Since the war years, Fort Macon has taken its place as one of North Carolina's top historical attractions. The park has maintained the highest public visitation of any North Carolina State Park since the 1950s. The old fort continues to be the centerpiece for visitation which approaches one and a half million visitors annually. In the decades which have followed World War II, a successive number of major programs have been carried on as funding would allow to promote the fort's interesting history and to ensure its continued existence for the enjoyment of visitors. The first efforts to interpret the fort's history began with the establishment of a small museum in the fort in 1950. The museum was expanded during an interpretive program of 1952–53, along with other historic restoration work. During 1976–77, a major fort restoration project funded by the North Carolina General Assembly took place which restored five casemates to original condition. During the period 1986 to 1996 a progressive historic restoration program was carried on with the aid of grants, public donation, and the Friends of Fort Macon support group. This program has thus far resulted in the creation of four restored period rooms, the rebuilding of the fort's 1836 Hot Shot Furnace, and the placement of a replica barbette cannon on the ramparts once again. Additional interpretative restoration is planned for the future.

By the late 1950s, there was a great deal of concern for the safety of the site of Fort Macon because the fort had become in danger of finally losing the battle with its age-old enemy, the sea. During the 1940s the shore erosion problem had abated somewhat, but then came a series of severe hurricanes during the 1950s which aggravated the problem. Severe shore erosion once again threatened the fort. Only by an expensive, multi-phased shore erosion project carried out jointly by North Carolina and the Federal Government between 1961 and 1970 was the problem finally stabilized to the point the fort is no longer considered to be in danger. Thus a problem which had so plagued and concerned a previous generation of engineers throughout the nineteenth century beginning with Lieutenant William A. Eliason and Captain John L. Smith had finally been put to rest.

Today Fort Macon remains one of the best-preserved examples of nineteenth century fortification in the country. Perhaps the greatest concern for Fort Macon for the immediate future, however, is its continued preservation and physical stabilization. Nineteenth century engineers created these seacoast forts to be permanent and Fort Macon has gone through more than a century and a half of exposure to the elements, storms, war, bombardment, and human impact, but not without a price. Just as these old forts are unique structures, so too are the problems associated with their preservation for the future. The constant assault of moisture and salt in the unforgiving coastal environment have taken their toll and will cause structural problems and concerns which at some point must be addressed if these old forts are to be preserved as part of our cultural heritage for the future. In the case of Fort Macon, it is hoped this book, in chronicling the rich history connected with the fort, will in some small measure help create an awareness of the unique importance of this structure, and foster the desire on the part of the State of North Carolina and the general public to see that this historic fort is always properly maintained and preserved for the enjoyment of future generations.

Appendix One

GARRISONS OF FORT MACON

DATE   **REGIMENT, COMPANY OR BATTERY**

Ante-Bellum Period

December, 1834 to   1st United States Artillery, Company G
February, 1836

July, 1842 to   3rd United States Artillery, Company F
January, 1844

February, 1844 to   3rd United States Artillery, Companies B and F
October, 1844

November, 1844   3rd United States Artillery, Company B

October, 1848 to   2nd United States Artillery, Company H
October, 1849

Civil War (Confederate)

April, 1861   1st North Carolina, Company A (Edgecombe Guards)
2nd North Carolina, Company K (Elm City Rifles)
4th North Carolina, Company F (Wilson Light Infantry)
12th North Carolina, Company F (Warren Guards)
13th North Carolina, Company C (Milton Blues)
27th North Carolina, Company A (Goldsboro Rifles)
27th North Carolina, Company B (Guilford Grays)
27th North Carolina, Company C (North Carolina Guards)
27th North Carolina, Company D (Goldsboro Volunteers)
27th North Carolina, Company G (Orange Guards)

May, 1861	2nd North Carolina, Company C (Old Topsail Rifles)
	2nd North Carolina, Company K (Elm City Rifles)
	4th North Carolina, Company F (Wilson Light Infantry)
	27th North Carolina, Company A (Goldsboro Rifles)
	27th North Carolina, Company B (Guilford Grays)
	27th North Carolina, Company D (Goldsboro Volunteers)
	27th North Carolina, Company G (Orange Guards)

June, 1861 — 1st North Carolina Artillery, Company G (Beaufort Harbor Guards)
2nd North Carolina, Company C (Old Topsail Rifles)
4th North Carolina, Company F (Wilson Light Infantry)
27th North Carolina, Company A (Goldsboro Rifles)
27th North Carolina, Company B (Guilford Grays)
27th North Carolina, Company D (Goldsboro Volunteers)
27th North Carolina, Company G (Orange Guards)

July, 1861 — 1st North Carolina Artillery, Companies B and G
27th North Carolina, Companies A, B and G

August, 1861 — 1st North Carolina Artillery, Companies B, F, G and H
27th North Carolina, Companies A, B and G

September, 1861 — 1st North Carolina Artillery, Companies B, F, G and H
3rd North Carolina Artillery, Company F
27th North Carolina, Company A, B and G

October, 1861 to February, 1862 — 1st North Carolina Artillery, Companies B, G and H
27th North Carolina, Companies A, B and G

March, 1862 to April, 1862 — 1st North Carolina Artillery, Companies B, F, G and H
3rd North Carolina Artillery, Company F

Civil War (Union)

April, 1862 to December, 1862 — 1st United States Artillery, Company C
3rd New York Artillery, Company I

December, 1862 — 1st United States Artillery, Company C
45th Massachusetts Infantry, Company G

January, 1863 to April, 1863 — 1st United States Artillery, Company C
45th Massachusetts Infantry, Companies G and I

April, 1863 to May, 1863	1st United States Artillery, Company C 45th Massachusetts Infantry, Company I 51st Massachusetts Infantry, Company C
May, 1863 to September, 1863	1st United States Artillery, Company C 81st New York Infantry, Companies B, D and G
September, 1863 to October, 1863	1st United States Artillery, Company C 2nd Massachusetts Heavy Artillery, Companies A, B, C and D
November, 1863 to February, 1864	1st United States Artillery, Company C 2nd Massachusetts Heavy Artillery, Companies A and B
February, 1864	1st United States Artillery, Company C 2nd Massachusetts Heavy Artillery, Companies A and D
March, 1864 to May, 1864	2nd Massachusetts Heavy Artillery, Companies A and D
May, 1864 to July, 1864	1st North Carolina Union Volunteers, Companies C, E, F and G
August, 1864 to November, 1864	1st North Carolina Union Volunteers, Companies B, C, E, F and G
November, 1864 to January, 1865	1st North Carolina Union Volunteers, Companies B, E, F and G
February, 1865 to March, 1865	1st North Carolina Union Volunteers, Companies B, D, E, F and G
March, 1865 to June, 1865	2nd Massachusetts Heavy Artillery, Company G

Reconstruction Era

June, 1865 to August, 1865	14th United States Colored Heavy Artillery, Companies H, I, L and M
August, 1865 to September, 1865	14th United States Colored Heavy Artillery, All Companies
September, 1865 to October, 1865	14th United States Colored Heavy Artillery, Companies A, D, E, G, H, K and L

November, 1865 to December, 1865	14th United States Colored Heavy Artillery, All Companies
December, 1865 to January, 1867	37th United States Colored Troops, Companies I and K
January, 1867 to March, 1867	8th United States Infantry, Company E
March, 1867 to April, 1867	40th United States Infantry, Companies B and E
May, 1867	40th United States Infantry, Companies B, E and I
June, 1867 to August, 1867	40th United States Infantry, Company I
September, 1867 to December, 1867	40th United States Infantry, Detachment (Companies I and H)
December, 1867	40th United States Infantry, Detachment (Companies B, I and H)
January, 1868 to August, 1868	40th United States Infantry, Companies B and I
August, 1868 to February, 1869	5th United States Artillery, Company H
February, 1869 to March, 1869	3rd United States Artillery, Company H
March, 1869	8th United States Infantry, Companies A and I 40th United States Infantry, Companies C and H
April, 1869	8th United States Infantry, Companies A and I 33rd United States Infantry, Company C
May, 1869	8th United States Infantry, Companies A and I 33rd United States Infantry, Companies C and F
June, 1869 to February, 1870	8th United States Infantry, Companies A and I
February, 1870 to November, 1872	4th United States Artillery, Companies K and L

November, 1872 to September, 1875	2nd United States Artillery, Companies E and L
September, 1875 to July, 1876	2nd United States Artillery, Companies I and L
August, 1876	2nd United States Artillery, Company L
September, 1876	2nd United States Artillery, Company L 2nd United States Artillery, Detachment (Companies D and E)
September, 1876 to April, 1877	2nd United States Artillery, Detachment (Companies D and E)

Spanish-American War

May, 1898	6th United States Artillery, Detachment (Company C)
June, 1898	6th United States Artillery, Detachment (Company C) Russell's Black Battalion, Companies A, B and C
July, 1898	6th United States Artillery, Detachment (Company C) 3rd North Carolina Volunteers, All Companies
July, 1898 to September, 1898	3rd North Carolina Volunteers, All Companies 2nd United States Artillery, Detachment (Battery I)
September, 1898 to October, 1898	2nd United States Artillery, Detachment (Battery I)

World War II

December, 1941 to August, 1942	244th Coast Artillery, Headquarters and Battery B
August, 1942	54th Coast Artillery, Battery G
September, 1942 to October, 1942	2nd Coast Artillery, Battery K
November, 1942 to March, 1944	2nd Coast Artillery, Headquarters and Battery K
March, 1944 to April, 1944	246th Coast Artillery, Battery B
May, 1944 to November, 1944	246th Coast Artillery, Battery A

Appendix Two

ARMAMENT OF FORT MACON

When Fort Macon was first designed, its intended armament was to be fifty guns, which included thirty guns and howitzers, and four mortars on the covertway, eight guns and howitzers on the citadel, and eight carronades in the casemates.[1] This plan of armament was slightly altered in 1835 with the following armament plan submitted by Engineer Lieutenant George Dutton:

	Covertway	Citadel
Front I	9 32-pounders	3 18-pounders
Front II	10 24-pounders	2 18-pounders
		3 8-inch howitzers
Front III	2 32-pounders	3 18-pounders
		7 24-pounders
Land Side	4 10-inch mortars	
In Casemates	8 18-pounder Carronades	

Total armament fifty-one guns.[2]

This was intended to be a full wartime armament for the fort. During the period of alteration and modification of the fort (1841–46), the intended armament changed again when permanent brick and stone gun mounts were constructed for forty-eight barbette guns and six carronades in the counterfire galleries. Soon afterward, in a report on fortifications by the Secretary of War to Congress on 8 December 1851, the intended armament was changed yet again to sixty-one guns consisting of twelve 32-pounders, twenty-two 24-pounders, four 18-pounders, four 12-pounders, six 8-inch howitzers, six flank howitzers, two 10-inch mortars, two Coehorn mortars, and three field pieces.[3]

As with most of the Third System forts, Fort Macon would never receive this full complement. In November, 1835, ten 24-pounders were sent to the fort, followed in January, 1836, by seven additional 24-pounders and ten barbette carriages.[4] These seventeen guns, along with three iron 6-pounder field guns left at the fort when its first garrison departed for the Seminole War in February, 1836, remained the only armament the fort possessed prior to the Civil War.

After the Civil War began, the Confederates acquired additional cannons for the fort from Charleston, Richmond and Norfolk. At the time of the siege of Fort Macon in April, 1862, the fort's armament is believed to have been as follows:

           2 10-inch columbiads
           5 8-inch columbiads
           1 5.82-inch Rifled columbiad
           4 Rifled 32-pounders (Navy pattern)
           18 32-pounders (Navy pattern)
           18 24-pounders
           6 32-pounder carronades

           Total 54 guns

Following its capture in 1862, Union forces added some guns to the armament, removed a few of the older guns, and kept the rest for years. The following table shows the state of the armament over successive years:

As of 31 December	1863	1864	1865	1866	1868	1871	1873
10-inch columbiad	2	2	2	2	2	2	2
8-inch columbiad	5	5	5	5	5	5	5
5.82-inch Rifled columbiad	1	1					
Rifled 32-pounder	4	4	4	4	4	4	4
32-pounder	18	18	18	18			
24-pounder	10	10	10	10			
32-pounder carronade	6	4					
10-inch siege mortar	2	2	2	2	2	2	2
100-pounder Parrott Rifle	3	2	2	2	2	2	2
24-pounder flank howitzer	6	6	6	6	6	6	6
12-pounder Napoleon						2	2[5]

In the last part of the nineteenth century, all the old, obsolete Civil War-era guns were disposed of by the Army with the exception of the two 100-pounder Parrott Rifles, two 10-inch siege mortars, and two 12-pounder Napoleons. These guns were remounted and used in the Spanish-American War of 1898. Between 1900 and 1902 these guns were also disposed of. The two 100-pounder Parrotts apparently went to war one more time. In 1900 they were donated as monuments to the city of Spartanburg, South Carolina, where they flanked a statue of Revolutionary War hero General Daniel Morgan. When World War II broke out, however, they were turned over to a scrap drive in September, 1942, and apparently melted down. Presumably their material went on in some other form to fight in World War II.[6]

Of all Fort Macon's guns, the only ones known to survive today are the two 10-inch siege mortars. In 1902 these were donated to the city of Raleigh, North Carolina, as monuments. Fortunately, they survived the smelting pots of World War II and were returned to Fort Macon in 1953. They have remained there ever since.

NINETEENTH CENTURY ARTILLERY

Unless someone has had occasion to take more than a passing glance into the world of muzzle-loaded artillery of the nineteenth century, such terminology as "32-pounder", "columbiad", and "Parrott Rifle" might seem quite strange when encountered in a book such as this. Yet when someone walks past one of these cannons on a town green or at a battlefield park, it is difficult not to wonder what these silent relics of another century are all about. The following section gives a brief review of this almost-forgotten period of weaponry.

Size: To begin with, cannons of the nineteenth century are categorized in size in two ways. Most are categorized by the weight of the solid shot projectile they fired. Thus, a 32-pounder fired a solid shot cannonball of that weight. Howevr, some cannons, particularly large-caliber cannons, are categorized by their bore diameter expressed in inches, i.e., 10-inch columbiad.

Class: The Army grouped different sizes of cannons into classes of artillery. *Field Artillery* comprised light, mobile cannons designed for use in the field to support soldiers in battle, such as 6- and 12-pounder smoothbores and 10-pounder rifles. *Siege and Garrison Artillery* comprised the largest cannons which could be moved conveniently by road, such as 18- and 24-pounder smoothbores and 30-pounder rifles. They could use large mobile carriages called siege carriages, or barbette carriages. Because of their weight they were used in forts or were carried along in the field in siege trains until needed. *Seacoast Artillery* comprised the largest caliber cannons for use by forts against ships such as 32- and 42-pounder smoothbores, columbiads and large-caliber rifles. Their great weight required a permanent installation.

Bore Type: Artillery of the period was of two bore types, smoothbore and rifled. Smoothbores were the oldest class of artillery going back to Medieval times. They fired a spherical projectile through a bore of smooth metal. Rifles utilized elongated projectiles and spiral grooves cut down the length of the bore to make the projectile spin. Spinning projectiles had greater range and accuracy than spherical projectiles and thus represented a great advance in artillery. Although rifling had been used with small arms for some time, it was only in the mid-nineteenth century that rifling was successfully applied to artillery. The innovation as so new the American Civil War was its first actual trial in combat. A number of artillery inventors and innovators in various countries were experimenting with and producing rifled weapons by the time of the Civil War. Included was Lieutenant Robert P. Parrott (1804–1877) of the U.S. Army, who created a whole system of rifled artillery for U.S. service from 10-pounders to 300-pounders. These guns bear his name and were the most famous and widely produced rifled cannons of the Civil War.

Ammunition: The artillery ammunition of the period was not unlike that of today. Solid iron projectiles called *solid shot* were used for battering, piercing armor or walls, and long-range firing. *Shells* were hollow projectiles filled with gunpowder and designed to explode by means of a fuse. They caused destruction with their blast and the fragments of the broken projectile which flew in all directions. Fragmentation ammunition such as *case shot* (shrapnel), *canister* and *grapeshot* used bullets and small metal shot to cause great destruction to enemy troops.

Special Types of Cannons: Other than just flat-trajectory artillery, there were other types of cannons in use. *Mortars* threw exploding projectiles into an arc from a high elevation to drop amidst enemy troops from above. They could lob shells behind walls and hills, and into trenches and battery positions where regular cannon could not. *Howitzers* also threw large explosive shells at high trajectories, although not as high as a mortar. They were employed frequently for flanking defense in fortifications. *Columbiads* were the heaviest cannons used by the Army and threw shot and shell at high elevations with large powder charges for long range. They were adopted in the mid-1840s and provided the main defense of seacoast forts.

Naval Cannons: Naval cannons usually tended to parallel Army cannons in caliber, including large-caliber shell guns which rivaled the Army's columbiads. Due to weight considerations aboard ships, Navy guns fre-

quently weighed less than their Army counterparts. One Navy cannon referred to in the text at times is the *carronade*. These were stubby, large-
caliber naval cannons used in the late eighteenth and early nineteenth
centuries which were designed as broadside guns to splinter the hulls of
enemy ships at close range. Although phased out of naval service in the
mid-1800s, the Army frequently employed them for flanking and interior
defense for forts where their large-caliber bores were particularly suited to
throwing anti-personnel ammunition into attackers.

Appendix Three
SOLDIER LIFE

The soldier of the nineteenth century faced living conditions which few today would consider tolerable. Those in permanent garrisons shared a range of miseries which were common from post to post, whether at Fort Macon or at any of the other seacoast forts or military camps across the country. General dampness, poor ventilation, the heat of summer and the cold of winter were all common conditions which pervaded almost every military post of the era, especially at Fort Macon where troops were housed in casemates rather than in barracks. The following items give the reader some idea of other living conditions faced by soldiers stationed at Fort Macon.

Number of Men per Casemate: The occupancy of a typical casemate fluctuated with the number of men stationed at the fort at any given time. Peacetime occupation was usually far less crowded than wartime occupation. In 1870, Fort Macon's Assistant Surgeon Elliott Coues (later one of the most renowned naturalists of the nineteenth century) recorded there were "twenty men in each casemate—there have never been fewer and sometime more . . ." Early in the Civil War, Confederate soldier James A. Graham noted there were about forty men in his casemate. During November to

December, 1865, the 14th U.S. Colored Heavy Artillery, whose companies averaged about seventy-four enlisted men each, somehow existed in the fort with each company occupying a single casemate![1]

Bunks: The bunks of soldiers at Fort Macon for most of the nineteenth century were typical four-man wooden bunks used throughout the Army. Two men slept at each level. Bedding consisted only of cotton bedsack mattresses with no pillows or linens, and only each soldier's individual blanket for warmth. Army regulations provided for a monthly allowance of straw to each soldier in garrison with which to stuff his bedsack. The bunks were made in such a manner as to be readily dismantled for weekly cleaning. In the mid-1870s, however, the old wooden bunks were finally replaced by individual bunks with iron bedsteads.[2]

Cleanliness: Army regulations of the period dictated the normal cleaning routine of the Army: "Ordinarily the cleaning will be on Saturdays. The chiefs of squads will cause bunks and bedding to be overhauled; floor dry rubbed; tables and benches scoured, arms cleaned; accoutrements whitened and polished, and everything put in order." In the case of Fort Macon, the following post order provides further illumination of how these regulations were actually carried out:

Headquarters, Fort Macon, NC
July 13th, 1864

General Orders
  No. 2

     I. From the frequent reports received of the uncleanliness of the fort (the quarters occupied by the troops in particular) it will be necessary to strictly enforce the following regulations:

     II. Commanding officers of Companies will be held strictly responsible that the quarters occupied by their companies are kept perfectly clean in every respect. A non-commissioned officer in each casemate should be designated daily to report any wilful neglect of any man to keep his quarters clean, that such men may be punished or furnished with less comfortable quarters.

III. The rooms will be swept as often as it may be necessary to keep them perfectly clean. The spit-boxes shall be emptied and clean sand placed in them each morning. The blankets shall be taken out of the fort, well shaken and aired twice each week. The bunks and floors shall be well scrubbed and rubbed dry twice each week.

IV. No food or eatables of any kind will be allowed in the quarters. Nothing but the army equipments and clothing of the men will be allowed in the casemates.

V. No spitting on the floor or on the walks in front of the casemates.

VI. All officers and soldiers will be held responsible that the above regulations are strictly observed.

By order of
Maj. C. C. Graves
Comm'dg. Post[3]

Bathing: Army regulations of the period provided that where conveniences for bathing were available, soldiers should bathe at least once a week and wash their feet twice a week. In 1870, Assistant Surgeon Elliott Coues reported at Fort Macon that: "There are no bath or wash-rooms—the men wash under a shed in the ditch at the postern gate . . . The sea affords constant bathing facilities in summer, there is no special provision for bathing in the winter."[4] The following order issued just after the close of the Civil War provides an idea of how this was carried out at Fort Macon:

Headquarters, Fort Macon, N.C.
June 26th, 1865

General Orders
<u>No 20</u>

    I. On Tuesdays, Thursdays and Saturdays between the hours of 7½ and 8½ a.m. the Garrison will bathe at the beach between the Sutler's shop and first point of Rocks East.

    II. The men will be formed by the 1st Sergeant and the whole will be conducted by the Officer of the Day to the beach who will cause every man to bathe.

    III. In case of bad weather on the days above mentioned the bathing will be on the succeeding day.

    IV. No man will be excused from bathing except by their Company Commander and it is recommended that no man be excused except in a case of the most urgent necessity.

    V. It is absolutely necessary that the most rigid cleanliness be observed not only for the comfort but health and even lives of all.

    VI. Company Commanders will see that their men change their underclothing at least twice a week and that the clothes are clean when changed.

    VII. Sufficient time is given between drill hours for all to wash and no excuses can be allowed for uncleanliness.

By order of Lt. Col. W. S. Poor, Com'dg.
Henry Hallem
1st Lt., 14th U.S.C.A. H., Post Hdqr.[5]

Sanitary Facilities: In 1870, Assistant Surgeon Coues wrote that "all slops and garbage are twice daily removed by the prisoners, in barrels, and thrown far out upon the beach, where they are partly devoured by birds and crabs, and partly washed away by the tide . . . " As for toilet facilities, he wrote that "a large and well-constructed sink (or privy) is located at the edge of the marsh, within high water-mark so that the excreta are constantly carried away by the tide."[6] The sink was about 200 yards from the fort's walls, which one officer inspecting the fort in 1869 found to be deplorable. In his official report the inspector wrote that "the officers themselves and the ladies of their families, are obliged, in obeying the calls of nature, to pass out by the guard and in full view of the entire command, to privies located at least two hundred yards from their quarters, and beyond the limits of the slope of the glacis. It is easy to perceive the inconvenience and indelicacy to which ladies are subjected by this disgraceful condition of things . . ."[7]

Drinking Water: The fort's four cisterns were intended to supply drinking water for the garrison. Early on, the water was found to be brackish and unsuitable for consumption despite all efforts to correct the condition. For a time, drinking water was furnished locally under contract. Afterward two surface wells were dug at the edge of the fort glacis which supplied the necessary water for fort garrisons. The water in the fort cisterns was used only for washing but was available under emergency or battle conditions.

Laundresses: Army regulations of the period allowed each company to have up to four washerwomen, or laundresses, who were hired to do the laundry of its soldiers. Laundresses received one ration per day and were paid according to a fixed amount set by the council of administration of each post. In the case of Fort Macon their pay was $1 per month per soldier. They usually also had quarters provided on post, although in the case of Fort Macon the quarters were usually in poor condition.[8] The women hired as laundresses might be the wives of enlisted men of a company or women living near the post. Women hired from outside the post were usually required to furnish certificates of good character to reduce the chance of prostitution taking place.

Daily Routine: The daily routine of a soldier at Fort Macon differed only slightly regardless of which period the fort was occupied. The following orders reflect a typical day in the life of a soldier at Fort Macon:

Headquarters, Fort Macon
May 10th, 1863

Order No. 2

Until further orders the following calls will be observed in this Garrison.

Reveille	At Sunrise	Roll Call
Breakfast	5:30 a.m.	
Drill (as Infantry)	6:00 "	
Recall	7:00 "	
Surgeon's Call	8:00 "	
Fatigue Call	8:30 "	
Drill (as Artillery)	9:00 "	
Recall	11:00 "	
Recall from fatigue	11:45 "	
1st Sergeant's Call	12:00 M	
Dinner	12:00 "	
Fatigue Call	1:00 p.m.	
Recall from fatigue	4:00 "	
Drill (as Artillery)	4:30 "	
Recall	5:30 "	
Supper	6:00 ^"	
Retreat	At Sunset	Roll Call
Tattoo	8:30 p.m.	Roll Call
Taps	9:00 "	

Immediately after Guard Mounting the Old Guard, superintended by the Sergeant of the Guard, will discharge their pieces at a target, and the best shot will be recorded.

Henry M. Stone
James L. Belden   Major, 3d N.Y. Artillery
  Post Adjutant   Com'g Post[9]

By contrast the soldier of the nineteenth century would have been very envious of his twentieth century counterpart stationed at Fort Macon in World War II. Although some of the fort's casemates in World War II were again used as soldier quarters for part of the troops stationed at the fort, the difference in living conditions was great. Casemates housed only ten to fifteen men each. Field cots were used early in the war but were afterward replaced by individual metal bunks. Bed linens were even provided once a week. The casemates were heated by coal-burning space heaters and were provided with electric lights. Part of the soldiers stationed at Fort Macon also lived outside the fort. In the early part of the war these men lived in tents but afterward were quartered in wooden barracks buildings. The troops had running water and sewage systems. Latrine buildings were located just outside the fort and, at about the middle of the war, one of the fort casemates was even turned into a latrine.

Appendix Four

CASEMATE USES

The twenty-six main casemates and five angle casemates of Fort Macon's citadel have been used at different times over the years for different purposes. In general they provided quarters for the fort's various garrisons, cells for prisoners, storage, and support facilities. The following plan shows casemate numbers and their uses over the years:

Casemate 1: is the main sally port.

Casemate 2: was the fort's guard room until after the Civil War when it became an office for the commandant or post adjutant.

Casemate 3: was used sometimes as an office, at other times as quarters for staff, and sometimes for storage.

Angle Casemate 3A: was usually used for storage and at times as an officers' mess.

Angle Casemate 4A: was used as the officers' kitchen. Its freestanding fireplace and oven was destroyed by the Army in World War II to create storage space.

Casemate 4: was usually used as the officers' mess room.

Casemate 5–8: were usually officers' quarters. Casemate 5 was the post commandant's quarters during Union occupation in the Civil War and

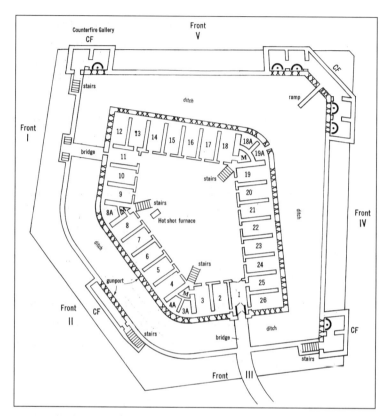

Diagram of Fort Macon showing casemate layout and numbering.

probably was also the quarters of Colonel Moses J. White during Confederate occupation. Casemate 6 was also used as the post library and
school for soldiers' children during the early 1870s.

Angle Casemate 8A: was used for officers' quarters, storage, and as a kitchen
in the 1870s. It was the Commanding Officer's office in World War II.

Casemate 9: was used for soldier quarters, at one point as a dispensary, and
as a company messroom in the 1870s.

Casemate 10: was used as soldier quarters or an office.

Casemate 11: was the main postern. It was utilized as a company messroom, and later as a prison messroom during the prison period.

Casemate 12: was the post bakehouse, fitted out with a large brick baking oven until it was destroyed by the Army in World War II to create storage space.

Casemate 13: was used as a kitchen. None of the kitchen facilities survive today.

Casemate 14: was used as quarters for enlisted men and at times as a company messroom.

Casemate 15–17: were always used as quarters for enlisted men.

Casemate 18: was used for ordnance storage, or quarters for enlisted men.

Angle Casemate 18A: was used for ordnance storage.

Angle Casemate 19A: is the rear postern with an entrance leading to counterfire galleries under the covertway. It was also used for ordnance storage.

Casemate 19: was used as a Quartermaster storeroom, as quarters for enlisted men, and as a prison cell during the prison period.

Casemate 20–22: were normally used as enlisted mens' quarters, and as prison cells during the prison period.

Casemate 23: was a kitchen and messroom into the Civil War and afterward was used as a prison cell during the prison period.

Casemate 24: was used as a Commissary Storeroom, and at times as a prison cell during the prison period.

Casemate 25: was used at times prior to the prison period as an Ordnance, Quartermaster or Commissary Storeroom. During the prison period it was used as a guard room.

Casemate 26: was originally intended as the fort's prison cell for prisoners of war and convicts. During the prison period, however, it was used as a Commissary or Quartermaster Storeroom.

Under the covertway are four rooms called counterfire galleries (CF) which defended the ditch against the possibility of assault parties crossing from the covertway to reach the citadel.

FOOTNOTES

Chapter 1

1. W. L. Saunders (ed.), *The Colonial Records of North Carolina,* (Raleigh: State of North Carolina, 10 volumes, 1886–90), II, 454, cited hereafter as *Colonial Records*; Walter Clark (ed.), *The State Records of North Carolina,* (Winston, Goldsboro, and Raleigh: State of North Carolina, 16 volumes, 1895–1914), XXV, 206, cited hereafter as *State Records*; Charles L. Paul, "Colonial Beaufort", *N. C. Historical Review,* XLII, April, 1965, 143–46.

2. *State Records,* XXV, 206–09; *Colonial Records,* III, 208, 336.

3. David Stick, *The Outer Banks of North Carolina, 1584–1958,* Chapel Hill, University of North Carolina Press, 1958, 35–36; *State Records,* XXII, iii; Charles L. Paul, "Beaufort, North Carolina: Its Development as a Colonial Town", *N.C. Historical Review,* XLVII, October, 1970, 379–80; Charleston *South Carolina Gazette,* November 7, 1741, January 9, 1742.

4. *Colonial Records,* V, 598.

5. *Colonial Records,* IV, 922; *State Records,* XXII, iii, 262–68.

6. *Colonial Records,* IV, 863–66, 922; *State Records,* XXIII, 292–96.

7. *Colonial Records,* V, 595.

8. *Colonial Records,* V, 345; *State Records,* XXIII, 293.

9. *Colonial Records,* V, 345.

10. *Colonial Records,* V, 597. This fort is not to be confused with another fort of the same name built near present-day Statesville, NC, to guard the colony's western frontier.

11. In addition to Fort Dobbs and Fort Johnston on the Cape Fear, Fort Granville was built on Portsmouth Island at Ocracoke Inlet with a similar construction to Fort Dobbs, only larger. Governor Dobbs also sent several petitions for a large fort to guard the harbor formed by the bight of nearby Cape Lookout, with which he was greatly impressed. The war ended before any action was taken on fortifying Cape Lookout. See *Colonial Records,* V, 345–47, 597–99, 646; *Ibid.,* VIII, 30–31.

12. *Ibid.,* V, 597, 803, 909.

13. *Ibid.,* V, 802–05, 974.

14. David Stick, *The Outer Banks of North Carolina, 1584–1958,* Chapel Hill, University of North Carolina Press, 1958, 45–47; *Colonial Records,* X, 549–50.

15. *State Records,* XI, xx; *Colonial Records,* X, 546–47; Hugh T. Lefler and Albert R. Newsome,

The History of a Southern State, North Carolina, Chapel Hill, University of North Carolina Press, 1973, 237–38.

16. *State Records,* XI, 632–33; David Stick, *The Outer Banks of North Carolina, 1584–1958,* Chapel Hill, University of North Carolina Press, 1958, 54–55; Hugh T. Lefler and Albert R. Newsome, *The History of a Southern State, North Carolina,* Chapel Hill, University of North Carolina Press, 1973, 237–38.

17. *State Records,* XI, 623–25, 774.

18. N.C. State Archives, General Assembly Session Records, November-December, 1777, House of Commons, Joint Papers, Petitions: "Petition of the Sundry Inhabitants of Carteret County, December 4, 1777"; *State Records.,* XII, 359–60.

19. New Bern, *North Carolina Gazette,* May 15, 1778.

20. *State Records,* XV, 215–18.

21. *Ibid.,* XXIV, 174.

22. *Ibid.,* XII, 614; *Ibid.,* XIII, 121–22, 126–27, 199, 311–13. Captain de Cottineau returned to France, where the *Ferdinand,* renamed the *La Pallas,* became part of the squadron of American Captain John Paul Jones. In the famous sea battle off Flamborough Head, England, on September 23, 1779, in which Jones in his ship *Bon Homme Richard* defeated the British frigate *Serapis,* Captain de Cottineau took a prominent part.

23. *Ibid.,* XV, 389.

24. Charles Biddle, *The Autobiography of Charles Biddle* (Philadelphia, E. Claxton and Company, 1883), 127.

25. *State Records,* XVI, 286.

26. Colonel Easton's detailed report of the British attack appears in N.C. State Archives, Governors' Papers, Thomas Burke, G.P. 8, 125–26. See also Jean B. Kell (ed.), *North Carolina's Coastal Carteret County During the American Revolution, 1765–1785,* Greenville, Era Press, 1975.

27. See *State Records,* XVI, 284–85, 290–91, 593–95, 601–02.

Chapter 2

1. *American State Papers, Military Affairs,* (Washington, D. C., Gales and Seaton, 1832–

1861, 7 volumes), I 61–4, 71–108, cited hereafter as *ASP; Statutes at Large and Treaties of the United States of America, 1789–1873,* (Boston, Little, Brown and Company, 1845–73), I, 345–47, cited hereafter as *Statutes at Large; Annals of Congress: Debates and Proceedings in the Congress of the United States . . . ,* (Washington, Gales and Seaton, 1834–56, 42 volumes), 3rd Congress, IV, 1423–24.

2. *Statutes at Large,* I, 554; *ASP,* I, 192–96.

3. *ASP,* I, 224.

4. *Annals of Congress: Debates and Proceedings in the Congress of the United States . . . ,* XV, 10th Congress, first session, 992–94; *Statutes at Large,* II, 453; *ASP,* I, 219–22. In addition to fortifications, the appropriation also would fund the construction of 257 wooden coastal gunboats to patrol the coast and inland waters.

5. *Statutes at Large,* II, 228; *Laws of North Carolina, 1807,* Chapter XVII, 11; *ASP,* II, 286. Of the three North Carolina sites selected in the Second System, Beaufort was the only one of new construction. The Cape Fear Site involved the completion of Fort Johnston, as yet unfinished from the First System. At Ocracoke, the engineers eventually decided against building any fortifications there.

6. National Archives Microfilm Collection, M417, Herbert Buell Collection of Engineer Records: Colonel Jonathan Williams to Secretary of War, February 29, 1808; Major Alexander Macomb to Secretary of War, August 10, 1808. RG (Record Group) 94, E 465, Outline Index of Military Forts and Stations and Reservations, Vol. H, p.27, National Archives, gives the origin of the name as being Colonel Andrew Hampton. However, the *Raleigh Observer,* August 2, 1877, cites the possibility of the fort being named after General Wade Hampton, the South Carolina cavalry officer distinguished in the Southern Campaigns of the Revolutionary War.

7. *Raleigh Observer,* August 2, 1877. No details of Fort Hampton's construction are known to exist beyond general procedures used by the Army Engineers at this time. However, an interesting account of how the Army Engineers built

tapia forts in this period was given by Lieutenant Joseph G. Swift, working on Fort Johnston, NC, in 1805. In his *Memoirs of Gen. Joseph Gardner Swift, LL.D., U.S.A., First Graduate of the United States Military Academy, West Point, Chief Engineer, U.S.A. from 1812 to 1818. 1800–1865* (Privately printed, 1890), 54, Swift wrote: "Soon after this the slaves . . . commenced the burning of lime in pens, called kilns, formed of sapling pines formed in squares containing from one thousand to one thousand two hundred bushels of oyster shells (alive) collected in scows from the shoals in the harbor—there abundant. These pens were filled with alternate layers of shells and 'light wood' from pitch pine and thus were burned in about one day—very much to the annoyance of the neighborhood by the smoke and vapor of burning shellfish, when the wind was strong enough to spread the fumes of the kilns. In the succeeding month of November I commenced the battery by constructing boxes of the dimensions of the parapet, six feet high by seven in thickness, into which boxes was poured the tapia composition, consisting of equal parts of lime, raw shells and sand, and water sufficient to form a species of paste, or batter, as the negroes term it." Fort Hampton would also have been built in this manner.

8. Two maps showing plans and profiles of Fort Hampton exist in the Cartographic and Architectural Branch of the National Archives, College Park, Md., in RG 77, Fortifications Files. Macomb's 1808 plan (Drawer 61, Sheet 2) is reproduced here since it shows more details of the fort. The second map, Drawer 61, Sheet 1, by Captain William T. Poussin in 1820, represents how the fort actually was built and is more accurate as to dimensions and measurement, which are cited here.

9. *ASP*, I, 246–47; *Ibid.*, II, 286; RG 153, E 56, North Carolina, National Archives; A. R. Newsome, "A Miscellany from the Thomas Henderson Letterbook, 1810–11", *North Carolina Historical Review*, October, 1929, 400.

10. *Carolina Federal Republican* (New Bern), July 25, August 8, November 14, 1812, December 4, 1813; *Raleigh Register*, November 20, 1812;

Sarah McCulloh Lemmon, *North Carolina in the War of 1812* (Raleigh, N.C. Department of Archives and History, 1971), 33–35, cited hereafter as *N.C. in the War of 1812*.

11. *Carolina Federal Republican*, May 29, December 4, 1813; *N.C. in the War of 1812*, 36.

12. *Carolina Federal Republican*, December 14, 1813.

13. *Ibid.*, July 17, July 24, July 31, November 27, 1813; *Raleigh Register*, July 23, July 30, August 6, 1813.

14. *Carolina Federal Republican*, November 27, 1813.

15. *Ibid.*, July 31, August 28, November 27, December 4, 1813; *Raleigh Register*, December 17, 1813. Bryant subsequently claimed in a letter to his father in Halifax a British frigate and sloop approached almost to within cannonshot of the fort, but the people of Beaufort denied this ever happened.

16. *Carolina Federal Republican*, July 24, July 31, November 27, 1813.

17. *Ibid.*, November 27, 1813.

18. *Ibid.*, November 27, December 4, 1813.

19. National Archives Microfilm Collection, M417, Herbert Buell Collection of Engineer Records: Lieut. Colonel W. K. Armistead to Secretary of War, January 25, 1814, National Archives.

20. *Carolina Federal Republican*, May 28, 1814.

21. *N.C. in the War of 1812*, 38; *Carolina Federal Republican*, July 9, July 16, July 23, July 26, 1814.

22. *Raleigh Register*, June 2, July 7, 1815.

23. *ASP*, II, 789.

24. See RG 77, Fortifications Files, Fort Macon, Drawer 61, Sheet 1, Cartographic and Architectural Branch, National Archives, College Park, Md.

25. See RG 77, Civil Works Map File, Maps H 28 and H 39, Cartographic and Architectural Branch, National Archives, College Park, Md.

26. See RG 77, Fortifications Files, Fort Macon, Drawer 61, Sheet 7, Cartographic and Architectural Branch, National Archives, College Park, Md.

Chapter 3

1. Bernard's appointment caused much criticism and even some resignations among officers of the Corps of Engineers who considered the choice of a foreign engineer to head the Board over native-born engineers an affront to their abilities and training. Nevertheless, Bernard remained as head of the Board for fifteen years before returning to France in 1831. Other Board members came and went over the years with one exception, the gifted Lieut. Colonel (later Brigadier General) Joseph G. Totten, who was to be one of the major driving forces behind Third System fortifications until his death in 1864.

2. See RG 77, Fortifications Files, Fort Macon, Drawer 61, Sheets 4 and 6, Cartographic and Architectural Branch, National Archives, College Park, Md.

3. RG 77, E 18: Lieut. W. A. Eliason to Maj. Gen. Alexander Macomb, March 25, 1826, E10, National Archives. Textual records and documents in the collection of the National Archives will hereafter be identified by record group (RG) number, followed by the entry (E) number within the record group where the records and documents may be found. For the identification of the various record groups and entries within them, consult the bibliography.

4. *Register of Debates in Congress* (Washington, Gales and Seaton, 1825–37, 14 volumes), I, 681.

5. *Ibid.*, 519, 667–70, 680–81.

6. RG 77, E 219: Maj. Gen. Alexander Macomb to Lieut. S. Tuttle, June 29, 1825, National Archives; *ASP*, III, 136.

7. *Ibid.*; RG 77, E 14: Lieut. W. A. Eliason to Maj. Gen. Alexander Macomb, November 3, 1825, E2609, National Archives.

8. RG 77, E 18: Lieut. W. A. Eliason to Maj. Gen. Alexander Macomb, January 1, 1826, E1, National Archives; RG 153, E 56: Reservations Files, Fort Macon, N.C., National Archives; *Laws of North Carolina*, 1825 Session (Raleigh, Bell and Lawrence, 1826), Chapter XXV, 15.

9. *Carolina Sentinel* (New Bern), January 7,

1826; RG 77, E 18: Lieut. W. A. Eliason to Maj. Gen. Alexander Macomb, January 1, 1826, E1, and March 25, 1826, E10, National Archives.

10. *Register of Debates in Congress* (Washington, Gales and Seaton, 1825–37, 14 volumes), 1825-26, II, part 1, 1233–37.

11. RG 77, E 14: Lieut. W. A. Eliason to Maj. Gen. Alexander Macomb, November 3, 1825, E2609; E 18: February 8, 1826, E2; March 25, 1826, E10, National Archives. See also RG 77, Fortifications Files, Fort Macon, Drawer 61, Sheets 7–9, Cartographic and Architectural Branch, National Archives, College Park, Md.

12. RG 77, E 18: Lieut. W. A. Eliason to Maj. Gen. Alexander Macomb, March 25, 1826, E10, National Archives. Not included in these figures was the cost of fort's intended armament of thirty-eight guns, four mortars and eight carronades, which totalled $26,394 (*ASP*, III, p. 258, Table B).

13. *Ibid.*

14. *Ibid.*

15. RG 77, E 18: Lieut. W. A. Eliason to Maj. Gen. Alexander Macomb, Memorial Accompanying the Yearly Report for September 30, 1826, E27, National Archives.

16. *Ibid.;* RG 77, E 18: Lieut. W. A. Eliason to Maj. Gen. Alexander Macomb, July 14, 1826, E16, National Archives.

17. RG 77, E 18: Lieut. W. A. Eliason to Maj. Gen. Alexander Macomb, August 5, 1826, E21; August 19, 1826, E 23; September 2, 1826, E24; Memorial Accompanying the Yearly Report for September 30, 1826, E27, National Archives; *Carolina Sentinel*, September 2, 1826.

18. *Laws of North Carolina,* 1825 Session (Raleigh, Bell and Lawrence, 1826), Chapter XXV, 15; RG 153, E 56, North Carolina, Fort Macon, National Archives.

19. *Laws of North Carolina,* 1826 Session (Raleigh, Bell and Lawrence, 1827), Chapter XX, 12–13; RG 77, E 18: Lieut. W. A. Eliason to Maj. Gen. Alexander Macomb, October 8, 1826, E31, National Archives.

20. RG 77, E 18: Lieut. W. A. Eliason to Maj. Gen. Alexander Macomb, November 9, 1826,

E32/33; June 15, 1827, E64, National Archives; *Carolina Sentinel*, December 23, 1826.

21. *Carolina Sentinel*, October 28, 1826; RG 77, E 18: Lieut. W. A. Eliason to Maj. Gen. Alexander Macomb, Memorial Accompanying the Yearly Report for September 30, 1826, E27, National Archives.

22. RG 77, E 18: Otway Burns to Secretary of War J. H. Eaton, October 19, 1829, B836/837; James Manney to Capt. John L. Smith, October 25, 1827, S304, Enclosure 4; Lieut. W. A. Eliason to Maj. Gen. Alexander Macomb, Yearly Report for September 30, 1826, E27; National Archives.

23. RG 77, E 18: Lieut. W. A. Eliason to Maj. Gen. Alexander Macomb, April 27, 1827, E57; June 15, 1827, E64, National Archives; *Carolina Sentinel*, June 30, 1827.

24. RG 77, E 18: Lieut. W. A. Eliason to Maj. Gen. Alexander Macomb, June 30, 1827, E65; February 23, 1828, E104; Captain John L. Smith to Maj. Gen. Alexander Macomb, Annual Memoir, October 25, 1827, S299, National Archives.

25. RG 77, E 18: Capt. John L. Smith to Maj. Gen. Alexander Macomb, July 26, 1827, S253; September 1, 1827, S273; Annual Memoir, October 25, 1827, S299, National Archives.

26. RG 77, E 18: Capt. John L. Smith to Maj. Gen. Alexander Macomb, Annual Memoir, October 25, 1827, S299; Capt. John L. Smith to Maj. Gen. Alexander Macomb, October 30, 1827, S304 and enclosures; November 5, 1827, S306; November 20, 1827, S313; January 7, 1828, S340, National Archives; *ASP*, III, 628.

27. *Raleigh Register*, September 11, 1827; RG 77, E 18: Capt. John L. Smith to Maj. Gen. Alexander Macomb, Annual Memoir, October 25, 1827, S299.

28. RG 77, E 18: Capt. John L. Smith to Maj. Gen. Alexander Macomb, Annual Memoir, October 25, 1827, S299; Lieut. W. A. Eliason to Brig. Gen. Charles Gratiot, October 18, 1828, E154, National Archives; *Carolina Sentinel*, August 31, September 26, November 3, 1827.

29. RG 77, E 18: Capt. John L. Smith to Maj. Gen. Alexander Macomb, November 28, 1827, S315; Lieut. W. A. Eliason to Brig. Gen. Charles Gratiot, October 18, 1828, E154, National Archives.

30. *Ibid.*; Lieut. W. A. Eliason to Brig. Gen. Charles Gratiot, October 25, 1829, E224, National Archives.

31. RG 77, E 18: Lieut. W. A. Eliason to Brig. Gen. Charles Gratiot, November 5, 1829, E229; January 23, 1830, E252; Otway Burns to Brig. Gen. Charles Gratiot, October 19, 1829, B836/837, National Archives.

32. RG 77, E 18: Lieut. W. A. Eliason to Brig. Gen. Charles Gratiot, October 25, 1829, E224, National Archives.

33. *Ibid.*; Lieut. W. A. Eliason to Brig. Gen. Charles Gratiot, November 5, 1829, E229; January 23, 1830, E252; Otway Burns to Brig. Gen. Charles Gratiot, October 19, 1829, B836/837, National Archives.

34. RG 77, E 18: Lieut. W. A. Eliason to Brig. Gen. Charles Gratiot, April 17, 1830, E268; Lieut. W. A. Eliason to Brig. Gen. Charles Gratiot, August 1, 1830, E280; Capt. John L. Smith to Brig. Gen. Charles Gratiot, August 17, 1830, S1084; August 18, 1830, S1085; October 24, 1830, S1129, National Archives.

35. RG 77, E 18: Capt. John L. Smith to Brig. Gen. Charles Gratiot, October 24, 1830, S1129, National Archives.

36. RG 77, E 18: Capt. John L. Smith to Brig. Gen. Charles Gratiot, October 23, 1831, S1428, National Archives.

37. RG 77, E 18: Capt. John L. Smith to Brig. Gen. Charles Gratiot, October 13, 1832, S1715, National Archives; *ASP*, IV, 728.

38. RG 77, E 18: Capt. John L. Smith to Brig. Gen. Charles Gratiot, October 24, 1830, S1129; October 23, 1831, S1428; October 13, 1832, S1715, National Archives.

39. RG 77, E 18: Capt. John L. Smith to Brig. Gen. Charles Gratiot, October 13, 1832, S1715; Lieut. George Dutton to Brig. Gen. Charles Gratiot, March 22, 1833, D938; April 14, 1833, D952; November 1, 1833, D1083, National Archives.

40. RG 92, E 225: Maj. R. M. Kirby to Adjutant General R. Jones, December 8, 1833; Maj.

R. N. Kirby to Maj. Gen. T. Jessup, December 8, 1833, K1, National Archives.

41. RG 77, E 18: Lieut. George Dutton to Brig. Gen. Charles Gratiot, October 14, 1834, D1338, National Archives.

42. RG 92, E 225: Maj. R. M. Kirby to Lieut. J. R. Irwin, January 1, 1835, I36, National Archives; *ASP*, V, 662. The other completed Third System forts were: Fort Pike, LA (1824); Fort Macomb, LA (1828); Fort Jackson, LA (1831); Fort Morgan, AL (1834); Fort Pickens, FL (1834); Fort Monroe, VA (1834); Fort Hamilton, NY (1831).

Chapter 4

1. RG 92, E 225: Maj. R. M. Kirby to Lieut. J. R. Irwin, January 1, 1835, I35, National Archives. Among the members of the newly-arrived company was 2nd Lieutenant John Bankhead Magruder, who was destined to achieve notoriety in the Civil War.

2. RG 77, E 18: Maj. R. M. Kirby to Maj. Gen. Alexander Macomb, January 16, 1835, K239 1/2; Lieut. George Dutton to Brig. Gen. Charles Gratiot, April 17, 1835, D1303, National Archives.

3. RG 77, E 18: Lieut. A. J. Swift to Brig. Gen. Charles Gratiot, November 25, 1835, S3036; November 27, 1835, S3042; December 15, 1835, S3057; January 20, 1836, S3105; January 28, 1836, S3115; February 4, 1836, S 3126; February 20, 1836, S3150, National Archives.

4. RG 94, E 12: Maj. R. M. Kirby to Adjutant General R. Jones, February 1, 1836, K10, National Archives; National Archives Microfilm Collection, M617, Rolls 718–19, Post Returns for Fort Macon, 1834–1898, February, 1836, cited hereafter as Post Returns.

5. RG 92, E 225: Ord. Sgt. Peter D. Stewart to Col. Henry Stanton, December 22, 1838, S311; Ord Sgt. Peter D. Stewart to Maj. Gen. T. Jessup, June 3, 1839, S167; October 28, 1839, S503, National Archives.

6. RG 77, E 18: Capt. A. J. Swift to Col. J. G. Totten, June 17, 1839, S703, National Archives; U.S. Congress, Congressional Documents Serial Set, House Document Number 2, *Annual Report*

of the Secretary of War, 1840 (Washington, Government Printing Office, 1841), Serial Set Number 382, 104–05, cited hereafter as *ARSW,* followed by the year.

7. RG 77, E 18: Capt. R. E. Lee to Col. J. G. Totten, January 7, 1841, L280, National Archives.

8. RG 77, E 18: Capt. R. E. Lee to Col. J. G. Totten, January 22, 1841, L286, National Archives.

9. Ibid.; Capt. George Dutton to Col. J. G. Totten, July 8, 1841, D1969; *ARSW,* 1841, 123.

10. RG 77, E 18: Capt. George Dutton to Col. J. G. Totten, July 8, 1841, D1969; September 16, 1841, D1555, National Archives.

11. RG 77, E 18: Capt. George Dutton to Col. J. G. Totten, September 16, 1841, D1555, National Archives.

12. RG 77, E 18: Capt. George Dutton to Col. J. G. Totten, July 8, 1841, D1969; Lieut. J. H. Trapier to Col. J. G. Totten, October 17, 1842, T604, National Archives; *ARSW,* 1842, 254.

13. RG 77, E 18: Capt. George Dutton to Col. J. G. Totten, July 8, 1841, D1969; Lieut. J. H. Trapier to Col. J. G. Totten, October 17, 1842, T604, National Archives; *ARSW,* 1842, 255.

14 RG 77, E 18: Capt. George Dutton to Col. J. G. Totten, July 8, 1841, D1969; Lieut. J. H. Trapier to Col. J. G. Totten, October 17, 1842, T604, National Archives; Post Returns, July, 1842.

15. RG 77, E 18: Lieut. J. H. Trapier to Col. J. G. Totten, October 6, 1843, T734, National Archives; *ARSW,* 1843, 104–05.

16. RG 77, E 18: Lieut. J. H. Trapier to Col. J. G. Totten, October 6, 1843, T734, National Archives; *ARSW,* 1843, 104–05.

17. RG 77, E 18: Lieut. D. P. Woodbury to Col. J. G. Totten, October 21, 1844, W450, National Archives; *ARSW,* 1844, 176–77. No record has yet been found as to when the second hot shot furnace was built other than a reference found in Lieut. J. H. Trapier to Col. J. G. Totten, March 20, 1843, T657, mentioning plans to build the furnace in October of that year. However it seems to have been overlooked in Woodbury's Annual Report of October 21, 1844.

18. RG 77, E 18: Lieut. D. P. Woodbury to Col. J. G. Totten, October 21, 1844, W450; October 15, 1846, W663, National Archives; *ARSW*, 1845, 254 and *Ibid.*, 1846, 124.

19. U.S. Congress, Congressional Documents Serial Set, House Executive Documents Number 5, *Report of the Secretary of War of December 8, 1851, on the Subject of Fortifications, in Answer to a Resolution of the House of Representatives of March 3, 1851*, Table A, (Washington, Government Printing Office, 1852), Serial Set #637, 32nd Congress, 1st Session.

20. RG 92, E 225: Lieut. A. P. Stewart to Maj. Gen. T. Jessup, October, 1842, S185; October 26, 1842, C650 and enclosure; November 24, 1842, S605, National Archives. Among the members of Company F were three officers who were to achieve notoriety in the Civil War: 1st Lieutenant Edward O. C. Ord, 2nd Lieutenant Alexander P. Stewart, and Bvt. 2nd Lieutenant Samuel G. French.

21. RG 92, E 225: Lieut. A. P. Stewart to Maj. Gen. T. Jessup, May 16, 1843, S224; RG 94, E 12: Lieut. E. O. C. Ord to Adjutant General R. Jones, April 28, 1843, O12, National Archives; Capt. J. R. Vinton to Mother, March 29, 1844, John Rogers Vinton Papers, William Perkins Library, Duke University, Durham, N.C., cited hereafter as Vinton Papers.

22. RG 92, E 225: Lieut. C. Q. Tompkins to Brig. Gen. W. K. Armistead, August 21, 1843, T130 and enclosures, National Archives.

23. *Ibid.*; Capt. W. Wall to Maj. Gen. T. Jessup, October 15, 1843, W218, National Archives.

24. RG 92, E 225: Capt. W. Wall to Maj. Gen. T. Jessup, February 16, 1844, W 291; RG 77, E 18: Lieut. Charles Thomas to Chief of Engineers, October 15, 1844, T97, National Archives; Post Returns, February, 1844.

25. See various letters in Vinton Papers.

26. RG 77, E 18: Lieut. D. P. Woodbury to Col. J. G. Totten, October 21, 1844, W450, National Archives; Capt. J. R. Vinton to Mother, February 19, 1844; September 21, 1844, Vinton Papers.

27. Post Returns, October and November, 1844. Included with Vinton's half-company was

a detachment of new recruits which had just arrived at Fort Macon only days before under 2nd Lieutenant Robert S. Garnett, later of Civil War fame (RG 94, E 12: Capt. J. R. Vinton to Adj. Gen. R. Jones, November 22, 1844, V78, National Archives). Captain John R. Vinton later had the unfortunate distinction of being one of the few American officers killed in the Mexican War, dying from a shell explosion at the siege of Vera Cruz, March 22, 1847.

28. RG 92, E 225: Capt. Henry Swartwout to Maj. Gen. T. Jessup, October 13, 1848, S130, National Archives.

29. Post Returns, October, 1848, and October, 1849.

30. See *ARSW*, 1850–1855; RG 77, E 18: Lieut. D. P. Woodbury to Col. J. G. Totten, August 16, 1854, W1447, National Archives; *A Compilation of Public Documents and Extracts from Reports and Papers relating to Lighthouses, Light-Vessels, and Illuminating Apparatus, and to beacons, buoys and fog signals, 1789–1871* (Washington, Government Printing Office, 1871).

31. See *ARSW*, 1856–1860; RG 77, E 18: Capt. J. G. Foster to Col. J. G. Totten, December 30, 1858, F1773; Ord. Sgt. Thomas Dailey to Col. J. G. Totten, September 14, 1857, D5444, National Archives.

32. *ARSW*, 1859-1860; RG 77, E 18: Capt. J. G. Foster to Col. J. G. Totten, June 25, 1859, F1809, National Archives.

Chapter 5

1. RG 156, E 3: Col. H. K. Craig to Ord. Sgt. William Alexander, April 12, 1861, Letterbook of Letters Setn, June 1860, to May, 1861, 569, National Archives.

2. RG 156, E 21: Ord. Sgt. William Alexander to Col. H. K. Craig, April 14, 1861, A108, National Archives.

3. RG 94, E 12: Ord. Sgt. William Alexander to Col. L. Thomas, April 26, 1861, A241 and enclosures; April 30, 1861, A243A, National Archives; *Raleigh North Carolina Standard*, April 24, 1861; *Charleston Mercury*, April 19, 1861; *Wilmington Daily Journal*, April 17, 1861.

4. U. S. War Department, *The War of Rebellion: A Compilation of the Official Records of the Union and Confederate Armies* (Washington, Government Printing Office, 1880–1901, 70 volumes in 128 parts), I, 476–77; LI, Part 2, 11. Cited hereafter as *OR*, all references being to Series I unless otherwise noted.

5. OR, I, 486; Ibid., Series III, I, 67–69, 72; Noble J. Tolbert, *The Papers of John Willis Ellis* (Raleigh, N.C. Department of Archives and History, 1964, two volumes), II, 612–13, 619, Cited hereafter as *John W. Ellis Papers; Raleigh North Carolina Standard,* May 1, 1861; "Wayne County Troops in the Civil War," Military Collections, Civil War Collection, Box 76, N. C. State Archives.

6. Record of the Corps of Engineers, Fort Macon, 1861, Alexander Justice Papers, Southern Historical Collection, University of N.C., Chapel Hill, p. 1–4, 19, Cited hereafter as Engineer Record.

7. Engineer Record, see various daily entries for work done.

8. *New Bern Daily Progress,* April 17–20, April 23–25, 1861; *Fayetteville Observer,* April 22, 1861; *Raleigh Register,* April 24, 1861; *Raleigh North Carolina Standard,* May 1, 1861; *Charlotte Western Democrat,* April 30, 1861; John A. Sloan, *Reminiscences of the Guilford Grays, Company B, 27th North Carolina Regiment* (Washington, D. C., R. O. Polkinborn, 1883), 22; Louis Manarin and Weymouth T. Jordan, Jr. (ed.) *North Carolina Troops, 1861–1865: A Roster* (Raleigh, N.C. Department of Archives and History, 1968–93), Vol. V, 308–09; Vol. VIII, 31, Cited hereafter as *NCT.*

9. *NCT,* I, 124; *New Bern Daily Progress,* April 24–27, April 30, 1861; Records of N. C. Adjutant General's Office, AG 13, pp. 13, 62, N.C. State Archives.

10. *Raleigh North Carolina Standard,* May 1, 1861; *New Bern Daily Progress,* April 25, April 29, April 30, 1861; *Hillsboro Recorder,* May 8, 1861.

11. James A. Graham to Mother, April 22, June 17, 1861, James A. Graham Papers, Southern Historical Collection, University of N. C., Chapel Hill; *Raleigh North Carolina Standard,* May 1, 1861; *Charlotte Western Democrat,* May 14, 1861.

12. *New Bern Daily Progress,* April 20, April 24, April 27, 1861; *Charlotte Western Democrat,* April 30, 1861; *Wilmington Daily Journal,* April 18, 1861; *Raleigh North Carolina Standard,* May 8, 1861; Mrs. John Huske Anderson, *North Carolina Women of the Confederacy* (Fayetteville, Mrs. John Huske Anderson, 1926), 110–111; John A. Sloan, *Reminiscences of the Guilford Grays, Company B, 27th North Carolina Regiment* (Washington, R. O. Polkinborn 1883) 22; James A Graham to Mother, May 8, 1861, James A. Graham Papers, Southern Historical Collection, University of N.C., Chapel Hill.

13. John A. Sloan, *Reminiscences of the Guilford Grays, Company B, 27th North Carolina Regiment* (Washington, R. O. Polkinborn, 1883), 22; *New Bern Daily Progress,* May 24, 1861.

14. *New Bern Daily Progress,* April 22, 1861; *Charleston Mercury,* April 17, 1861; *John W. Ellis Papers,* II, 721..

15. *OR,* LI, Part 2, 13–14; *Charleston Courier,* April 19, 1861; *New Bern Daily Progress,* April 22, 1861; *John W. Ellis Papers,* II, 622, 628; Engineer Record, 17.

16. RG 109, Department of North Carolina, Wilmington Command, Chapter II, Volume 331, Letterbook of Letters Sent and Orders, April–May, 1861, pp. 39–40, 42, 52, National Archives; *John W. Ellis Papers,* II, 721; Engineer Record, 43, 51, 53, 56, 57, 63, 65, 68; *New Bern Daily Progress,* June 11, 1861; *Raleigh Register,* September 11, 1861.

17. *John W. Ellis Papers,* II, 696; *OR,* I, 488; LI, Part 2, 60; Engineer Record, 57.

18. Engineer Record, 69,70, 74. 75, 80, 81.

19. *OR,* I, 486–87; LI, Part 2, 84, 85; Engineer Record, 24, 65, 68, 72–74, 82–83, 86, 89.

20. Statement of Deficiencies and Wants of Ordnance and Ordnance Stores at Fort Macon, May 31, 1861, Papers of Governor John W. Ellis, G.P. 151, N.C. State Archives; *OR,* LI, Part 2, 116, 120.

21. *New Bern Daily Progress,* June 4, June 18, July 1, 1861; Journal of Company B, 10th North Carolina, William A. Hoke Papers, Vol. V, Southern Historical Collection, University of N.C. ,

Chapel Hill, Cited hereafter as Journal of Company B.

22. Walter Clark (ed.), *History of Several Regiments and Battalions from North Carolina in the Great War, 1861–65; Written by Members of the Respective Commands* (Raleigh and Goldsboro, Nash Brothers, 1901, 5 volumes), Vol. II, 425–27, Cited hereafter as *NCR*; *NCT*, I, 40; III, 379; Capt. Pride Jones to Gov. H. T. Clark, July 17, 1861, Asa Biggs to Gov. H. T. Clark, July 18, 1861, Papers of Governor Henry T. Clark, G.P. 152, N.C. State Archives; Journal of Company B. Colonel Tew would later be killed at the battle of Sharpsburg, September 17, 1862.

23. *OR*, Series IV, I, 402–04; *Raleigh North Carolina Standard*, September 25, 1861; Capt. H. T. Guion to John D. Whitford, July 13, July 15, 1861, John D. Whitford Papers, #89.3, N.C. State Archives, Cited hereafter as Whitford Papers; Engineer Records, 82, 83, 86, 89, 105.

24. *Raleigh North Carolina Standard*, September 25, 1861; Engineer Record, 94; U.S. Navy Department, *Official Records of the Union and Confederate Navies in the War of Rebellion* (Washington, Government Printing Office, 1894–1927, 30 volumes), VI, 713–14, Cited hereafter as *NOR*, all references being to Series I.

25. Engineer Record, see various entries, pages 65–96.

26. *New Bern Daily Progress*, August 26, 1861; NCR, I, 500; National Archives Microfilm Collection, M270, Compiled Military Service Records of Confederate Soldiers, North Carolina, 10th Regiment (1st Artillery), Record of Events for Companies F and H, Cited hereafter as M270, 10th N.C. Service Records.

27. Engineer Record, 105; Records of N.C. Adjutant General's Office, AG 22, 352, N.C. State Archives; Col. J. A. J. Bradford to Gov. H. T. Clark, August 20, 1861, Papers of Governor Henry T. Clark, G.P. 153, N.C. State Archives.

28. A good account of this first battle appears in John G. Barrett, *The Civil War in North Carolina*, Chapel Hill, University of N.C. Press, 1963, pp. 36–45.

29. *Charlotte Western Democrat*, October 8, 1861; *NOR*, VI, 713–14; *OR*, IV, 638.

30. *Charlotte Western Democrat*, October 8, 1861; NCT, VI, 118–19; William H. Parker, *Recollections of a Naval Officer, 1841–1865* (New York, Charles Scribner's Sons, 1883), 213–14.

31. *OR*, LI, Part 2, 269–70; David Thompson to Sister Mary, September 1, 1861, Frank Nash Papers, Folder 10, Southern Historical Collection, University of N. C., Chapel Hill, Cited hereafter as Nash Papers; M270, 10th N. C. Service Records, Record of Events for Company G; *Fayetteville Observer*, September 5, 1861.

32. *OR*, LI, Part 2, 269–70.

33. *Fayetteville Observer*, September 9, 1861; *OR*, IV, 642–43, 645; H. K. Burgwyn to Gov. H. T. Clark, September 6, 1861, Papers of Governor Henry T. Clark, G.P. 154, N.C. State Archives; William H. Parker, *Recollections of a Naval Officer, 1841–1865* (New York, Charles Scribner's Sons, 1883), 217; William K. Scarborough (ed.), *Diary of Edmund Ruffin* (Baton Rouge, Louisiana State University Press, 1976), Vol. II, 126–29.

34. *NCT*, I, 427; IV, 394; VII, 455; NCR, I, 362–63; II, 306-07, 750; Records of Tredegar Iron Works, Foundry Sales Book, VIII, 3, p. 131, Virginia State Library, Richmond; David Thompson to Mother, September 13, 1861, Frank Nash Papers.

35. *OR*, IV, 643; LI, Part 2, 270, 274; Thomas Scharf, *History of the Confederate States Navy from its Organization to the Surrender of its Last Vessel* (New York, Rogers and Sherwood, 1887), 383–84; William H. Parker, *Recollections of a Naval Officer, 1841–1865* (New York, Charles Scribner's Sons, 1883), 215–20; H. K. Burgwyn to Gov. H. T. Clark, September 6, 1861, Papers of Governor Henry T. Clark, G. P. 154, N. C. State Archives.

36. *NOR*, VI, 726; David Thompson to Mother, September 22, 1861, Frank Nash Papers; Brig. Gen. Richard Gatlin to J. D. Whitford, September 23, 1861; Capt. H. T. Guion to J. D. Whitford, September 23, 1861, Whitford Papers.

37. David Thompson to Mother, September

22, 1861, Frank Nash Papers; *OR*, LI, Part 2, 310–11; Lieut. Col. J. L. Bridgers to Gov. H. T. Clark, September 24, 1861, Papers of Governor H. T. Clark, G.P. 154, N. C. State Archives.

38. George W. Cullum, *Biographical Register of the Officers and Graduates of the U. S. Military Academy at West Point, N.Y. From Its Establishment in 1802, to 1890 With the Early History of the United States Military Academy* (Boston, Houghton-Mifflin and Company, 1891, 3 volumes), II, 700; RG 109, E 193: Carded Records Showing Military Service, National Archives; Journal of Company B.

39. W. N. Geffroy to Thomas Bragg, September 27, 1861, Papers of Gov. H. T. Clark, G. P. 154, N. C. State Archives; Engineer Record, 101–02; *NCT*, I, 101, 269, 427.

40. *OR*, IV, 663, 666–67, 682–83, 687; Letterbook of Gov. H. T. Clark, G.L.B. 46, pp. 99–100, 124, 165, N.C. State Archives.

41. *OR*, IV, 575, 576, 685–86, 690, 693; LI, Part 2, 352; W. N. Geffroy to Thomas Bragg, September 27, 1861, Papers of Gov. H. T. Clark, G. P. 154, N. C. State Archives; J. D. Whitford to Gov. H. T. Clark, October 13, 1861; Brig. Gen. Richard Gatlin to J. D. Whitford, October 16, 1861, Whitford Papers; Certificates and Receipts, J. M. Eason and Brother to the State of N. C., November 29, 1861, James A. Bryan, Bryan Family Papers, Series II, Southern Historical Collection, University of N. C., Chapel Hill..

42. *NOR*, VI, 222–23, 240, 242.

43. Capt. H. T. Guion to J. D. Whitford, September 23, 1861; Brig. Gen. Richard Gatlin to J. D. Whitford, October 27, 1861, Whitford Papers; J. D. Whitford to Gov. H. T. Clark, Papers of Governor H. T. Clark, October 13, 1861, N.C. State Archives; Letterbook of Gov. H. T. Clark, G.L.B. 46, p. 162, N. C. State Archives.

44. *OR*, LI, Part 2, 357; Brig. Gen. Richard Gatlin to J. D. Whitford, October 27, 1861, Whitford Papers.

45. *NOR*, VI, 242.

46. *Ibid.*, 242, 269.

47. *Ibid.*, 269–70.

48. RG 92, E 1428, Miscellaneous Lists Related to Chartered, Hired or Seized Vessels; Repairs and Services of Vessels; Vessels for Various Expeditions, 1861–65, National Archives; *OR*, LI, Part 2, 369; *NOR*, VI, 689; *Charlotte Western Democrat*, November 12, 1861; *Fayetteville Observer*, November 7, November 11, 1861; David Thompson to Mother, November 4, 1861, Frank Nash Papers.

49. *NCT*, II, 455; *NOR*, VI, 416, 478, 689, 690, 695; *Fayetteville Observer*, November 11, November 21, 1861; Capt. William Martin to Hugh Leach, December 11, 1861, Soldier Letters File, Fort Macon State Park; Col. Z. B. Vance to Brig. Gen. L. O'B Branch, December 5, 1861, Lawrence O'B. Branch Papers, University of Virginia, Charlottesville, Cited hereafter as Branch Papers.

50. *New Bern Daily Progress*, September 21, October 3, 1861; Capt. William Martin to Hugh Leach, December 11, 1861, Soldier Letters File, Fort Macon State Park; *NCR*, I, 489, 502; II, 307.

51. *NCT*, IV, 394; VII, 455; *NCR*, I, 489–90, 502.

52. *NCT*, I, 113, 427; M270, 10th N. C. Service Records, Company G, Josiah Pender.

53. Invoices of Ordnance Stores, October 25, 1861, James A. Bryan, Bryan Family Papers, Series II, Southern Historical Collection, University of N. C., Chapel Hill; Brig. Gen. L. O'B. Branch to Brig. Gen. Richard Gatlin, December 11, 1861, Brig. Gen. L. O'B. Branch to Col. M. J. White, December 14, 1861, Branch Papers.

54. RG 109, Department of North Carolina, Chapter II, 262 1/2, Letters and Telegrams Sent, pp. 89–90, National Archives; Engineer Record, 107.

Chapter 6

1. *OR*, IV, 576, 717.

2. For the formation and organization of the expedition see: *Battles and Leaders of the Civil War, Being for the Most Part Contributions by Union and Confederate Officers* (New York, *Century Magazine*, 1887, 4 volumes), I, 660–61, Cited hereafter as

Battles and Leaders; OR, V, 36; Series III, Vol. I, 500, 535–36; U. S. 37th Congress, 3rd Session, *Joint Committee Report on the Conduct of the War*, Vol. IV, Part 3, 333.

3. *OR*, IX, 352.

4. *Ibid.*, 74–80, 354–60; *Battles and Leaders*, I, 660–68.

5. *OR*, IV, 576–77.

6. *OR*, LI, Part 2, 434, 442, 448; Brig. Gen. L. O'B. Branch to "All Commanders of Posts", January 11, 1862, Branch Papers; Records of Tredegar Iron Works, Foundry Sales Book, VIII, 3, pp. 186, 187, Virginia State Library, Richmond.

7. Brig. Gen. L. O'B. Branch to Colonel [M. J. White], February 12, 1862, Branch Papers.

8. *OR*, IV, 577; LI, Part 2, 475, 480–81; IX, 441; David Thompson to Mother, February 25, 1862, Frank Nash Papers; Journal of Company B; *NCT*, I, 101; IV, 394; VII, 455; VIII, 1.

9. *NOR*, I, 332–35, 747–48; *Raleigh State Journal*, March 5, March 15, 1862; W. C. Whittle, "The Cruise of the C. S. Steamer *Nashville*," *Southern Historical Society Papers*, XXIX, 208.

10. *OR*, IX, 55–56, 442; LI, Part 2, 486–87; Journal of Company B.

11. *NCR*, I, 504; Journal of Company B; *Raleigh State Journal*, April 9, 1862; *New York Times*, April 10, 1862; *OR*, IX, 278; John K. Burlingame, *History of the 5th Rhode Island Heavy Artillery During Three and a Half Years of Service in North Carolina* (Providence, Snow and Farnham, 1892), 53–54, Cited hereafter as Burlingame; G. H. Allen, *Forty-Six Months in the 4th Rhode Island Volunteers* (Providence, J. A. and R. A. Reid, 1887), 99, Cited hereafter as Allen.

12. *OR*, IX 278; *NOR*, I, 818; VII, 136–39; *New York Daily Tribune*, March 28, 1862; W. C. Whittle, "The Cruise of the C. S. Steamer *Nashville*," *Southern Historical Society Papers*, XXIX, 210; D. H. Hill, Jr., *Bethel to Sharpsburg* (Raleigh, Edward and Broughton Company, 1926, 2 Volumes), I, 256; RG 24, Logs of *State of Georgia* and *Gemsbok*, March 23–24, 1862, National Archives. The embarrassment caused to the U.S. Navy Department by the *Nashville*'s easy to escape from Union warships was enormous. The Northern press and public was enraged, and the incident was dubbed as "Bull Run to the Navy."

13. *Battles and Leaders*, I, 652, 669; *New York Daily Tribune*, March 27, 1862; *New York Times*, April 10, 1862.

14. *OR*, IX, 281–82; *Providence Daily Journal*, April 4, April 10, 1862; *Philadelphia Inquirer*, April 5, 1862.

15. *OR*, IX, 277, 282; *Philadelphia Inquirer*, April 5, 1862; Hilliard Bryant Ferriss to Brother, April 2, 1862, H. B. Ferriss Papers, Connecticut State Library, Hartford, Cited hereafter as Ferriss Papers.

16. *OR*, IX, 276–77, 282; William A. Croffut and John M. Morris, *Military and Civil History of Connecticut During the Recent War* (New York, Ledyard Bell, 1868), 178, Cited hereafter as Croffut and Morris.

17. *OR*, IX, 277–78, 286.

18. *Ibid.*, IX, 277–80, 282; Edwin W. Stone, *Rhode Island in the Rebellion* (Providence, George H. Whitney, 1864), 309; Allen, 101–04; *Providence Daily Journal*, May 3, 1862; RG 94, E 159: Brig. Gen. J. G. Parke to Brig. Gen. A. E. Burnside, March 27, 1862, A. E. Burnside Papers, National Archives.

19. RG 24, Log of *State of Georgia*, March 27–28, 1862; Log of *Albatross*, March 28, 1862, National Archives; *OR*, IX, 278–80; Allen, 111; *Providence Daily Journal*, April 17, 1862; *NOR*, VII, 173-74.

20. Burlingame, 53–54; *New York Times*, April 10, 1862.

21. *OR*, IX, 286; *New York Times*, April 16, 1862.

22. *OR*, IX, 281, 283; LI, Part 1, 620–21; *NOR*, VII, 185, 204; *New York Herald*, April 16, 1862; Burlingame, 57, 59; J. M. Drake, *History of the 9th New Jersey Veteran Volunteers* (Elizabeth, Journal Printing House, 1889), 71; Henry Hall, *Cayuga in the Field, A Record of the 19th New York Volunteers, All the Batteries of the 3rd New York Artillery, and the 75th New York Volunteers, Comprising an*

Account of Their Organization, Camp Life, Marches, Battles, Losses, Toils and Triumphs in the War for the Union, With Complete Rolls of Their Members (Auburn, Syracuse, Truair, Smith and Company, 1873) , 121–22, Cited hereafter as Hall; Allen, 111.

23. Journal of Company B; David Thompson to Mary, September 1, 1861, Frank Nash Papers; *NCR*, I, 503–04.

24. Journal of Company B; *NCR*, I, 503.

25. *New York Times*, April 10, 1862; RG 24: Log of the *Gemsbok*, March 26–28, 1862, National Archives; *NCR*, I, 503–04.

26. *New York Herald*, April 12, April 16, 1862; *New York Daily Tribune*, May 5, 1862; *OR*, IX, 293.

27. *NCR*, I, 505–06; Journal of Company B.

28. *NCR*, I 506; *OR*, IX, 293; Journal of Company B; RG 94, E 159: Brig. Gen. J. G. Parke to Maj. Gen. A. E. Burnside, April 10, 1862, A. E. Burnside Papers, National Archives.

29. Journal of Company B; *NCR*, I, 507–08; A. C. Evans to Mother, April 9, 1862, A. C. Evans Papers, Southern Historical Collection, University of N.C., Chapel Hill; *OR*, IX, 458.

30. *OR*, IX, 283; *New York Daily Tribune*, April 23, 1862; *Philadelphia Inquirer*, April 22, 1862; *New York Herald*, April 22, 1862; Journal of Company B; RG 24: Logs of *State of Georgia* and *Albatross*, April 11, 1862, National Archives.

31. *Philadelphia Inquirer*, April 22, 1862; *New York Times*, April 26, 1862; Hilliard B. Ferriss to A. G. Ferriss, April 15, 1862, Ferriss Papers; *OR*, IX, 283; Croffut and Morris, 179; Journal of Company B.

32. RG 24: Logs of *State of Georgia*, *Albatross* and *Gemsbok*, April 12, 1862, National Archives.

33. *OR*, IX, 284, 286, 291; Burlingame, 60; Hall, 122–23; *New York Herald*, May 4, 1862; Jared Wheeler to Friend Delia, April 19, 1862, Manuscript Collection, Connecticut State Library, Hartford.

34. *OR*, IX, 272, 283, 286; *Providence Daily Journal*, April 26, 1862; Burlingame, 61; U.S. 37th Congress, 3rd Session, *Joint Committee Report on the Conduct of the War*, Vol. IV, Part 3, 335.

35. *OR*, IX, 273, 286; *New York Herald*, May 4, 1862; *New York Daily Tribune*, May 5, 1862.

36. *OR*, IX, 272–73; *Philadelphia Inquirer*, April 26, 1862; *New York Daily Tribune*, May 5, 1862.

37. Croffut and Morris, 180; *Litchfield Enquirer*, May 15, 1862.

38. *New York Times*, April 26, 1862; *New York Herald*, April 22, April 26, 1862; *New York Daily Tribune*, May 5, 1862.

39. *OR*, IX, 293; Journal of Company B; *New York Herald*, April 26, 1862.

40. Journal of Company B; *New York Daily Tribune*, May 5, 1862; RG 24, Log of the *Gemsbok*, April 22–24, 1862; *OR*, IX, 291; Burlingame, 62-63.

41. *OR*, IX, 272, 274; *New York Daily Tribune*, May 5, 1862.

42. *New York Herald*, May 4, 1862; *New York Times*, May 5, 1862; *New York Daily Tribune*, May 5, 1862; Daniel R. Larned to Mrs. A. E. Burnside, April 25, 1862, D. R. Larned Papers, Manuscript Collection, Library of Congress, Cited hereafter as Larned Papers; Journal of Company B; M270, 10th N. C. Service Records, Capt. H. T. Guion to Col. J. A. J. Bradford, May 29, 1862, Record of Events for Company B, April, 1862, Cited hereafter as Battle Report Company B.

43. Journal of Company B; Battle Report Company B; *New York Herald*, May 4, 1862; *New York Daily Tribune*, May 5, 1862; D. R. Larned to Mrs. A. E. Burnside, April 25, 1862; D. R. Larned to Sister, April 22–28, 1862, Larned Papers.

44. *OR*, IX, 273, 287, 289.

45. *Providence Daily Journal*, May 9, 1862; *New York Herald*, May 4, 1862; *New York Daily Tribune*, May 5, 1862; RG 24: Log of *Daylight*, April 24, 1862; Journal of Company B; *OR*, IX, 289.

46. *OR*, IX, 289–90.

47. *Ibid.*, 287; *Litchfield Enquirer*, May 15, 1862; *Grier's Almanac, 1862*, Grier's Almanac Publishing Company, Atlanta, Georgia.

48. James M. Hollowell's hourly record of the bombardment of Fort Macon, April 25–26, 1862, J. M. Hollowell Papers, P.C. 1388, N. C. State Archives, Cited hereafter as Hollowell; *OR*, IX, 294.

49. *OR*, IX, 284, 289; *New York Times*, May 5,

1862. The time of the first shot varies in some reports.

50. Hall, 124; D. R. Larned to Sister, April 22–28, 1862; *New York Daily Tribune,* May 5, 1862.

51. *New York Daily Tribune,* May 5, 1862; *New York Times,* May 5, 1862; Hollowell; Journal of Company B; *OR,* IX, 287.

52. Hall, 124; *OR,* IX, 290.

53. Hollowell; *New York Daily Tribune,* May 5, 1862.

54. *NOR,* VII, 279; RG 24: Logs of *State of Georgia, Daylight, Chippewa,* and *Gemsbok,* April 25, 1862, National Archives. Statistics and additional information on these ships can be found in *NOR,* Series II, Vol. I, 57 ,72, 91, and 214.

55. *NOR,* VII, 279-80; RG 24: Logs of *Daylight, Chippewa, Gemsbok* and *State of Georgia,* April 25, 1862, National Archives.

56. Hollowell; Journal of Company B; Battle Report Company B; *NOR,* VII, 279–81; RG 24: Logs of *Daylight, Chippewa, Gemsbok* and *State of Georgia,* National Archives.

57. *OR,* IX, 276; *New York Daily Tribune,* May 5, 1862; *New York Herald,* May 4, 1862.

58. *OR,* IX, 287, 289; *New York Daily Tribune,* May 5, 1862.

59. Hall, 125.

60. *OR,* IX, 287, 292.

61. *New York Herald,* May 4, 1862; *New York Daily Tribune,* May 5,1862; Capt. Herman Biggs to Wife, April 27, 1862, Herman Biggs Papers, Southern Historical Collection, University of N. C., Chapel Hill, Cited hereafter as Biggs Papers; *OR,* IX, 292.

62. *New York Herald,* May 4, 1862; *New York Daily Tribune,* May 5, 1862; *NCR,* I, 510; *OR,* IX, 290; Hollowell.

63. *New York Herald,* May 4, 1862; *New York Daily Tribune,* May 5, 1862; *New York Times,* May 5, 1862.

64. *OR,* IX, 288; Burlingame, 64; *New York Herald,* May 4, 1862.

65. Burlingame, 64.

66. *New York Daily Tribune,* May 5, 1862; RG 24: Log of the *Chippewa,* April 25, 1862, National Archives; *OR,* IX, 285.

67. *OR,* IX, 289, 290; *New York Herald,* May 4, 1862; *New York Daily Tribune,* May 5, 1862.

68. *New York Daily Tribune,* May 5, 1862.

69. Journal of Company B; *Raleigh State Journal,* May 3, 1862.

70. Journal of Company B; Battle Report Company B.

71. *OR,* IX, 284; Hollowell; Journal of Company B; Battle Report Company B; *New York Herald,* May 4, 1862; *New York Daily Tribune,* May 5, 1862.

72. *OR,* IX, 294; Journal of Company B; Battle Report Company B; Hollowell; *NCR,* I, 510.

73. *OR,* IX, 274; Herman Biggs to Wife, April 27, 1862, Biggs Papers; D. R. Larned to Henry, April 26, 1862; D. R. Larned to Mrs. A. E. Burnside, April 27, 1862, Larned Papers.

74. *OR,* IX, 276. Commander Lockwood was not present, but signed the terms later in the day when the blockading squadron entered Beaufort Harbor (See RG 24: Log of *Daylight,* April 25, 1862, National Archives). He sandwiched his signature in between those of Parke and White.

75. *New York Daily Tribune,* May 5, 1862; *New York Herald,* May 4,1862; D. R. Larned to Sister, April 22-28, 1862; D. R. Larned to Henry, April 26, 1862; D. R. Larned to Mrs. A. E. Burnside, April 27, 1862, Larned Papers; J. M. Hollowell, *War-Time Reminiscences, and Other Selections* (Goldsboro, *Goldsboro Herald,* 1939), 51.

76. Burlingame, 65–66; *New York Herald,* May 4, 1862; *New York Daily Tribune,* May 5, 1862.

77. *New York Daily Tribune,* May 5, 1862; Burlingame, 66; RG 24: Logs of *Chippewa, Gemsbok* and *State of Georgia,* April 25, 1862, National Archives; D. R. Larned to Henry, April 26, 1862; D. R. Larned to Sister, April 22–28, 1862, Larned Papers.

78. Burlingame, 67; *New York Daily Tribune,* May 5, 1862; Paul Branch, "Confederate Flags of Fort Macon" (Unpublished monograph, Fort Macon State Park, 1994). After being sent to Rhode Island for presentation to the Rhode Island General Assembly, Fort Macon's large garrison flag was subsequently cut up into pieces

for each politician as a souvenir. In 1994, Fort Macon State Park reacquired a surviving piece of this flag, part of the blue field containing one star. The storm flag taken by General Parke and his staff was carried home to Connecticut after the war by Lieutenant Moses A. Hill and, although altered at some point by the removal of its lower red bar, has made its way to the North Carolina Museum of History, where it resides today.

79. Journal of Company B; *OR,* IX, 294; *New York Herald,* May 4, 1862; *New York Daily Tribune,* May 5, 1862; D. R. Larned to Sister, April 22–28, 1862; Herman Biggs to Wife, April 27, 1862, Biggs Papers; *New York Herald,* May 2, 1862; RG 24: Log of *Chippewa,* April 26–27, 1862, National Archives.

80. *OR,* IX, 274, 288, 290, 294; *New York Daily Tribune,* May 5, 1862.

81. *NOR,* VII, 281; *New York Daily Tribune,* May 5, 1862; RG 24: Log of *Chippewa,* April 25, 1862, National Archives.

82. *OR,* IX, 275, 294.

Chapter 7

1. *OR,* IX, 383, 384; U.S. 37th Congress, 3rd Session, *Joint Committee Report on the Conduct of the War,* Vol. IV, Part 3, 336–37.

2. *NOR,* VII, 281, 292, 569; VIII, 477, 505.

3. *OR,* IX, 382.

4. See RG 156, E 102, *Quarterly Summary Statement of Ordnance and Ordnance Stores at Forts, Permanent Batteries and Garrisons,* September, 1862; and E 100, *Quarterly Summary Statement of Ordnance and Ordnance Stores at Forts, Permanent Batteries and Garrisons,* 1838–64, National Archives; Post Returns, July, 1862.

5. Albert W. Mann, *History of the 45th Regiment of Massachusetts Volunteer Militia* (Boston, W. Spooner, 1908), 199, 202, 392, 393, Cited hereafter as Mann.

6. See Post Returns, July, 1862, and subsequent post returns showing the numbers of prisoners confined monthly.

7. RG 393, Part V, Post Headquarters Records

of Fort Macon, E 12: "Instructions to the Sergeant of the Provost Guard", February 11, 1863; Special Order Number 5, April 26, 1863, National Archives; *OR,* Series II, Vol. V, 361–62.

8. *NOR,* X, 137–38; Post Returns, August, 1864; *NCT,* V, 374–75.

9. Mann, 203; *OR,* XVIII, 512, 514, 530.

10. *OR,* XVIII, 700; XXXIII, 289–91.

11. See *OR,* XXXIII, 84–94.

12. *OR,* XXXIII, 51, 77, 78; *NOR,* IX, 455–56, 459. The Union Department (later District) of North Carolina was divided into "Sub-Districts" in 1863. The Sub-District of Beaufort included the posts of Newport Barracks, Morehead City, Beaufort, and Fort Macon.

13. See *OR,* XXXIII, 47–103, for reports related to the operations against New Bern.

14. *OR,* XXXIII, 260–61, 290–93, 613–14, 635–36, 672, 706–07, 740, 748–49, 768–69; *NOR,* IX, 522, 583.

15. *OR,* XXXIII, 289, 291, 949; *NOR,* IX, 664, 681.

16. See *OR,* XXXVI, Part 2, 3–5; John G. Barrett, *The Civil War in North Carolina* (Chapel Hill, University of N. C. Press, 1963), 221–25; Leslie S. Bright, William H. Rowland and James C. Bardon, *C.S.S. Neuse, A Question of Iron and Time* (Raleigh, N.C. Department of Archives and History, 1981), 14–15.

17. *OR,* XXXIII, 865–70, 948, 960, 1010; XXXVI, Part 2, 626–27, 693.

18. *OR,* XLVI, Part 2, 272; XLVII, Part 2, 111–13; XLVII, Part 3, 443; Post Returns, April, 1865; June, 1865.

Chapter 8

1. Post Returns, November, 1865; RG 393, Part V, Post Headquarters Records, Fort Macon, E 6: General Orders Number 34, November 6 1865, National Archives.

2. See Post Returns, 1865–1877.

3. *Circular Number 4, Report on Barracks and Hospitals with Descriptions of Military Posts* (Washington, War Department, Surgeon General's Office, 1870), pp. 88–90; RG 159, E 15: Inspec-

tion of Fort Macon, April 19–20, 1870, A 11; Inspection of Fort Macon, April 18, 1871, A 10, National Archives.

4. Jane Coues to Sister, March 13, 1869, April 16, 1869; Jane Coues to "Louise", June 14, 1869, August 30, 1869, October 5, 1869, Jane Augusta (McKenny) Coues Papers, Private Collection of Mr. David F. Dean, Rochester, New York. Mrs. Coues' husband Elliott already had established a considerable reputation as a naturalist when he served at Fort Macon from 1869 to 1870. Afterward he became one of the most famous ornithologists of the 19th Century. Among the dozens of works he published is a five-part series of papers submitted to the National Academy of Sciences entitled "Notes on the Natural History of Fort Macon, N.C. and Vicinity."

5. 1870 Federal Census, Carteret County, N. C.; Jane Coues to Louise, June 14, 1869, Jane Augusta (McKenny) Coues Papers, Private Collection of David F. Dean, Rochester, New York; RG 92, E 225: Report of an Inspection of Public Quarters, November 18, 1872, National Archives; RG 159, E 15: Inspection of Fort Macon, April 18, 1871, A10, National Archives.

6. RG 94, E 547: Volume 197, Medical Records of the Post, Fort Macon, see various entries, National Archives; RG 393, Part V, Post Headquarters Records of Fort Macon, E 2: Maj. John D. Wilkins to Bvt. Col. J. H. Taylor, October 1, 1869; Maj. H. A. Allen to Maj. J. H. Taylor, September 17, 1873; Capt. John I. Rodgers to Assistant Adjutant General, Department of the South, September 10, 1874, National Archives.

7. RG 393, Part V, Post Headquarters Records of Fort Macon, E 2: Lieut. Col. W. S. Poor to Capt. S. E. Carter, July 6, 1865; Lieut. Col. W. S. Poor to Lieut. Col. J. A. Campbell, July 15, 1865; Capt. G. M. Brayton to Bvt. Col. J. H. Taylor, June 2, 1869, National Archives.

8. *Circular Number 4, Report on Barracks and Hospitals With Descriptions of Military Posts* (Washington, War Department, Surgeon General's Office, 1870), 89; RG 159, E 15: Inspection Report of Fort Macon, April 20, 1870, A 11, Na-

tional Archives; RG 92, E 225: Report of an Inspection of Public Quarters by the Commanding Officer and Post Quartermaster, November 18, 1872, National Archives; RG 393, Part V, Post Headquarters Records of Fort Macon, E 2: Capt. G. M. Brayton to Bvt. Col. J. H. Taylor, June 2, 1869; Maj. J. D. Wilkins to Assistant Adjutant General, Department of the South, September 11, 1869; Maj. Joseph Stewart to Maj. J. H. Taylor, September 21, 1872, National Archives.

9. RG 393, Part V, Post Headquarters Records of Fort Macon, E 2: Lieut. Col. W. S. Poor to Lieut. Col. J. A. Campbell, July 15, 1865, National Archives.

10. U.S. Congress, Congressional Documents Serial Set, 39th Congress, 2nd Session, U.S. House, Annual Report of the Chief of Engineers to the Secretary of War, 1866, Document Number One, (Washington, Government Printing Office, 1867), Serial Set Number 1285, 427, (Annual Reports of the Chief of Engineers will be cited hereafter as *Annual Report of the Chief of Engineers*, followed by the year); RG 92, E 225: Lieut. Col. Q. A. Gillmore to U.S. Engineer Office, October 13, 1875, 5th Endorsement of Lieut. John McGilvray to Chief Quartermaster, Department of the South, September 1, 1875, #4305, National Archives.

11. RG 156, E 3: Letters Sent, 1866, pp. 167, 209; Letters Sent, 1867, p. 490, National Archives; RG 393, Part V, Post Headquarters Records of Fort Macon, E 2: Capt. C. B. Gaskill to Bvt. Maj. Gen. A. B. Dyer, May 11, 1867; Capt. C. B. Gaskill to Lieut. Stivers, August 10, 1867; Capt. C. B. Gaskill to Bvt. Maj. Gen. A. B. Dyer, October 29, 1867, National Archives.

12. RG 156, E 113, Register of Cannon and Carriages Required, on Hand, and Supplied to Forts, Batteries, etc., 1861–1873, National Archives; RG 393, Part V, Post Headquarters Records of Fort Macon, E 2: Capt. John I. Rodgers to Assistant Adjutant General, Department of the South, December 13, 1872, National Archives.

13. *Annual Report of the Chief of Engineers*, 1871–75; RG 393, Part V, Post Headquarters

Records of Fort Macon, E 2: Maj. Joseph Stewart to Maj. J. H. Taylor, September 21, 1872; Capt. J. I. Rodgers to Mr. Daniels, June 11, 1873; Maj. H. A. Allen to Maj. J. H. Taylor, September 17, 1873; Capt. J. I. Rodgers to Assistant Adjutant General, Department of the South, September 10, 1874, National Archives; RG 92, E 225: Lieut. J. A. Campbell to Chief Quartermaster, Department of the South, July 26, 1873, #3904, National Archives.

14. RG 92, E 225: Case of Proposed New Quarters at Fort Macon, #5898, National Archives; RG 393, Part V, Post Headquarters Records of Fort Macon, E 2: Capt. J. I. Rodgers to Assistant Adjutant General, Department of the South, September 10, 1874; Lieut. M. Crawford to Assistant Adjutant General, Department of the South, September 12, 1876, National Archives.

15. RG 393, Part V, Post Headquarters Records of Fort Macon, E 2: Capt. J. I. Rodgers to Assistant Adjutant General, Department of the South, September 13, 1875, National Archives.

16. RG 94, E 12: Case of Application for Change of Station of Company L, 2nd Artillery, Fort Macon, N C., September 4, 1876, #5142, National Archives; Post Returns, September, 1875; September, 1876; April, 1877.

17. RG 77, E 18: Capt. P. C. Hains to Brig. Gen. R. Delafield, January 3, 1866, H2047, National Archives.

18. See *Annual Report of the Chief of Engineers,* for the years 1867-70 and 1874–77.

19. RG 92, E 225: Lieut. Bishop Aldrich to Bvt. Maj. Gen. R. O. Tyler, June 6, 1867, A3687, National Archives.

20. RG 393, Part V, Post Headquarters Records of Fort Macon, E 12: Returns of Prisoners Confined in the Military Prison at Fort Macon, N.C., 1869–70; RG 94, E 12: Maj. Gen. G. G. Meade to Bvt. Maj. Gen. E. D. Townsend, October 21, 1868, A503, National Archives.

21. RG 393, Part V, Post Headquarters Records of Fort Macon, E 2: Maj. James Stewart to Maj. J. H. Taylor, January 27, 1872, National Archives.

22. RG 393, Part V, Post Headquarters Records of Fort Macon, E 2: Capt. C. B. Gaskill to Capt. J. W. Clous, July 24, 1867, National Archives.

23. Post Returns, 1867–68; RG 393, Part V, Post Headquarters Records of Fort Macon, E 2: Capt. C. B. Gaskill to Bvt. Capt. William Prince, May 25, 1867, National Archives; RG 94, E 12: Proceedings of a Board of Officers Convened at Fort Macon, N. C., October 2, 1868, A503/S932, National Archives.

24. NRG 393, Part V, Post Headquarters Records of Fort Macon, E 2: Capt. G. M. Singer to Bvt. Maj. D. T. Wells, October 22, 1866; Capt. S. B. Husted to Bvt. Maj. D. T. Wells, October 31, 1866, National Archives.

25. RG 393, Part V, Post Headquarters Records of Fort Macon, E 2: Lieut. Charles Snyder to Assistant Adjutant General, Raleigh, N.C., February 5, 1867.

26. RG 94, E 12: Proceedings of a Board of Officers Convened at Fort Macon, N.C., October 2, 1868, A503/S932, National Archives.

27. RG 393, Part V, Post Headquarters Records of Fort Macon, E 12: Return to the AAG, Department of the South of Prisoners Escaped from the Post of Fort Macon, N.C., February 9, 1869, National Archives; RG 393, Part V, Post Headquarters Records of Fort Macon, E 2: Maj. G. P. Andrews to Bvt. Brig. Gen. R. C. Drum, March 3, 1869, National Archives; RG 393, Part V, Post Headquarters Records of Fort Macon, E 6: Special Orders No. 69, March 12, 1869, National Archives.

28. RG 393, Part V, Post Headquarters Records of Fort Macon, E 2: Capt. Alfred Smith to Adjutant General, U.S. Army, March 30, 1869, National Archives; Jane Coues to Sister, April 16, 1869, Jane Augusta (McKenny) Coues Papers, Private Collection of David F. Dean, Rochester, N. Y.

29. RG 393, Part V, Post Headquarters Records of Fort Macon, E 2: Maj. H. A. Allen to Assistant Adjutant General, Department of the South, February 22, 1874, National Archives.

30. RG 393, Part V, Post Headquarters

Records of Fort Macon, E 2: Maj. G. P. Andrews to Bvt. Brig. Gen. R. C. Drum, February 12, 1869, National Archives; RG 94, E 12: Maj. Gen. G. G. Meade to Bvt. Maj. Gen. E. D. Townsend, October 21, 1868, A503, National Archives.

31. Post Returns, 1870-76; RG 393, Part V, Post Headquarters Records, E 2: Lieut. M. Crawford to Assistant Adjutant General, Department of the South, September 12, 1876, National Archives.

32. See RG 92, E 225: R. H. Bradley's Application to the Quartermaster Department, May 11, 1877, #2207; A. Oaksmith to Secretary of War, May 18, 1877, #2273; A. Oaksmith to Chief Quartermaster, Department of the South, July 2, 1878, #4180, National Archives.

33. RG 92, E 225: Ord. Sgt. Adolphus Smith to Assistant Adjutant General, Department of the South, August 21, 1879, #5328, National Archives.

34. RG 92, E 225: Lieut. Col. R. Jones to Assistant Adjutant General, Department of the East, March 28, 1884, National Archives.

35. See *Annual Report of the Chief of Engineers,* 1881–89.

36. For reports of the Endicott Board see 49th Congress, 1st Session, *House Executive Documents,* #49; and 49th Congress, 2nd Session, *House Executive Documents,* Appendix 3.

37. RG 77, E 103: C. L. Abernathy and E. W. Hill to Senator Marion Butler, February 15, 1898, #24605, National Archives; 55th Congress, 3rd Session, *House Executive Documents,* Appendix 4-J, 693.

38. *Raleigh News and Observer,* April 7, 1898; RG 77, E 103: #25373; RG 156, E 25, Forts and Posts, Fort Macon, #26293-1, National Archives.

39. *Raleigh News and Observer,* April 7, April 15, 1898; 55th Congress, 3rd Session, *House Executive Documents,* Appendix 4-J, 692-93; RG 77, Fortifications Files, Fort Macon, Drawer 252, Sheet 25–12, Cartographic and Architectural Archives, Archives II, College Park, Md.

40. *Raleigh Morning Post,* April 19, May 1, 1898.

41. RG 77, E 103: Capt. W. E. Craighill to Brig.

Gen. John Wilson, April 25, 1898, and enclosures, #25463, National Archives; *Kinston Daily Free Press,* May 27, 1898; National Archives Microfilm Collection, M617, Roll 192, Post Returns of Fort Caswell, N.C., May, 1898; RG 77, Fortifications Files, Fort Macon, Drawer 252, Sheet 25–13, Cartographic and Architectural Archives, Archives II, College Park, Md.

42. Willard B. Gatewood, Jr., "North Carolina's Negro Regiment in the Spanish-American War," *North Carolina Historical Review,* October, 1971, 372–75; Willard B. Gatewood, Jr., *Smoked Yankees and the Struggle for Empire: Letters from Negro Soldiers, 1898–1902* (Urbana, University of Illinois Press, 1971), 8–11. North Carolina was one of only several states to muster in all-black volunteer military units during the war. The Ninth Ohio Battalion was actually mustered in with all black officers before the North Carolina Battalion but its companies were National Guard units which were already established and had been in service since the 1870's.

43. *Raleigh News and Observer,* May 3, 1898.

44. *Fayetteville Observer,* May 28, 1898; *Kinston Daily Free Press,* May 30, June 9, 1898; *Raleigh Morning Post,* June 2, 1898.

45. Willard B. Gatewood, Jr., "North Carolina's Negro Regiment in the Spanish-American War," *North Carolina Historical Review,* October, 1971, 375–77; *Kinston Daily Free Press,* June 25, 1898; *Fayetteville Observer,* June 16, June 23, 1898; National Archives Microfilm Collection, M617, Roll 192, Post Returns of Fort Caswell, N.C., July–October, 1898.

46. *Kinston Daily Free Press,* August 20, August 25, 1898.

47. Willard B. Gatewood, Jr., "North Carolina's Negro Regiment in the Spanish-American War," *North Carolina Historical Review,* October, 1971, 381; *Kinston Daily Free Press,* September 15, 1898; *New Bern Weekly Journal,* September 13, September 16, 1898.

48. RG 156, E 990: Statement of Guns, Howitzers, and Mortars on Hand at the Various Forts, Office of the Chief of Ordnance, October 20, 1899, National Archives; E 25: Forts and Posts,

Fort Macon, #26293; E 25: Relics, #19958; E 28: Mayor Arch B. Calvert to Secretary of War, February 22, 1900, #19958, National Archives; 56th Congress, 2nd Session, *Annual Report of the Chief of Ordnance*, Appendix 3, 50–51; Governor C. B. Aycock Papers, G.P. 307: Brig. Gen. William Crozier to Senator F. M. Simmons, May 15, 1902; Senator F. M. Simmons to Mayor A. M. Powell, May 16, 1902; Brig. Gen. William Crozier to Senator F. M. Simmons, May 28, 1902; G. G. Thompson, Jr. to Col. Fred A. Olds, August 7, 1902, N.C. State Archives.

49. RG 94, E 25: #424830, National Archives; RG 156, E 25: Forts and Posts, Fort Macon, # 26293-7, National Archives; RG 92, E 89: #182639, National Archives.

50. RG 94, E 25: #494307, National Archives; T. Michael O'Brien and Dennis L. Noble, "Soldiers of Surf and Story: The Light and Lifesavers of Cape Lookout, N.C.," (Unpublished Manuscript, no date), 642-43.

51. RG 94, E 25: #494307, #490729, National Archives.

52. RG 94, E 25: #494307, National Archives; RG 156, E 27: Forts and Posts, Fort Macon, #26293-(11–25), National Archives.

Chapter 9

1. RG 77, E 103: #48169, #59190, National Archives; *Annual Report of the Chief of Engineers,* 1904–06; *Annual Report of the United States Lifesaving Service for the Fiscal Year Ending June 30, 1904* (Washington, Government Printing Office, 1905), 45.

2. RG 159, E 7: #10743, National Archives; RG 156, E 27, Forts and Posts, Fort Macon, #26293-(26–27), National Archives.

3. RG 153, E 56: Reservation Files, Fort Macon, N.C., National Archives; *Annual Report of the Chief of Engineers,* 1907–08.

4. See 59th Congress, 1st Session, *Senate Documents,* No. 248, February 27, 1906.

5. RG 77, E 103, #66521-(1–14), National Archives; RG 107, E 80: #15236, National Archives; RG 156, E 27, Forts and Posts, Fort Macon, #26293-28, National Archives.

6. RG 77, E 103, #66521-(1–14), National Archives; RG 107, E 80: #15236, National Archives.

7. RG 77, E 103: #96697-113; #66521-(17–23), National Archives; RG 153, E 56: Reservations Files, Fort Macon, National Archives.

8. RG 77, E 103: #96697-113, National Archives.

9. RG 94, E 25: #2533191; E 26: 552582642 and #2597601 of file #2529741.

10. *Beaufort News,* April 26, 1923; *General Orders and Bulletins, War Department, 1923,* Bulletin No. 7, pp. 18–21.

11. *Beaufort News,* January 17, 1924; Gov. Cameron Morrison Papers, G. P. 426: J. H. Pratt to Gov. Cameron Morrison, November 26, 1923, N. C. State Archives.

12. *Beaufort News,* April 26, May 17, July 26, 1923; January 17, 1924.

13. Gov. Cameron Morrison Papers, G.P. 426: J. H. Pratt to Gov. Cameron Morrison, November 26, 1923; Gov. Gameron Morrison to J. H. Pratt, December 12, 1923, NC State Archives; *Beaufort News,* January 17, 1924; *Raleigh News and Observer,* January 20, 1924.

14. Gov. Cameron Morrison Papers, G.P. 435: Gov. Cameron Morrison to Thomas P. Ivy, February 26, 1924; Secretary of War J. W. Weeks to Senator F. M. Simmons, April 28, 1924, N.C. State Archives; *Congressional Record,* 68th Congress, 1st Session, House of Representatives, p. 9128, Senate, pp. 9301–02; *Raleigh News and Observer,* May 23, May 28, 1924. Abernathy's amendment was initially opposed by a Texas congressman, but on May 21 the congressman happened to be absent. Abernathy then cleverly seized the moment to offer his amendment and it passed without objection, *Raleigh News and Observer,* May 23, 1924.

15. *Beaufort News,* June 9, 1924, Gov. Cameron Morrison Papers, G.P. 437: Acting Secretary of War Dwight Davis to Gov. Cameron Morrison, September 18, 1924, N.C. State Archives.

16. *Beaufort News,* July 9, July 16, July 23, 1925; *Raleigh News and Observer,* July 16, July 18, 1925.

17. Records of N.C. Department of Conservation and Development, Activities of the Board of Conservation and Development, Boxes 3–4, Monthly Reports of J.S. Holmes, State Forester, 1926–33, N.C. State Archives.

18. *Public Laws and Resolutions Passed by the General Assembly at its Session of 1933,* pp. 968–69; Records of the Department of Conservation and Development, Administrative and Director's Office, Box 2, Report of the Forestry Division to the Board of Conservation and Development for the Biennium ending June 30, 1934, N.C. State Archives; *Beaufort News,* February 1, 1934.

19. *Beaufort News,* March 8, March 22, April 5, 1934; Records of the Department of Conservation and Development, Administrative and Director's Office, Box 2, Report of the Forestry Division to the Board of Conservation and Development for the Biennium ending June 30, 1934, N.C. State Archives; Department of Conservation and Development, State Parks Division, 85.4, Miscellaneous Records of the Parks Division, 1930–70 (Cited hereafter as Miscellaneous Records of the Parks Division, 85.4), Box 2, Emergency Conservation Work, Monthly Work Progress Reports, April, June, 1934, Old Records Center, Raleigh, N.C.

20. Miscellaneous Records of the Parks Division, 85.4, Box 2: Specifications for Restoration of Fort Macon, ECW Camp, NC-SP1, U.S. Department of the Interior, National Park Service, State Park Emergency Conservation Work, N.C., Department of Conservation and Development; C.C.C. Narrative Reports, November, 1934, to Autust, 1935; C.C.C. Monthly Work Progress Reports, April, 1934, to August, 1935. Department of Conservation and Development, State Parks Division, 85.1, State Parks and Lakes Files, 1930–70 (Cited hereafter as State Parks and Lakes Files, 85.1), Box 4: Orin M. Bullock, Jr. to J. S. Holmes, November 1, 1934; Walter D. Toy to J. S. Holmes, January 23, 1935; H. E. Weatherwax to J. S. Holmes, April 16, 1935, Old Records Center, Raleigh, N.C.

21. Miscellaneous Records of the Parks Division, 85.4, Box 2: C.C.C. Narrative Reports, November, 1934, to August, 1935; C.C.C. Monthly Work Progress Reports, April, 1934, to August, 1935.

22. *News and Observer,* April 19, April 26, April 30, May 1, May 2, 1936; *Beaufort News,* April 16, April 30, 1936.

23. Records of the Department of Conservation and Development, Administrative Reports and Correspondence, 1936–41, Box 5, Semiannual Reports of the Forestry Division, Branch of State Parks, to the Board of Conservation and Development, 1936–1940, N.C. State Archives.

24. *Ibid.,* 1939–1941; *Beaufort News,* January 18, February 8, February 15, 1940.

25. Brig. Gen. R. L. Tilton to R. B. Etheridge, December 17, 1941; Office Memo, Subject: Use of Fort Macon State Park by United States Army, December 22, 1941, U.S. Army Occupation of Park, 1941–46: Reports and Correspondence File, Fort Macon State Park.

26. Mrs. L. W. Humphrey to T. W, Morse, December 19, 1941, U.S. Army Occupation of Park, 1941–46: Reports and Correspondence File, Fort Macon State Park.

27. Brig. Gen. Rollin L. Tilton, *History of the Chesapeake Bay Sector* (Fort Monroe, Va., 1945), pp. 21–22, Appendix 2, p. 1.

28. "World War II Veteran Remembrances Related to the Restored World War II Barracks", World War II Veteran Information and Remembrance Files, Fort Macon State Park; Lieut. Col. (ret.) Charles E. H. Jones to Paul Branch, October 20, 1981; Lieut. Col. (ret.) J. Norman Worsham to Paul Branch, November 6, 1986, World War II Veteran Information and Remembrance File, Fort Macon State Park.

29. *Beaufort News,* December 25, 1941, October 10, 1946; *News and Observer,* January 8, 1942; Lieut. Col. (ret.) J. Norman Worsham to Paul Branch, November 6, 1986, World War II Veteran Information and Remembrance File, Fort Macon State Park. The incident was first mentioned in the *Riplely's Believe It or Not* column of July 19, 1945, and has subsequently been mentioned in books on oddities of the Civil War as well.

30. "World War II Information from Joseph D. Sebes, Beaufort, N.C., Commander of Battery B, 244th Coast Artillery, Obtained from Various Telephone and Personal Interviews," World War II Veteran Information and Remembrance File, Fort Macon State Park; Brig. Gen. Rollin L. Tilton, *History of the Chesapeake Bay Sector* (Fort Monroe, Va., 1945), p. 23.

31. Gov. J. M. Broughton Papers, Box 77: Ist Lieut. T. I. Wesley, Jr., to State of N.C., April 27, 1942, enclosing Lease No. W2287 ENG 47, N. C. State Archives; Brig. Gen. R. L. Tilton to R. B. Etheridge, January 5, 1942; A. L. Martin to R. B. Etheridge, February 7, 1942, U.S. Army Lease of Park, 1941–46 File, Fort Macon State Park.

32. Maj. J. C. Mazzie to T. W. Morse, January 13, 1942; Office Memorandum, Thomas Morse, June 28, 1943, U.S. Army Occupation of Park, 1941–46: Reports and Correspondence File, Fort Macon State Park; T. W. Morse to W. F. Williams, May 9, 1946, and attachments, U.S. Army Lease of Park, 1941–46 File, Fort Macon State Park.

33. "World War II Veteran Remembrances Related to the Restored World War II Barracks," World War II Veteran Information and Remembrance File, Fort Macon State Park; "World War II Information from Joseph D. Sebes, Beaufort, Commander of Battery B, 244th Coast Artillery, Obtained fiom various Telephone and Personal Interviews", World War II Veteran Information and Remembrance File, Fort Macon State Park.

34. Brig. Gen. Rollin L. Tilton, "Notes on Fort Monroe, 1930–1946" (Unpublished Manuscript, Fort Monroe, Va., 1946), Operations, 1942, p. 13.

35. Personal Diary of Brig. Gen. Rollin L. Tilton, Casemate Museum, Fort Monroe, Va., pp. 174, 176, 181, 182, 188, 196; Gov. J. M. Broughton Papers, Box 77: Telegram, Gov. J. M. Broughton to Gen. George C. Marshall, July 30, 1942; Acting Chief of Staff Joseph McKenney to Gov. J. M. Broughton, August 1, 1942, N.C. State Archives; *Directory of the Army of the United States,* August, 1942, Office of the Chief of Military History, Washington, D. C.

36. RG 77, E 1007, Harbor Defense Files, 1918–1945, Beaufort Inlet, National Archives.

37. *Ibid.*; Interview with Raymond D. Robbins, November 9, 1994, Fort Historian's Log, Fort Macon State Park; R. J. Pearse to J. C. Horne, May 16, 1945, U.S. Army Lease of Park, 1941–46 File, Fort Macon State Park.

38. Brig. Gen. Rollin L. Tilton, *History of the Chesapeake Bay Sector* (Fort Monroe, Va., 1945), p. 76; *Station List of the Army of the United States, Fourth Service Command,* March, 1944; November, 1944, Office of the Chief of Military History, Washington, D. C.; Gov. J. M. Broughton Papers, Box 77: Col. W. S. Pritchard to Gov. J. M. Broughton, October 24, 1944, N. C. State Archives; U.S. Army, *History of the Eastern Defense Command, and of the Defense of the Atlantic Coast of the United States in the Second World War,* (New York, G-3 Section, Eastern Defense Command, 1945), 28.

39. See file: U.S. Army Lease of Park, 1941–46 File, Fort Macon State Park; Walter F. Williams to Tom [Morse], October 1, 1946, and attachments, U.S. Army Lease of Park, 1941 16 File, Fort Macon State Park.

Appendix Two

1. RG 77, E 18: Lieut. W. A. Eliason to Maj. Gen. Alexander Macomb, March 25, 1826, E10, National Archives; *ASP,* III, 258.

2. RG 77, E 18: Lieut. George Dutton to Brig. Gen. Charles Gratiot, April 17, 1835, D1303, National Archives.

3. U.S. Congress, Congressional: Documents Serial Set, House Executive Document Number 5, *Report of the Secretary of War of December 8, 1851, on the Subject of Fortifications, in Answer to a Resolution of the House of Representatives of March 3, 1851,* Table A (Washington, Government Printing Office, 1852), Serial Set Number 637, 32nd Congress, 1st Session.

4. RG 77, E 18: Lieut. A. J. Swift to Brig. Gen. Charles Gratiot, November 25, 1835, S3036; January 28, 1836, S3115, National Archives.

5. RG 156, E 113, *Register of Cannons and Car-*

riages Proposed, on Hand, and Supplied to Forts, Batteries, etc., 1861–1873, pp. 236–37, National Archives.

6. *Spartanburg Herald,* September 29, 1942.

Appendix Three

1. *Circular # 4, A Report on Barracks and Hospitals with Descriptions of Military Posts* (War Department, Office of the Surgeon General, 1870), p. 88; James A. Graham to his mother, April 22, 1861, James A. Graham Papers, Southern Historical Collection, University of N.C., Chapel Hill; Past Returns, November to December, 1865; RG 393, Part V, Post Headquarters Records, E 6: General Orders Number 34, November 6, 1865, National Archives.

2. *Circular # 4, A Report on Barracks and Hospitals with Descriptions of Military Posts* (War Department, Office of the Surgeon General, 1870), p. 88; Circular # 8, *A Report the Hygiene of the United States Army, with Descriptions of Military Posts* (War Department, Office of the Surgeon General, 1875), p. 154.

3. RG 393, Part V, Post Headquarters Records, E 6, National Archives.

4. *Circular # 4, A Report on Barracks and Hospitals with Descriptions of Military Posts* (War Department, Office of the Surgeon General, 1870), pp. 88, 90.

5. RG 393, Part V, Post Headquarters Records, E 6, National Archives.

6. *Circular # 4, A Report on Barracks and Hospitals with Descriptions of Military Posts* (War Department, Office of the Surgeon General, 1870), pp. 88, 90.

7. RG 159, E 15: Inspection Report of Post of Fort Macon and Garrison, N.C., November 19–27, 1869, S17, National Archives.

8. RG 159, E 15, Inspection Report of Port Macon, April 18, 1871, A10, National Archives.

9. RG 393, Part V, Post Headquarters Records, E 12, National Archives.

BIBLIOGRAPHY

Unpublished Sources

1. National Archives:
   Record Group 24-Records of the Bureau of Naval Personnel.
   Deck Logs of U.S. Navy Vessels:
   Albatross
   Chippewa
   Daylight
   Gemsbok
   State of Georgia

   Record Group 77-Records of the Office of the Chief of Engineers
   Entry 14-Letters Received, 1819–1825.
   Entry 18-Letters Received, 1826–1866.
   Entry 103 General Correspondence, 1894–1923
   Entry 219-Letters, Reports and Records Relating to Forts, 1810–1869.
   Entry 1007-Harbor Defense Files, Geographic Files, 1918–1945.

   Record Group 92-Records of the Office of the Quartermaster General.
   Entry 89-General Correspondence, 1890–1914.

   Entry 225-Consolidated Correspondence File, 1794–1889.
   Entry 1428-Miscellaneous Lists Related to Chartered, Hired or Seized Vessels; Repairs and Services of Vessels; Vessels for Various Expeditions, 1861–65.

   Record Group 94-Records of the Office of the Adjutant General.
   Entry 12-Letters Received, 1805–1889.
   Entry 25-General Correspondence, 1890–1917.
   Entry 26-Record Cards, 1890–1917.
   Entry 159-Generals' Papers and Books.
   Entry 465-Outline Index of Military Forts and Stations and Reservations.
   Entry 547-Medical Histories of Posts.

   Record Group 107-Records of the Office of the Secretary of War
   Entry 80-General Correspondence, 1890–1913.

   Record Group 109-War Department Collection of Confederate Records.
   Chapter II, Vol. 262 1/2-Department of North Carolina, Letters and Telegrams Sent.

Chapter II, Vol. 331-Department of North Carolina, Wilmington Command, Letterbook of Letters Sent and Orders, April–May, 1861.
Entry 193-Carded Records Showing Military Service.

Record Group 153-Records of the Office of the Judge Advocate General.
Entry 53-Reservations File, 1809–1942.

Record Group 156-Records of the Office of the Chief of Ordnance.
Entry 3-Letters Sent from the Chief of Ordnance.
Entry 21-Letters Received, 1812–1894.
Entry 25-Record Cards for General Correspondence, 1890–1903.
Entry 27-Synopses and Copies of General Correspondence, 1904–1910.
Entry 28-General Correspondence, 1894–1913.
Entry 100-Quarterly Summary Statement of Ordnance and Ordnance Stores on Hand at Forts and Batteries, 1838–1864.
Entry 102-Summary Statement of Ordnance and Ordnance Stores on Hand at Forts on September 30, 1862.
Entry 113-Register of Cannon and Carriages Required, on Hand and Supplied to Forts and Batteries, 1861–1873.
Entry 990-Applications for Condemned Ordnance, 1895–1900.

Record Group 159-Records of the Office of the Inspector General.
Entry 7-Inspection Reports, 1891–1907.
Entry 15-Letters and Reports Received, 1863–1894.

Record Group 393-U.S. Army Continental Commands, 1821–1920.
Part V-Records of Army Posts:
Post Headquarters Records of Fort Macon:
Entry 2-Letters Sent, 1865–1877.
Entry 6-General Orders, Special Orders and Circulars, 1864–1870.

Entry 12-Miscellaneous Records, 1862–1873.

Cartographic and Architectural Branch.
Record Group 77-Fortifications File.
Record Group 77-Civil Works File.

Microfilm Collections:
M270-Compiled Military Service Records of Confederate Soldiers.
M417-Herbert Buell Collection of Engineer Records.
M617-Returns of Military Posts, 1800–1916.

2. North Carolina State Archives.
A. Government Agencies:
Adjutant General's Records:
AG 13-Letterbook of Orders, 1847–1861.
AG 22-Record of Issues, May, 1861–July, 1862.

Department of Conservation and Development Records:
Administrative and Director's Office.
Administrative Reports and Correspondence.
Activities of the Board of Conservation and Development.

State Parks Division Records, Department of Conservation and Development:
85.1 State Parks and Lakes Files, 1930–1970.
85.4 Miscellaneous Records of the Parks Division, 1930–1970.

N.C. General Assembly:
Session Records.

B. Governors' Papers:
Charles B. Aycock
J. M. Broughton
Thomas Burke
Henry T. Clark
John W. Ellis
Cameron Morrison

C. Military Collections:
Civil War Collection

D. Personal Papers:
   D. H. Hill
   James M. Hollowell
   John D. Whitford

3. Southern Historical Collection, Library of the
   University of North Carolina, Chapel Hill:
   A. Personal Papers:
      Herman Biggs, #2351
      Bryan Family Papers, #96
      A. C. Evans, #2991
      James A. Graham, #283
      William A. Hoke, #345
      Alexander Justice, #1308
      Frank Nash, #539

4. Casemate Museum, Fort Monroe:
   Personal Diary of Brig. General Rollin L.
   Tilton
   Tilton, Rollin L. "Notes on Fort Monroe,
   1930-1946." Unpublished Manuscript. Fort
   Monroe, 1946.

5. Connecticutt State Library, Hartford:
   Hilliard Bryant Ferris Letters
   Jared Wheeler Letter

6. Duke University, Durham:
   John Rogers Vinton Papers

7. Fort Macon State Park:
   A. Fort History Files:
      Soldier Letters File
      U.S. Army Occupation of Park, 1941–46:
      Reports and Correspondence
      U.S. Army Lease of Park, 1941-46
      World War II Veteran Information and
      Remembrance File
   B. Monographs:
      Branch, Paul. "Confederate Armament of
      Fort Macon." Unpublished Manu-
      script: Fort Macon State Park, 1995.
      ———. "Confederate Flags of Fort Ma-
      con." Unpublished Manuscript: Fort
      Macon State Park, 1994.
      ———. "Confederate Garrison Strength
      of Fort Macon." Unpublished Manu-
      script: Fort Macon State Park, 1997.

8. Library of Congress:
   Daniel R. Larned Papers

9. North Carolina Maritime Museum, Beaufort, N.C.:
   O'Brien, T. Michael and Dennis L. Noble.
   "Soldiers of Surf and Story: The Light
   and Lifesavers of Cape Lookout, North
   Carolina." Unpublished Manuscript, no
   date.

10. Office of the Chief of Military History, Wash-
    ington, D. C.:
    U.S. Army. *Directory of the Army of the United
    States.* Washington: Adjutant General's
    Office, August, 1942.
    U.S. Army. *Station List of the Army of the United
    States, 4th Service Command.* Washington:
    Adjutant General's Office, March, No-
    vember, 1944.

11. University of Virginia, Charlottesville:
    Lawrence O'Brien Branch Papers

12. Virginia State Library, Richmond:
    Records of the Tredegar Iron Works:
    Foundry Sales Book, 1860-1867

13. Private Collections:
    David F.Dean Collection, Rochester, N. Y.:
    Papers of Jane Augusta (McKenny) Coues

Published Sources

Allen, G. H. *Forty-Six Months In the Fourth Rhode
Island Volunteers.* Providence: J. A. and R. A. Reid,
1887.
American State Papers, Military Affairs. 7 Volumes. Washington: Gales and Seaton, 1832–
1861.
Anderson, Mrs. John Huske. *North Carolina
Women of the Confederacy.* Fayetteville: Mrs. John
Huske Anderson, 1926.
*Annals of Congress: The Debates and Proceedings
in the Congress of the United States: with an Appendix containing important state papers and public
documents; and all the laws of a public nature, with
a copious index, compiled from authentic materials.*
42 Volumes. Washington: Gales and Seaton,
1834–56.

Annual Report of the U.S. Lifesaving Service, 1904. Washington: Government Printing Office, 1905.

Barrett, John G. *The Civil War in North Carolina.* Chapel Hill: University of N.C. Press, 1963.

Biddle, Charles. *The Autobiography of Charles Biddle.* Philadelphia: E. Claxton and Company, 1883.

Bright, Leslie, William H. Rowland, and James C. Bardon. *C.S.S. Neuse, A Question of Iron and Time.* Raleigh: N.C. Department of Archives and History, 1981.

Burlingame, John K. *History of the Fifth Regiment of Rhode Island Heavy Artillery During Three and a Half Years of Service in North Carolina.* Providence: Snow and Farnham, 1892.

Carteret County Federal Census, 1870.

Circular #4, Report on Barracks and Hospitals with a Description of Military Posts. Washington: War Department, Surgeon General's Office, 1870.

Circular #8, Report on Hygiene of the United States Army, with a Description of Military Posts. Washington: War Department, Surgeon General's Office, 1875.

Clark, Walter, ed. *The State Records of North Carolina.* 16 Volumes. Winston-Salem, Goldsboro and Raleigh: State of North Carolina, 1895–1914.

Clark, Walter, ed. *The Histories of Several Regiments and Battalions from North Carolina in the Great War, 1861–65; Written by Members of the Respective Commands.* 5 Volumes. Raleigh and Goldsboro, Nash Brothers, 1901.

Compilation of Public Documents and Extracts from Reports and Papers Relating to Lighthouses, Light Vessels, and Illuminating Apparatus, and to Beacons, Buoys and Fog Signals, 1789–1871. Washington: Government Printing Office, 1871.

Congressional Record. 68th Congress, 1st Session, 1923-24.

Croffut, William A., and John M. Morris. *The Military and Civil History of Connecticut During the Recent War.* New York: Ledyard Bell, 1868.

Cullum, George W. *Biographical Register of the Officers and Graduates of the United States Military Academy at West Point, New York, From Its Estab-* lishment in 1802 to 1890, With the Early History of the United States Military Academy. 3 Volumes. Boston: Houghton, Mifflin and Company, 1891.

Gatewood, Jr., Willard B. "North Carolina's Negro Regiment in the Spanish-American War," *North Carolina Historical Review,* October, 1971.

Gatewood, Jr., Willard B. *Smoked Yankees and the Struggle for Empire: Letters from Negro Soldiers, 1898–1902.* Urbana: University of Illinois Press, 1971.

Grier's Almanac. Atlanta: Grier's Almanac Publishing Company, 1862.

Hall, Henry and James Hall. *Cayuga in the Field, A Record of the 19th N. Y. Volunteers, All the Batteries of the 3rd New York Artillery, and 75th New York Volunteers, Comprising an Account of Their Organization, Camp Life, Marches, Battles, Losses, Toils and Triumphs in the War for the Union, With Complete Rolls of Their Members.* Syracuse: Truair, Smith and Company, Printers, 1873.

Hill, Daniel Harvey. *A History of North Carolina in the War Between the States, Bethel to Sharpsburg.* 2 Volumes. Raleigh: Edwards and Broughton, 1926.

Hollowell, James M. *War-Time Reminiscences, and Other Selections.* Goldsboro: *The Goldsboro Herald,* 1939.

Johnson, Robert U., and Clarence C. Buell. *Battles and Leaders of the Civil War, Being for the Most Part Contributions by Union and Confederate Officers.* 4 Volumes. New York, *Century Magazine,* 1887.

Laws of North Carolina

Lefler, Hugh T., and Albert R. Newsome. *The History of a Southern State: North Carolina.* Chapel Hill: University of North Carolina Press, 1973.

Lemmon, Sarah McCulloh. *North Carolina in the War of 1812.* Raleigh, N.C. Department of Archives and History, 1971.

Manarin, Louis, and Weymouth T. Jordan, ed. *North Carolina Troops, 1861–1865.* 13 Volumes (to date). Raleigh: N.C. Department of Archives and History, 1968–1993.

Mann, Albert W. *The History of the 45th Regiment of Massachusetts Volunteer Militia.* Boston: W. Spooner, 1908.

Newsome, A. R. "A Miscellany from the Thomas Henderson Letterbook, 1810–1811. *North Carolina Historical Review*. October, 1929.

Parker, William H. *Recollections of a Naval Officer, 1841-1865.* New York, Charles Scribner's Sons, 1883.

Paul, Charles L. "Beaufort, N.C.: Its Development as a Colonial Town." *North Carolina Historical Review*, October, 1970.

Paul, Charles L. "Colonial Beaufort." *North Carolina Historical Review*, April, 1965.

Public Laws and Resolutions Passed by the General Assembly at its Session of 1933.

Register of Debates in Congress. 14 Volumes. Washington: Gales and Seaton, 1825–1837.

Saunders, W. L. *The Colonial Records of North Carolina.* 10 Volumes. Raleigh: State of North Carolina, 1886-1890.

Scarborough, William K., ed. *The Diary of Edmund Ruffin.* 2 Volumes. Baton Rouge: Louisiana State University Press, 1976.

Scarf, Thomas. *The History of the Confederate States Navy From it Organization to the Surrender of its Last Vessel.* New York: Rogers and Sherwood, 1887.

Sloan, John. *Reminiscences of the Guilford Grays, Company B, 27th North Carolina Regiment.* Washington: R. O. Polkinborn, 1883.

Statutes At Large and Treaties of the United States of America, 1789–1873. Boston: Little, Brown and Company, 1845–1873.

Stick, David. *The Outer Banks of North Carolina, 1584–1958.* Chapel Hill: University of North Carolina Press, 1958.

Stone, Edwin. *Rhode Island in the Rebellion.* Providence: George H. Whitney, 1864.

Swift, Joseph G. *Memoirs of Gen. Joseph Gardner Swift, LL.D., U.S.A., First Graduate of the United States Military Academy, West Point, Chief Engineer, U.S.A. from 1812 to 1818. 1800–1865.* Privately Printed, 1890.

Tilton, Rollin L. *The History of the Chesapeake Bay Sector.* Fort Monroe, 1945.

Tolbert, Nolbert J. *The Papers of John Willis Ellis.* 2 Volumes. Raleigh: N.C. Department of Archives and History, 1964.

U.S. Army. *History of the Eastern Defense Command and of the Defense of the Atlantic Coast of the United States in the Second World War.* New York: G-3 Section, Eastern Defense Command, 1945.

U.S. Congress. Congressional Documents Serial Set.

U.S. Navy Department. *The Official Records of the Union and Confederate Navies in the War of Rebellion.* 30 Volumes. Washington: Government Printing Office, 1894–1927.

U.S. War Department. *General Orders and Bulletins, War Department, 1923.*

U.S. War Department. *The War of Rebellion: A Compilation of the Official Records of the Union and Confederate Armies.* 70 Volumes in 128 parts. Washington: Government Printing Office, 1880–1901.

Whittle, W. C. "The Cruise of the C. S. Steamer *Nashville*." *Southern Historical Society Papers,* Volume XXIX.

Newspapers

Beaufort News
Carolina Federal Republican (New Bern)
Carolina Sentinel (New Bern)
Charleston Courier
Charleston Mercury
Charlotte Western Democrat
Fayetteville Observer
Hillsboro Recorder
Kinston Daily Free Press
Litchfield Inquirer
New Bern Daily Progress
New Bern Weekly Journal
New York Daily Tribune
New York Herald
New York Times
Philadelphia Inquirer
Providence Daily Journal
Raleigh Morning Post
Raleigh News and Observer
Raleigh North Carolina Standard
Raleigh Register
South Carolina Gazette (Charleston)
Wilmington Daily Journal

INDEX

Abernathy, Congressman Charles L., 203, 220, 221

Albatross, U.S.S., 110, 111, 137, 138, 139, 148

Albemarle, C.S.S., 174, 176, 177

Alexander, Ord. Sgt. William, 80, 84, 85, 87, 130

Alexander, Lieut. W. S., 197

Alice Price, 145, 146, 147, 161, 162, 165

Allen, Major John, 127, 130, 131, 133

Alliance, 127

Ammon, Capt. John H., 133, 140, 148, 149, 158, 170

Anderson, Brig. Gen. Joseph R., 91, 92, 102

Andrews, Lieut. William S., 155

Appelman, Major Hiram, 141, 143

Armistead, Brig. Gen. W. K., 31, 77

Barden, Congessman Graham A., 231

Baxter, Lieut. Bejamin D.,153

Beaufort, 6, 7, 8, 9, 24, 25, 38, 41, 44, 46, 5O, 53, 54, 61, 68, 76, 77, 78, 79, 84, 85, 87, 91, 105, 106, 110, 119, 122, 124, 129, 132, 133, 136, 146, 155, 159, 164, 165, 166, 171, 173, 175, 177, 178, 183, 204, 207, 210, 211, 215, 216, 219; early history, 2, 3; Spanish attack on, 4, 5; Revolutionary War and, 10–19; War of 1812 and, 27–32; Union occupation, 130, 131, 135; U.S.

Naval Station established at, 169, 170

Beaufort, C.S.S., 103

Beauregard, Brig. Gen. P. G. T., 92

Bell, Col. Joseph, 8

Bellona Foundry, 93

Bernard, Brig. Gen. Simon, 32, 36, 38, 46, 50, 157, 167, 190, 202

Biggs Capt. Herman, 146, 147

Bishop, Lieut. Harry G., 192, 206, 207, 208

Blount, Capt. Richard H., 113, 123, 151, 152

Bogue Banks Lighthouse, 81, 134

Bradford, Col. James A. J., 98, 100

Branch, Brig. Gen. Lawrence O'B., 112, 114, 121, 122, 123, 125, 134, 165

Bread Incident, 135, 136

Bridgers, Lieut. Col. John L., 96, 102, 104, 105

Broughton, Governor J. Melville, 231

Brown, Capt. Earl I., 216

Bryan, Congressman John H., 46, 53

Bryant, Capt. Joseph, 27, 29

Burns, Capt. Otway, 52, 53, 56, 57, 58

Burnside, Maj. Gen. Ambrose E., 117, 118, 119, 120, 121, 122, 125, 126, 127, 128, 131, 141, 145, 146, 147, 148, 153, 157, 161, 162, 163, 164, 165, 169

Butler, Senator Marion, 203

289